DRINKERS, DRIVERS, AND BARTENDERS

DRINKERS, DRIVERS, AND BARTENDERS

Balancing Private Choices and Public Accountability

Frank A. Sloan, Emily M. Stout,
Kathryn Whetten-Goldstein,
Lan Liang

THE UNIVERSITY OF CHICAGO PRESS
Chicago & London

FRANK A. SLOAN is the J. Alexander McMahon Professor of Health Policy
Management and Economics and director of the Center for Health Policy, Law,
and Management at Duke University. Emily M. Stout is an associate in research at
Duke University. Kathryn Whetten-Goldstein is an assistant professor in the Department
of Public Policy at Duke University. Lan Liang is an assistant professor
in the Department of Economics at the University of Illinois, Chicago.

THE UNIVERSITY OF CHICAGO PRESS, CHICAGO 60637
THE UNIVERSITY OF CHICAGO PRESS, LTD., LONDON

09 08 07 06 05 04 03 02 01 00   1 2 3 4 5

ISBN: 0–226–76280–7 (cloth)
ISBN: 0–226–76281–5 (paper)

Library of Congress Cataloging-in-Publication Data

Drinkers, drivers, and bartenders : balancing private choices and public accountability /
Frank A. Sloan ... [et al.].
     p.   cm.
Includes bibliographical references and index.
ISBN 0-226-76280-7 (cloth : alk.) — ISBN 0-226-76281-5 (pbk : alk.)
   1. Liquor laws—United States.   2. Bars (Drinking establishments)—Law and
legislation—United States.   3. Drunk driving—United States.   4. Drinking and
traffic accidents—United States.   5. Liability for traffic accidents—United States.
6. Criminal liability—United States.   I. Sloan, Frank A.
KF1293.5.D75   2000
345.73'0247—dc21   99-057260

Contents

v

CONTENTS

CONTENTS

Preface

The key feature of a capitalist economy like that of the United States is that the various participants in the market have freedom of choice. To determine demand, firms rely on consumers' wants; they enter the market when they see opportunities for profit and exit when they do not. The owners of such firms supply equity capital with the intention of earning a profit; employees select their place of work based on a combination of pecuniary and nonpecuniary benefits. Specific public policies—for example, antitrust enforcement—are designed to ensure that the flow of resources among sectors is not impeded by various noncompetitive restraints. This is the model for the overwhelming majority of goods and services.

Drinking alcohol may cause major harm to individual drinkers, their families, and others in society. Although there may be long-term risks to personal health and to family well-being, the risk that excessive consumption causes to others on the road is immediate. Such "negative externalities" (in economic jargon) provide the rationale for public intervention.

Drinking in public places is a particular problem because it is so likely that the individual will drive after drinking. The dilemma for public policy is how to weigh the rights of free consumers to spend their funds as they wish, for firms to operate as businesses, for employees of such firms to enjoy the benefits of gainful employment, and for everyone to navigate safe roadways.

Several assumptions have provided the basis for regulating commercial servers of alcohol since the nineteenth century. First, individual drinkers are not always well positioned to monitor their own consumption of alcohol. Second, commercial servers are efficient monitors of excessive drinking, so sanctions for failure to monitor alcohol consumption have been placed on them. Third, these sanctions are effective in inducing servers to monitor drinking, and such monitoring in fact makes our roadways safer.

The first assumption can be taken at face value. There is empirical evidence that a great deal of drinking and driving emanates from places were alcohol is sold by the drink. Before this study was conducted, evidence was sparse on the effectiveness of server monitoring and of public regulation of the server. Policymaking in this sphere, as in many others, was largely based on the presumed logic of the underlying assumptions.

In recent years, using a time series of state cross sections, a few studies, including work by one of us, have found that imposing tort liability on commercial servers reduced mortality from motor vehicle accidents and that few of the other regulatory interventions appeared to be as effective as tort. Although intriguing, this finding was far from conclusive. Researchers had observed the relevant end point, reduction in motor vehicle fatalities, but not the intervening steps. By surveying owners and managers of commercial alcohol service establishments (bars) and their employees, we hoped to determine whether, in fact, servers' monitoring changed in response to changes in tort law as well as in administrative and criminal law and regulation. As in other studies, the diversity of laws and regulations among the states of the United States provided a basis for studying variation in server behavior. Overall, our work confirms the effectiveness of imposing tort liability on commercial servers of alcohol that the previous studies suggested.

Although not a primary focus, this book contains new evidence about the effect of social host liability on motor vehicle mortality, binge drinking, and drinking and driving. To our knowledge, ours is the first national study to present empirical data concerning this developing and controversial area of tort law. The rights of servers, consumers, and the public at large conflict in the area of commercial server liability, and the conflict is even more apparent when people's rights to drink and serve alcohol in their homes do not coincide with the general public interest.

In view of the burden that heavy drinking imposes on society, both in the United States and in other countries, the empirical analysis of how law and regulation influence the behavior of servers and consumers is important in its own right. The impetus for our research was broader than this. Tort law is currently under attack in America. Trial lawyers who represent plaintiffs in tort cases, and even the plaintiffs themselves, are often portrayed as greedy. Claims are widely seen as not meritorious and as motivated largely by personal financial gain. In North Carolina in 1998, for example, one of the candidates for the United States Senate mounted a campaign in which he criticized his opponent by referring to him as a "personal injury lawyer."

At the same time, tort is seen as ineffective in eliciting socially optimal levels of precaution. With a very few notable exceptions, empirical evidence is lacking on the effectiveness or ineffectiveness of tort law as a deterrent of careless behavior in any field. Our work adds to the research base on this important topic. We leave it to readers to decide how far one can generalize about tort from the empirical evidence in this context.

Perhaps to a lesser extent, regulation is also under attack. Conversely, policymakers and their constituents appear to have faith that criminal laws will achieve the desired effects. Using information we obtained from surveys of regulatory agencies (state insurance departments and alcoholic beverage commissions) and police departments, our analysis adds to existing knowledge about the efficacy of these forms of public oversight as well.

Our book has several intended audiences. First, many people have an interest in alcohol control policy, either as public officials or as private citizens. To illustrate the importance of the latter, one need only check the Mothers Against Drunk Driving Web site (<www.madd.org>). We found this to be a valuable source of information for our work. Second, many scholars are active in the fields of addiction and alcohol control policy, working in both public health and mental health. Although regulating commercial servers of alcohol is not typically their primary research interest, our issue is of sufficient public policy importance to merit their interest. A third target audience is scholars in law and economics, mostly in law schools, economics departments, and schools of public policy. Fourth, the book should be of interest to scholars in health economics. Patterns of consuming goods that are not beneficial to health, such as excessive alcohol or cigarettes, are of growing interest to scholars in this specialized area of economics.

Finally, we hope you enjoy reading about our research as much as we enjoyed doing it. For those of you who are researchers, we hope our findings stimulate further work on this important public policy topic.

Acknowledgments

This study was supported in part by a grant from the National Institute on Alcohol Abuse and Alcoholism (NIAAA). The current grant to Duke University is a continuation of a grant that was originally funded while Frank Sloan was on the faculty of Vanderbilt University. A finding that dram shop liability decreased motor vehicle fatalities and excessive consumption of alcohol provided the impetus for this book, which focuses on commercial servers of alcohol. We appreciate the support of Susan Martin of NIAAA, who has been our project officer from the time the research began at Vanderbilt.

Philip Cook, a colleague at Duke University, participated in conceptualizing our study of commercial servers, helped design our surveys of commercial establishments and employees, was an observer at one of the focus group meetings, and made helpful comments after the data were collected. About the time the survey began, he became acting director and then director of Duke's Sanford Institute of Public Policy Studies. Because of his additional administrative duties, he could not continue as an active researcher on the study. We greatly appreciate his intellectual contribution. He has been a productive investigator in alcohol research. Thomas Metzloff, a colleague at Duke Law School, conducted research on dram shop cases in North Carolina. Although the material he gathered was not used for this book, it helped our understanding of this area of the law.

Although we refer to the surveys of bar owners or managers and of employees as "our surveys," more precisely they were conducted for our purposes by Mathematica Policy Research, a consulting firm in Princeton, New Jersey. MPR is highly experienced in survey research, but surveying bars (which is very uncommon) was a first for the staff. Taking it as an interesting challenge, they were highly successful in obtaining a good response rate and, judging from the many screens we performed after receiving the data, obtained accurate data. We thank Maureen Martella, then on MPR's staff, who directed the surveys. We also thank Richard Strouse, who worked with us on these surveys and several previous ones.

Several Duke students helped with data collection. Robert Carroll conducted the Survey of Police Departments. He also did pilot interviews of bar owners and employees and, as a passive observer, watched their behavior. He developed an informational brochure for bar owners and managers that described the purposes and nature of our surveys. He performed the Survey of State Insurance Departments and of the Survey of Dram Shop Insurers. Jennifer Davis completed these two surveys. Brandon Ehrhart also conducted the Survey of Police Departments. Nishant Vajpayee did background research on state alcoholic beverage commissions and reviewed the law and regulation literature.

Randall Bovbjerg, a partner of long standing in our medical malpractice research, helped us decide on a title for the book.

Katherine Taylor, our administrative assistant at the Center for Health Policy, Law, and Management, helped prepare the manuscript for publication. During the final stages of the study, Hester Haverkamp Davies, a research associate at our Center, read the chapters and provided commentary on both content and readability.

Finally, we are grateful to the respondents to our various surveys, who gave of their time and expertise so that we would all have a better picture of alcohol control policies and their success or failure. In the end, it is these individuals who made this book possible.

1

Setting the Stage

Ever since its invention, excessive consumption of alcohol has been a problem, causing social and medical harm. In most countries moderate use of alcoholic beverages is not viewed as harmful, and it may even provide a health benefit (Ferrence and Kozlowski 1995; Thun et al. 1997). Among the most costly results of excessive use today are alcohol-related roadway injuries and fatalities. Law and public policy aim to alleviate these social effects by influencing the behavior both of individual drinkers and of others who might be in a position to limit their drinking, such as commercial servers of alcohol.

To combat such social harms, many countries have long had laws to control the production, distribution, and consumption of alcohol. Beginning with the settlement of Jamestown, Virginia, in 1607, the colonies in the United States adopted many such laws, particularly those designed to curb excessive drinking. With the invention of the automobile, the new combination of cars and alcohol shifted the focus away from drinking itself to reducing the number of drunk driving incidents and related deaths. In the early 1980s states again began to emphasize regulating the serving of alcoholic beverages not only as a way to control excessive consumption but also as a method of controlling drunk driving at its source.

Setting the stage for our analysis, this chapter covers a number of topics. We examine recent trends in alcohol consumption and the social costs of drunk driving in the United States. The high social cost of excessive drinking, as well as the view that heavy alcohol use is morally wrong, has led to various forms of regulation. That development provides a rationale for this book's in-depth empirical analysis of the behavior of those who work in bars and their responses to policies designed to encourage them to curb excessive drinking on their premises. These policies include administrative, criminal, and tort laws and regulations. The chapter concludes with a road map of the following chapters.

PRODUCTION AND CONSUMPTION OF ALCOHOLIC BEVERAGES

Production of alcoholic beverages in the United States has declined in recent years for all major categories (table 1.1). Nevertheless it remains a large industry. In 1995 the value of beer shipments was $17.3 billion (1996 dollars). Alcohol producers and other sellers of alcohol represent a potent political force.

Recent Trends in Alcohol Consumption in the United States

By several measures, alcohol consumption has declined in the United States since 1980 (table 1.2). Since 1984, the percentage of Americans who drink at all or who binge drink has declined (figs. 1.1 and 1.2). This information was obtained from the Behavioral Risk Factor Survey, a national survey of adults aged eighteen and over conducted annually by state health departments under the direction of the U.S. Centers for Disease Control and Prevention. Responses reflect self-reports of drinking at all and binge drinking within the month before the survey. The survey defines binge drinking as having five or more drinks on a single occasion. Total consumption fell as measured in gallons of alcohol consumed annually per capita by the adult population, as did consumption of beer, wine, and dis-

Table 1.1 Production of Alcoholic Beverages in the United States

	1980	1985	1990	1995
Beer				
Breweries (number)	86	103	286	879
Production (millions of barrels of thirty-one wine gallons)[b]	193	194	202	200
Value of shipments (billions of dollars)	17.8	12.2	18.2	17.3[a]
Wines				
Production (millions of wine gallons)	982	622	577	412
Whiskey				
Production (millions of tax gallons)[c]	87	65	77	69

Source: U.S. Bureau of Alcohol, Tobacco, and Firearms as reported in *Statistical Abstract of the U.S. 1997*, table 1232.

[a]Extrapolated from 1994 data on value of shipments.

[b]A wine gallon is the United States equivalent of 231 cubic inches.

[c]For spirits of one hundred proof or over, a tax gallon is equivalent to the proof gallon; for spirits of less than one hundred proof, the tax gallon is equivalent to the wine gallon. A proof gallon is the equivalent of a United States gallon at sixty degrees Fahrenheit, containing 50 percent ethyl alcohol by volume.

Table 1.2 Trends in Alcohol Consumption per Capita in the United States: 1850–1995

Measure	1850[a]	1860[a]	1870[a]	1880[a]	1890[a]	1895[a]	1900[a]	1905[b]	1910[b]	1915[b]	1920[b]	1925[b]	1930[c]
Alcoholic beverages (adult population, gallons)	4.09	6.42	7.70	8.79	13.19	16.96	17.01	20.20	21.86	19.99	2.95	0.12	0.11
Beer	1.58	3.22	5.31	6.93	11.37	15.20	15.53	17.34	19.81	18.40	2.61	—	—
Wine	0.27	0.34	0.32	0.47	0.48	0.39	0.36	0.47	0.62	0.33	0.12	0.03	0.03
Distilled spirits	2.24	2.86	2.07	1.39	1.34	1.37	1.12	1.39	1.43	1.26	0.22	0.09	0.08
Total ethanol (gallons)	2.1	2.53	2.07	1.72	1.99	2.23	2.06	2.39	2.6	2.56	1.96	—	—

Measure	1935[d]	1940[e]	1945[d]	1950[f]	1955[f]	1960[g]	1965[h]	1970[i]	1975[i]	1980[i]	1985[i]	1990[i]	1995[i]
Alcoholic beverages (adult population, gallons)	11.45	20.66	20.81	27.81	26.76	27.27	29.13	35.8	39.7	42.8	40.7	40.0	35.9
Beer	10.45	18.22	18.86	24.99	23.88	24.00	25.50	30.6	33.9	36.6	34.6	34.9	31.6
Wine	0.30	0.96	0.73	1.34	1.30	1.40	1.50	2.2	2.7	3.2	3.5	2.9	2.6
Distilled spirits	0.70	1.48	1.22	1.48	1.58	1.87	2.13	3.0	3.1	3.0	2.6	2.2	1.8
Total ethanol (gallons)	1.2	1.56	2.25	2.04	2	2.07	2.32	2.61	2.69	2.76	2.62	—	—

Sources:

[a] Statistical Abstract of the United States 1955, table 1011.
[b] Statistical Abstract of the United States 1960, table 1084.
[c] Statistical Abstract of the United States 1966, table 1159.
[d] Statistical Abstract of the United States 1965, table 1141.
[e] Statistical Abstract of the United States 1969, table 1118.
[f] Statistical Abstract of the United States 1976, table 1317.
[g] Statistical Abstract of the United States 1984, table 1392.
[h] Statistical Abstract of the United States 1985, table 1364.
[i] Statistical Abstract of the United States 1997, table 232.

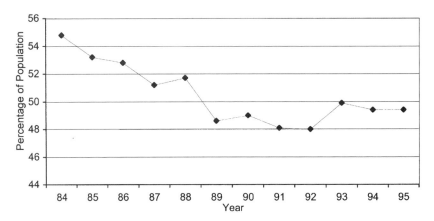

Fig. 1.1 Percentage of the United States population who drink. Source: Unpublished data from annual Behavioral Risk Factor Survey.

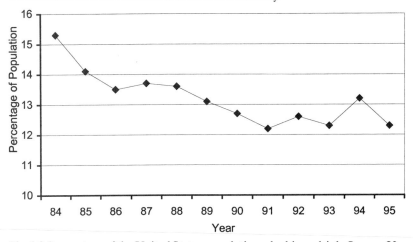

Fig. 1.2 Percentage of the United States population who binge drink. Source: Unpublished data from annual Behavioral Risk Factor Survey.

tilled spirits. The percentage of persons aged twelve and over who have ever used alcohol or are current users has also declined (table 1.3). In 1995 slightly over half of the United States population over age twelve considered themselves current users, in contrast to over three-fifths of the population in 1980.

Consumption of alcoholic beverages increased through the twentieth century. It was appreciably higher in the second half of the century than in the first half (see table 1.2). For example, per capita consumption was almost twice as high in 1995 as eighty years earlier, just before national pro-

Table 1.3 Alcohol Use in the United States

	1979	1985	1990	1995
Use of alcohol by those twelve years and older (%)				
Ever used	88.5	84.9	82.2	82.3
Current user	63.2	60.2	52.6	52.2

Source: U.S. Statistical Substance Abuse and Mental Health Administration, *Statistical Abstract of United States 1997,* table 220.

hibition was enacted. Alcohol consumption began to rise appreciably during the 1960s and 1970s. Consumption of beer grew dramatically during this period, reflecting the increase in production among domestic brewers, and wine consumption grew as the production of domestic wines increased. Consumption of distilled spirits has declined since 1970 and returned to its level in 1850.

By the mid-1970s, total consumption of absolute alcohol per capita reached forty gallons a year, the highest level since the 1850s, driven up by the combination of new drinkers, fewer abstainers, and increases in intake by veteran drinkers. After reaching a high in 1980, consumption has fallen in the 1990s, perhaps influenced by tighter alcohol control, as discussed in this book.

Limits on Exercise of Market Power

Producers of alcoholic beverages engage in price competition, and they seek to establish brand identity and consumer loyalty through advertising in order to enhance their individual market shares. One method of measuring a firm's market share is to measure demand for its product if prices are raised only by that firm. Although the price sensitivity of demand for the products of individual alcohol producers is not known, logically it should be high. Estimates for beer and distilled spirits vary as a whole, but clearly such demand is price sensitive (Leung and Phelps 1993; Saffer, Grossman, and Chaloupka 1998; Cook and Moore n.d.).

Potential competition from different types of alcoholic beverages (e.g., the competition beer sellers face from wine and spirits and conversely) constrains the market power of individual sellers, as does competition from nonalcoholic beverages. In the United States the dominant beverage group is soft drinks. Tea, the cheapest beverage except water, ranks fifth in consumption. Water, once a nearly zero-price beverage, is now moving into corporate focus as bottled water gains popularity. In the United States the major growth markets for beverages have been soft drinks and beer.

5

SOCIAL COST OF EXCESSIVE USE OF ALCOHOL

Many social problems accompany alcohol consumption. The National Institute of Alcohol Abuse and Alcoholism estimated the total cost of alcohol abuse and dependence at $163.4 billion for 1996. Based on comprehensive analysis of the external costs, Manning and coauthors (1991) estimated the lifetime external costs of excessive drinking at $60,100 per heavy drinker (1996 dollars). External costs are those not borne by the drinker or the drinker's household. This cost translated to $1.70 per excess ounce of alcohol consumed, or $0.77 per excess drink—that is, five or more drinks of any type of alcoholic beverage per day. This cost was estimated to increase to $180 billion by 1996. A large portion of this amount can be attributed to drunk driving and its associated costs. Alcohol-related traffic crashes cost society $45 billion annually in hospital costs, rehabilitation expenses, and lost productivity (Hingson 1996).

The U.S. Public Health Service estimated the mortality-increasing effects of alcohol through a variety of diseases and events, including highway collisions. According to this source, 110,000 deaths occur annually because of alcohol, including deaths from highway crashes, cirrhosis, home drownings, fires, job injuries, and cancer (McGinnis and Foege 1993). Also, 9,000 homicides and suicides annually are attributable to alcohol. The Public Health Service estimated a total of 2.7 million potential life years are lost annually owing to alcohol, of which about a quarter are inflicted on others through collisions and homicides while the remaining three-quarters of the losses are carried directly by alcohol consumers and their families. Estimates for other countries are correspondingly high (see, e.g., Maynard and Godfrey 1994 for the United Kingdom).

DRUNK DRIVING IN THE UNITED STATES
The Social Burden of Drunk Driving

Alcohol-related motor vehicle accidents impose substantial costs on various segments of society. Often injury and illness are self-inflicted because a person fails to act in a way that prevents future loss. Society typically is concerned about self-inflicted loss, especially when the injured person for one reason or another is not well positioned to make a rational, informed choice. In motor vehicle accidents drunk drivers pose a threat not only to themselves but also to the safety and property of others. These external threats provide the primary rationale for public intervention, although society is concerned about the safety of the drunk driver as well.

Motor Vehicle Collisions

Motor vehicle collisions are a significant cause of deaths. In 1996 the National Highway Traffic Safety Administration estimated that alcohol-related traffic fatalities in the United States exceeded 17,000. This was a 32 percent decrease from 1982, the first year such data were collected in a comparable form. Deaths both for young people, those aged fifteen to twenty (fig. 1.3), and for adults, those twenty-one to sixty-four (fig. 1.4), generally decreased from 1984 to 1995. Alcohol-related motor vehicle deaths are those attributed to alcohol on the police accident report. Although reporting has improved, these incidents are still underreported. Therefore many researchers use motor vehicle fatalities involving one vehicle and occurring after 8:00 P.M. as a proxy for alcohol-related traffic deaths. The annual number of traffic deaths from alcohol-related causes exceeds the number of Americans (58,000 total) who died each year in the Vietnam War.

In 1996, 40.9 percent of motor vehicle fatalities were estimated to have been alcohol related, compared with 57.3 percent in 1982 (Bedard 1998). There were about one million alcohol-related crashes in 1995, and about

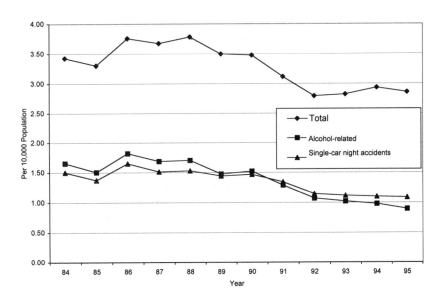

Fig. 1.3 Motor vehicle fatality rates in the United States: ages fifteen to twenty. Source: Unpublished data from the Fatal Accident Reporting System.

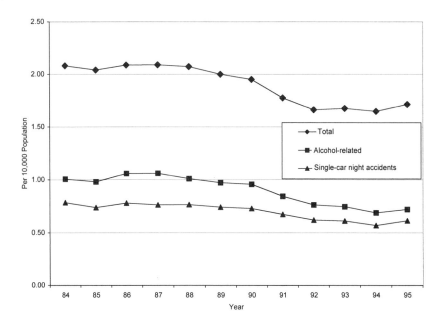

Fig. 1.4 Motor vehicle fatality rates in the United States: ages twenty-one to sixty-four. Source: Unpublished data from the Fatal Accident Reporting System.

30,000 persons each year suffer permanent disabilities from this cause (Miller et al. 1997).

Alcohol Abuse and Crime Rates

Excessive alcohol use has consequences besides those on the roadway. It is linked to crime rates. For example, among victims of violence who were able to describe the offender's use of drugs or alcohol, two-thirds reported that the offender had been drinking at the time of the crime. Among the 11.1 million victims of violence in the United States each year, one in four were certain the offender had been drinking before committing the crime (Greenfeld 1998).

POLITICAL RESPONSES TO THE PROBLEM

In response to the high social costs of drunk driving, grassroots organizations have been formed that aim to publicize the harm caused by drunk driving, prevent drunk driving through education, and most important, lobby politicians to pass stricter alcohol-related legislation. One such organization is

Mothers Against Drunk Driving (MADD), a nonprofit organization with more than six hundred chapters in the United States. MADD was formed by a small group of California women in 1980 after a hit-and-run drunk driver killed a thirteen-year-old girl. He had been out on bail only two days when he was arrested for another hit-and-run drunk driving crash. This driver also had three previous drunk driving arrests and two convictions. He was allowed to plea bargain to vehicular manslaughter. Although he was sentenced to two years in jail, the judge allowed the offender to serve his time in a work camp and later a halfway house (MADD Web site: <www.madd.org>).

A large percentage of the United States population supports legal measures to deter excessive alcohol use in general and drunk driving in particular, but there appears to be appreciable disagreement about specifics. In one survey, 96 percent of respondents favored an educational program for drunk drivers (Applegate et al. 1995). Over half wanted legislatures to support various specific policies, but there was also vocal opposition. Fines of over $2,000 were opposed by 61 percent of citizens. Mandatory jail terms for driving under the influence of alcohol (DUI) were opposed by 30 percent. Extending responsibility to parties other than the drunk driver is a very unpopular alternative: 82 percent of United States citizens opposed making it legal for injury victims from alcohol-related motor vehicle accidents to sue bar owners. Respondents were reluctant to support policies that intruded on their own rights or conveniences. In fact, however, a huge amount of legislation has been enacted to deal with DUI. Between 1980 and 1990, over five hundred laws were passed in the United States that dealt with drunk driving (Chaloupka, Saffer, and Grossman 1993). One such law was the Federal Uniform Drinking Act of 1984. The act virtually compelled all states to raise the minimum drinking age to twenty-one by limiting federal highway funding to states that did not comply. Substantial legislative activity continued throughout the 1990s (MADD Web site: www.madd.org).

It would be misleading to imply that political forces favoring restrictions on alcohol use and on DUI have the upper hand. For example, attempts to lower the national blood alcohol content (BAC) standard from 0.10 to 0.08 have been successfully opposed in many states by organizations representing alcohol producers and commercial establishments.

Drinking and Driving and Government Policy: An Analytic Framework
Alcohol Control Policies

Societies have implemented various alcohol policies to mitigate the social cost of excessive alcohol consumption as well as to raise revenue for the public sector. The most influential types of regulation are alcohol taxation, laws to deter drunk driving, the establishment of a minimum age for buying and drinking alcohol, alcohol advertising laws, limitations on alcohol availability, and tort law that aims to make drivers and servers of alcohol more cautious (Saffer, Grossman, and Chaloupka 1998).

Administrative, criminal, and tort laws influence the behavior of individual drinkers and commercial servers. Administrative agencies have primary responsibility for taxation, for enforcing advertising bans, and for limiting the availability of alcohol, both in liquor stores ("off site") and in bars and restaurants ("on site"). Criminal agencies, which in this context are sometimes linked to administrative organizations, are responsible for enforcing the criminal laws, mainly those specifically aimed at reducing drunk driving and serving alcohol to minors.

Tort law is derived from a system of common law and statutes aimed to deter injuries, compensate injury victims, and provide orderly redress of wrongdoing. A tort is any wrongful act, other than breach of contract, for which a private person may bring a lawsuit. The principles of tort law are also applied to insurance claims. Auto and liquor liability insurance tends to blunt individual drinkers' and commercial servers' incentives to exercise due care, especially if premiums do not vary with adverse experience, including tort liability claims, accidents, or violations of law.

Social Objectives of Regulation

In view of the external costs that drunk drivers impose on others, there is a clear rationale for public intervention before and after harm results. Public intervention in alcohol regulation has several goals.

By far the most important goal is *deterrence* of reckless behaviors that cause injury to persons and property. Deterrence may be achieved in a variety of ways: education; rehabilitation, taxation, controls over availability of alcohol, and punishment. Irrespective of the policy instrument used, deterrence is efficient when preventive activity is set at the level that minimizes the sum of prevention cost and injury cost. The underlying effectiveness of particular policies is incorporated in this criterion. Thus, if a policy is ineffective, it adds to prevention cost without reducing injury cost and therefore should not be instituted.

A second goal is *compensation* of injury victims. Policies most clearly directed at this goal involve tort law and insurance. Problems with the effectiveness of these policies occur when a drunk driver is insolvent or is uninsured.

A third goal is *retribution and justice.* It seems only fair that the injurer be punished for the harm imposed on others. Without formal mechanisms for punishment, individuals may seek retribution on their own.

A fourth goal is *revenue generation* to benefit the public sector. As we document in chapter 2, both the federal and state governments obtain substantial funds from taxes imposed on alcohol and on enterprises that sell alcoholic beverages. Insofar as taxation reduces consumption, public funds can be used to pay for the care of injured victims, and heavy alcohol users pay higher taxes, potentially reducing the traffic accident rate. Such taxation tends to be regressive if the demand for alcoholic beverage is price inelastic, however, and it therefore burdens not only the consumers of alcohol but also other members of their households. On the other hand, if higher taxes on alcohol reduce an adult's consumption, the person's productivity on the job and in the home may increase. Such changes would in turn be beneficial to the other family members.

On Whom Should Regulation Be Imposed?

To further the deterrence objective, on grounds of efficiency, policy should encourage the least costly methods of prevention. Parties are likely to differ in their ability to prevent alcohol-related injury to persons and property. In this context, a number of candidates come to mind: the individual drinker; the drinker's family; the drinker's school or employer, depending on the person's age and work status; correctional institutions; commercial sellers of alcohol; other servers of alcohol; manufacturers of motor vehicles; and producers of alcoholic beverages.

Among the regulatory targets, some parties seem more relevant than others. For example, in democratic societies, in contrast to totalitarian regimes, there is a reluctance to hold family members liable for the acts of their relatives. An exception might be a case in which a family member was also directly involved in the act, such as in serving alcohol to a relative who subsequently drove and injured someone. This reluctance to impose liability on close family members remains, even though it may be an efficient deterrent.

Similarly, schools and employers are less likely liability candidates than servers and drinkers. If these institutions were held responsible for the drunk driver, they might prescreen and possibly reject potential students and employees based on their drinking habits. However, employers have been held liable for acts of intoxicated employees while at work when they should have known about or anticipated the employees' intoxication. Because students and employees are there only part time, these institutions may be inefficient monitors of excessive drinking. An exception is colleges and universities where students, many of them under the legal drinking age, live full time. In the past, such institutions have been found liable for harm caused by intoxicated students.

Among other parties who may be held liable, three are typically not assigned responsibility for curbing excessive use of alcohol. Motor vehicle manufacturers are not, largely because no cost-effective technology exists to aid in preventing drunk driving accidents, such as a Breathalyzer to prevent intoxicated drivers from starting their automobiles. This admittedly has not stopped the United States government from imposing laws it may be impossible to comply with. One such example is the mandatory production of cars with maximum fuel efficiency.

The second party that typically escapes liability is the producer of alcoholic beverages. Although liability may be imposed on tobacco manufacturers, this is not true of alcoholic beverage producers, for whom imposing user taxes and requiring warning labels appear to suffice. Perhaps the difference lies in the possibly beneficial effects of moderate drinking (Ferrence and Kozlowski 1995; Thun et al. 1997), whereas consumption of tobacco at any level has been deemed harmful. Yet the external costs of heavy drinking far exceed those attributable to smoking (Manning et al. 1989, 1991).

Finally, as a practical matter, correctional institutions are not held liable for failing to rehabilitate those who undergo alcohol education programs while incarcerated. In any case, only a very small proportion of heavy drinkers are incarcerated. Additionally, rehabilitation centers or outpatient programs are generally not held liable for failing to rehabilitate their patients.

After we eliminate many of the possibly liable parties, the individual drinker, the seller of alcohol, and the noncommercial server (social host) remain potentially liable. This book addresses policies aimed at the individual drinker and the commercial server. As we explain in chapter 5, regulation of social hosts is in its infancy.

Carrots versus Sticks

Conceptually, it should be possible to achieve deterrence by both positive methods ("carrots") and negative methods ("sticks"). In practice, sticks have dominated the methods of control over the drunk driver and commercial server. Certainly, offering financial incentives for persons not to drink and drive would violate most citizens' canons of equity. This does not eliminate education, but often it is difficult to find an audience for such intervention, particularly with adults. For this reason carrots are sometimes combined with sticks, such as in "safe driving school" for traffic offenders.

Alternative Regulatory Approaches

To combat the drunk driving problem, policies are primarily designed to deter the drunk driver and prevent accidents. Three types of law—administrative, criminal, and tort—are employed to carry out the objectives of anti–drunk driving policies. Administrative rules have been imposed on sellers, criminal liability has been imposed on both individual consumers and sellers, and when an injury occurs, tort law has been imposed on consumers, sellers, and noncommercial servers.

Why are three approaches employed where one might suffice? Conceptually, imposing tort liability—that is, assessing monetary damages— alone should suffice. In this scenario injury victims could seek compensation from injurers. If injurers are made to pay, this should deter actions leading to harm. In a tort case, the defendant may be the injurer or, in the context of drunk driving, a third party who could have prevented the injury, such as a server. It is comparatively efficient to impose liability on someone in a position to prevent the drinker from becoming intoxicated.

Several reasons may be advanced for not relying totally on tort. First, some injurers may not have the funds to fully compensate victims for their loss (Beard 1990; Schwartz 1997). Posner (1986, 205) expressed the views of most experts in law and economics in stating that "the criminal law is primarily designed for the nonaffluent; the affluent are kept in line by tort law." In technical terms, injurers may be "judgment proof." An injurer who can declare bankruptcy after a lawsuit and hence escape payment will not be affected by the threat of tort liability. Second, victims may not seek compensation through tort even when they are entitled to it, sometimes because of the high cost of litigation. Underclaiming means potential injurers have insufficient incentive to take optimal precautions. There is thus considerable reason to doubt Posner's statement (and the opinion of many other experts in the law and economics field) that the affluent are kept in line by tort law.

In addition to tort liability, a drunk driver or server may also face criminal liability, which is imposed on a server who sells alcoholic beverages to either an obviously intoxicated or an underage person. There are several reasons for imposing criminal liability.

First, when victims do not know who injured them or when identifying and apprehending violators is difficult, it may be desirable to rely on public enforcement rather than on private enforcement by means of contract or tort law (Polinsky and Shavell 1999). It would be difficult for private parties to fully capture the benefit of developing information systems that may be needed to identify and apprehend violators. Second, much of public enforcement is general in that several types of violators may be detected with the same screen. For example, a waiting policeman may apprehend drunk drivers, speeders, or those who litter. By contrast, an injury victim will enforce only the tort that caused the specific injury. A barrier to private enforcement is that the state does not generally allow private parties to use force in apprehending violators. Motorists are not allowed to chase and arrest reckless drivers. Third, except where fines are imposed, criminal liability is not subject to the "judgment proof" problem—that is, lack of resources to pay the financial penalty. Instead of paying a fine, indigent criminals may be incarcerated, or alternative penalties such as driver license revocation may be imposed. But incarceration is costly. If scarce resources are allocated to this type of punishment, fewer resources can be devoted to other goods and services that satisfy social needs.

All states impose administrative regulation of off-site (stores) and on-site vendors of alcohol (bars and restaurants that serve alcohol). By restricting availability and regulating seller practices, administrative regulation aims to decrease consumption and subsequently reduce the consequences of excessive use. Unlike tort and criminal liability, however, availability restrictions are imposed on all commercial establishments rather than focusing on the heavy drinker or abuser. Also, administrative restrictions are a double-edged sword. To the extent that they reduce alcohol abuse and drunk driving, they produce a desirable outcome. But when output restrictions increase the market power of sellers, they carry a welfare cost.

An alternative or complement to any of the regulations above is taxing alcoholic beverages. Taxation is aimed, albeit imperfectly, at the heavy drinker, since taxes rise in proportion to consumption. Yet, as with administrative regulation, there is no distinction between the drinker who exercises care and one who does not. Both pay the tax, holding the quantity of consumption constant. Although estimates of the price elasticity of demand for alcoholic beverages vary widely, there is a consensus that consumption falls as price rises.

Levels of Authority

In the system of federalism that exists in the United States, individual jurisdictions, primarily the states and local communities, determine and administer the laws that apply to drunk driving (see, e.g., Lawrence 1988).

Enforcing criminal laws is largely a local responsibility. Local jurisdictions have a large role in regulating alcohol availability; much of the legislative function is at the state level.

Over time the federal government has become more active in influencing traffic safety and drunk driving policy. Before 1950 it was inactive in highway safety issues. More recently Congress has successfully used financial incentives to persuade the states to enact specific legislation or programs to address the problem of driving under the influence (Lawrence 1988).

SOCIAL CONTROL

A distinction can be made among three forms of social control: special deterrence, which is directed at preventing recidivism by the individual offender; general deterrence, which uses the threat of sanctions to provide a disincentive for undesirable conduct; and informal sanctions or social norms. Snortum (1988) cautioned that these controls are not mutually exclusive. For example, sobriety checkpoints may be intrusive and intimidating; such checkpoints could detect violations by persons both with and without a history of DUI. Further, there are likely to be important interactions, such as between the probability of detection and the level of punishment.

Special deterrence may take the form of higher criminal penalties or, in this context, alcohol-abuse treatment programs. Many of the alcohol-related administrative, criminal, and tort laws are directed at general deterrence. A convenient assumption in modeling individual and firm responses to a legal threat is that these actors are rational. So far as the assumption of rationality predicts behavior that appears consistent with the data, it does not seem fruitful to dwell on the realism of the assumption.

Social norms may dictate drinking patterns and influence the propensity to drink and drive beyond any effect that law and market forces may have on incentives. We do not specifically measure changes in social norms here, although some behaviors, such as the trend toward less drinking and driving, controlling for the influence of laws and prices, may reflect changes in norms. Peer pressure brought about by the efforts of Mothers Against Drunk Driving aims to improve roadway safety through social norms. The state binary and time trend variables in our analysis in chapter 9, using data on motor vehicle fatalities, to some extent reflect social norms.

Lessig (1998) (and several other articles in the *Journal of Legal Studies,* June 1998) described behavior as regulated by four types of constraint, with law being one type. First, law threatens sanctions ex post if certain rules are not obeyed. Concepts of specific and general deterrence fall under this heading. Markets regulate behavior through price as the second type of constraint. The third type, "nature" or "architecture," also affects behavior. Because of these physical constraints, we cannot look through walls, for example. To a seller of alcoholic beverages distance is a constraint of architecture, although it might be seen as a form of price.

Social norms, the fourth category, regulate individual behavior, but not through the marketplace or by government decree. For example, a racist's jokes may be less acceptable now and are therefore told less frequently. Binge drinking may be a socially acceptable custom in some settings but not in others. Some forms of behavior, such as tipping a waiter at a highway diner, could be explained only by social norms, certainly not by financial incentives. Lessig goes on to characterize social norms as behavior that becomes internalized and so does not require social enforcement. People adhere to it of their own accord.

It is important to recognize that neither incentives nor social norms explain all behaviors, certainly not in the context of this study. Although social norms undoubtedly influence behavior, there is no precise theory about how norms are formed and evolve. Existing theories describe behavior given social norms (see, e.g., Hirshi 1969). The publicity surrounding the legislative process and the passage of a new law may influence social norms as well as creating incentives to be lawful. Social norms may increase the deterrent effect of a law if someone has strong ties to persons who would disapprove of the violation (Snortum 1988).

PUBLIC HEALTH AND ALCOHOL CONTROL

Public health values the well-being of the community above the well-being of the individual. Therefore some public health motives aim to identify and control hazards and dangers that threaten the community as a whole rather than focusing on the problems of a minority of people who are particularly subject to difficulties. The thrust of some public health policy is achieving social justice. Tort attempts to achieve the same end, maximizing social welfare, but through a different means—perfecting the market by changing individuals' incentives. Public health advocates seek to ensure that all hazards and essential goods are controlled by fair and equitable community rules so as to minimize the risk of death and disability (Beauchamp 1980). The aim is to limit the damaging effects of alcohol on an entire community. Community alcohol problems are a predictable and expected consequence of the consumption ethic, which urges the maximum legal availability of alcohol as a consumer product, and of commercial pressures to integrate alcohol into everyday life. Many of the problems with alcohol can be traced to growth in the alcohol industry and in personal consumption. Prevention of alcohol-related injuries and illnesses is needed to minimize the number who suffer early disability and death. Public health options include creating rules to minimize groups' exposure to hazards as well as providing safeguards against damage if hazardous exchanges do occur.

The initiative and burden for controlling injury and death lie within the community and society in general. Both private and public sectors ideally should work together to strengthen methods for controlling consumption and affirming norms for minimal alcohol use. This control must be undertaken primarily by government or nongovernment agencies through organized, nonvoluntary actions. These policies are universal in their effects, distributing benefits in the form of lower risk of alcohol-related injury.

At the state level, government authority to regulate for the people's protection is based on "police power"—the power to provide for the health, safety, and welfare of the people (*Jacobsen v. Massachusetts,* 197 U.S. 11 [1905]). Federal power to regulate public health rests largely on the commerce power granted by article 1, section 8, clause 3 of the United States Constitution, which gives Congress the power to "regulate commerce with foreign nations, and among the several states and with the Indian tribes." Public health powers are also granted by the taxing and spending power under article 1, section 8, clause 1, which grants the power to collect taxes and provide for the general welfare of the United States. Authority over interstate commerce allows Congress to regulate commerce between the states as well as whatever affects that commerce. Many federal interests in public health matters do not involve direct federal regulatory control but rather operate through, or in conjunction with, the states and their local governments. The federal power used in this context is the power to tax and spend for the general welfare.

There has been massive federal participation in public health through a variety of grant-in-aid programs. These programs involve a grant of federal funds to a state or to a municipal government for a particular legislatively defined purpose. The state or local government may obtain the funds and spend them for the designated purpose if it accepts the conditions of the grant. The conditions generally require the state to comply with certain federal requirements or to carry out the purpose of the grant in prescribed ways.

Overview of the Book

This book reports on empirical analyses of the effects of policies to curb excessive alcohol use and driving under the influence of alcohol. A substantial part of our analysis focuses on commercial servers of alcohol and on the role of various public policies in regulating commercial servers. Most research on this topic has examined individuals; we present what is to our knowledge the first in-depth analysis of the viewpoints and behaviors of commercial servers, both owners or managers and employees of such establishments.

Although many policies affect drinking and driving, we emphasize the role of tort and criminal laws. Theoretical analysis of the effects of imposing different liability rules on behavior is reasonably well developed. In sharp contrast, there is a paucity of empirical evidence on such important issues as whether tort and criminal law are effective deterrents. Our book presents new information on this important topic.

Chapter 2 is the first of four chapters on various forms of regulation that affect drivers and commercial alcohol servers. This chapter analyzes the role and performance of administrative agencies, such as the alcoholic beverage commission, the alcohol law enforcement agency, and the department of revenue. Administrative oversight of commercial on-site (bars and taverns) and off-site (stores) sellers of alcohol includes control over entry and practices of the regulated firms. Control over entry may reduce excessive alcohol use by making purchases of alcohol less accessible, by preventing the adverse consequences of a high density of alcohol sellers, or both. But if the history of regulation in other sectors generalizes to this sector, entry regulation is often captured by the industry the public agency seeks to regulate.

In chapter 2 we describe the evolution of administrative regulation in the United States, which has included a period when there was an absolute prohibition on the sale of alcoholic beverages. We study the effectiveness of such regulation as an entry barrier to off-site and on-site commercial establishments and examine how far administrative rules translate into commercial servers' perceptions of the probability of being cited for serving obviously intoxicated adults or minors.

Chapter 3 examines the role of criminal law in regulating the behavior of commercial servers of alcohol. As we stated above, state legislatures have been active in enacting legislation, much of it affecting criminal liability of private parties. The trend has been toward stiffer mandatory penalties for various manifestations of heavy drinking. But such sanctions will deter only to the extent that they are enforced. Local police departments have many priorities, only some of which involve enforcing alcohol laws. In this chapter we report the results of our survey of local police departments regarding their resources in total and their allocation of effort to controlling excessive alcohol use and its effects. We assess how far extra resources translate into differences in the probabilities of a citation as perceived by commercial servers.

Chapters 4 and 5 assess the role of tort liability. Tort in this context has two targets: the driver and the commercial server. Chapter 4 discusses the effects of tort liability and insurance on individual drunk drivers and reviews the literature on how automobile liability insurance affects drivers' behavior. Although insurance offers the advantage of risk pooling and hence risk reduction to individuals, it also has the disadvantage of moral hazard. In this context drivers who have liability coverage may be less careful. An exception might be when insurers base premiums on drivers' accident records and on chargeable violations. One lesson from previous research is that compelling drivers to purchase experience-related liability insurance is effective in inducing them to drive more carefully.

Chapter 5 focuses on tort liability for commercial servers, including bars, restaurants, and liquor stores. In a handful of states, tort is being applied to social hosts. As with other forms of liability, tort has been extended beyond the individual to parties that should be positioned to monitor their behavior, presumably because heavy drinkers lack either the capacity or the inclination to abide by the rules.

In chapter 5 we describe the history of tort law in this context. An intriguing finding from previous research (such as Chaloupka, Saffer, and Grossman 1993; Sloan, Reilly, and Schenzler 1994a, 1994b, 1995; and Ruhm 1996) is that one of the most effective policies in reducing motor vehicle fatalities and drinking and driving has been dram shop liability. "Dram shop" is an old English term for bar or tavern. An important contribution of this study is to look inside the "black box" to determine whether dram shop liability really influences the behavior of commercial servers. We report on servers' perceptions about such laws and how these laws have affected serving practices and discuss what the servers said they do in response to these laws.

Chapter 6 discusses liability insurance for commercial servers. Much of the effect of tort liability may be mitigated by liability insurance. Such insurance serves the usual role of risk diversification by risk pooling. In most states, purchasing minimum levels of general liability insurance is compulsory. This type of liability insurance protects against general injuries such as the classic "slip and fall." Purchasing dram shop insurance, which protects against suits brought by those injured by an intoxicated customer of the establishment, is never compulsory, but most establishments have it. The chapter also presents new results from our survey on the dram shop liability insurance market and on commercial servers' demand for such insurance.

Chapter 7 is the first of two chapters that present results from our Survey of Commercial Servers, a national survey of almost eight hundred bar owners, managers, and employees. The key question addressed in both chapters is whether making servers liable for serving obviously intoxicated adults or minors really makes them more careful. Insofar as there is a deterrent effect, specifically which deterrents work? We examine the effects of policies we described in chapters 2 through 5.

Whereas chapter 7 focuses on responses of owners or managers of commercial server establishments, chapter 8 focuses on employees of these same establishments. The employees were asked some of the same questions as their bosses, with the bosses not present. Thus we revisit the questions about deterrence, substituting responses of employees for those of owners or managers. We also examine patterns of employee compensation. In particular, we ask and answer whether there are financial incentives for employees to engage in bad serving practices.

Chapter 9 presents our analysis of the effects of various policies on the decisions to drink, to binge drink, and to drive drunk. We also examine the effects of various policies on motor vehicle death rates. Here the observational unit is the individual driver rather than the commercial server. As we indicate elsewhere in this book, several empirical studies of this issue have been conducted with the same data. Ours is a somewhat richer analysis with a more comprehensive set of policy variables. As Ruhm (1996) demonstrated, failure to incorporate a rather complete set of policy variables has led to reporting of some biased results in past research.

Chapter 10 is the final chapter, in which we summarize our key findings, compare them with earlier findings when such comparisons are feasible, and explore the implications of our results for public policy. Our most important finding is that imposing tort liability in this context is an effective deterrent. Thus, given the controversy surrounding tort and tort reform, we ask whether our findings generalize to other contexts.

The appendix describes the surveys we conducted for our study. Our main data collection effort was our Survey of Commercial Servers. In addition, to assess how laws are implemented in practice, we surveyed state alcoholic beverage commissions and local police departments in the jurisdictions served by the bars we surveyed. To learn more about the market for dram shop liability insurance and about regulation of this insurance, we surveyed state insurance departments and some property casualty insurers. The results of these surveys not only were of interest in their own right but also were used to construct explanatory variables for our empirical analysis of servers' behavior.

2

Administrative Regulation of Alcohol Consumption

Statutes governing the regulation of alcohol consumption have three ostensible goals: to control availability, and thereby consumption, of alcohol; to regulate business practices affecting the distribution and sale of alcoholic beverages; and to raise revenue for the public sector. Liquor regulations aim to control two types of problems presented by alcoholic beverages. By controlling availability and sales practices, the public sector hopes to protect the community from alcohol-related accidents and deaths, thereby mitigating social costs resulting from excessive consumption, including drunk driving, property damage, industrial accidents, lost work productivity, disturbance of the peace, an increase in major crimes, alcoholism, and alcohol-related diseases. Availability and regulation of business practices are controlled by restricting market entry of commercial sellers of alcoholic beverages, promulgating rules sellers must abide by, and enforcing penalties for violating such rules.

From the standpoint of the individual consumer, administrative regulation, if effective, raises the full price of alcohol. The full price includes the price charged for the beverage plus costs incurred in obtaining it, including taxation, the cost of travel time, and related travel expenses. One goal of administrative regulation is to limit heavy drinking, thereby reducing incidents of driving under the influence of alcohol and other deleterious effects. Price, either monetary or nonmonetary, may be influenced by administrative agencies and may thereby affect alcohol consumption. Revenue is raised by taxing alcohol at the consumption, distribution, and manufacturing levels, as well as through licensing fees and, in some states, by operating off-site sales outlets as a public monopoly.

Aside from the potential public health benefits of alcohol regulation, some have argued that restrictions on entry and business practices ensure the orderly marketing and stability of the alcohol industry. Since national prohibition, such regulation has focused on the distribution of alcohol at both the retail and wholesale levels rather than on production. The need for order and stability are classic arguments of proponents of entry regulation and are not unique to this sector (Breyer 1982).

Both state and federal governments raise revenue by taxing alcoholic beverages. In 1994 the federal government raised $8 billion (1996 dollars) by taxing the alcohol industry. In the same year state and local governments received $4.1 billion (1996 dollars) in revenue from alcoholic beverages through taxation and state-operated liquor store revenue (U.S. Bureau of the Census 1997). There was an appreciable range in state dependence on tax revenue. In sixteen states, public enterprises control liquor sales at the wholesale or the retail level (or both), as opposed to a system of licensing only independent private businesses that sell alcoholic beverages. Profits from these public enterprises accrue to state and local governments.

CHAPTER OVERVIEW

This chapter describes the administrative regulation of sellers of alcoholic beverages and discusses its role both in curbing excessive alcohol use and in determining the performance of retail sellers. It addresses four sets of pertinent issues. First, how has administrative regulation in this sector evolved throughout the history of the United States? Public concern with problems and consequences of alcohol use predate the founding of the country. Our account thus begins with the history of alcohol regulation, both before and after the brief period of national prohibition. We then describe the current structure of regulation of alcohol sales in the United States.

Alcohol regulation is widespread throughout the world. However, although the theoretical issues discussed below are broadly applicable, there are important institutional differences in how this is done. For example, in the United Kingdom brewers own bars (Slade 1998). In the United States such vertical integration is very rare.

The impetus of alcohol regulation over the years has been to reduce the social costs of heavy drinking. In recent years opposition to public regulation has grown, perhaps in small part owing to the writings of influential scholars who view regulation as subject to capture by the regulated industry. Therefore as a second focus we review these theories of regulation, asking several questions: What do the states regulate? What is the scope of such regulation, and how does this vary among states? Which organizations are charged with enforcement? Unlike other sectors, such as transportation and communications, there has been no impetus to deregulate commercial sales of alcohol. In fact there is remarkable stability of regulation in this sector.

Third, we assess how well administrative rules are actually enforced. What penalties are imposed formally by statute or regulation? In practice, which of these penalties are enforced? What resources are spent on enforcement? Our Survey of State Alcoholic Beverage Commissions and our Survey of Commercial Servers provide information on how administrative regulation works in practice.

The Survey of State Alcoholic Beverage Commissions (ABC Survey) was conducted in 1996 by our staff at Duke University by mail, telephone, and fax. We obtained responses from state alcoholic beverage commissions (ABCs) or their equivalent in forty-three states dealing with enforcement and the licensing process.

The Survey of Commercial Servers, conducted from September 1996 until February 1997, surveyed owners, managers, and employees of 778 bars and restaurants throughout the United States about their alcohol serving practices, liability claims, insurance, and alcohol policy enforcement. The sample was drawn from the *American Yellow Pages,* 1996 edition. A random sample of establishments listed as standard industrial classification (SIC) code 5813 was selected. This classification includes establishments labeled as bars, beer gardens, beer parlors, beer taverns, bottle clubs, cabarets, cocktail lounges, discotheques, nightclubs, saloons, taverns, and wine bars (U.S. Executive Office of the President 1987).

The survey was conduced by Mathematica Policy Research (MPR) from its Princeton, New Jersey, office. The survey inquired about practices in bars aimed at preventing alcohol abuse and its effects, perceptions of being sued or cited for various bad practices related to alcohol service, promotions and pricing practices, competition the bar faced, and various characteristics of the establishment. At the end of the survey of bar owners or managers, the respondents were asked for the names of bartenders and wait staff. MPR then randomly selected bartenders and wait staff for interviews. We discuss the Survey of Employees in greater detail in chapter 8. Area variables, including state laws, were merged with the data from individual bars. More details concerning these surveys are supplied in the appendix.

Fourth, judging from what can be observed about administrative regulation, is such regulation likely to be effective? There are both benefits and costs of any regulation. In this context, the potential benefits are largely weighed in terms of mitigating the social costs of excessive alcohol consumption and the costs of reducing consumption by groups not able to make an informed decision, particularly minors.

Restricting availability and curbing certain business practices, however, confers market power on sellers. This is a major cost of such regulation. Some types of regulation are ineffective; in such cases both benefits and costs may be minimal.

This chapter's discussion of benefits versus costs of regulation of the retail sector of the alcohol industry includes both a literature review and some original research. The literature deals with the few studies that report research on the effectiveness of such regulation. We present new results on how regulation affects market entry of sellers of alcoholic beverages. Using information from our Survey of Commercial Servers, we report how regulation has affected their business practices and their perceptions of the probability of being cited by regulatory agencies for serving obviously intoxicated patrons and minors. Our evaluation of the effects of regulation on servers' behavior is one of the subjects addressed in chapters 7 and 8.

EVOLUTION OF ALCOHOLIC BEVERAGE CONTROL REGULATION
Three Phases

Administrative regulation of alcoholic beverage sales in the United States dates back to before the founding of the republic and can be conveniently divided into three phases (Cooprider 1940). Before national prohibition, responsibility for liquor control was generally left to local officials. During Prohibition, federal law prohibited sales of alcoholic beverages; since its repeal, the tendency has been to follow a middle course and centralize control at the state level, with varying participation by local public authorities. Interstate differences in administrative law that evolved in the 1930s, with some exceptions, have been largely maintained through the 1990s.

Regulation before National Prohibition

For two hundred years after the founding of Jamestown, Virginia, in 1607, there were few organized attempts to restrict the normal use of alcoholic beverages (Krout 1925). Most government attempts concentrated on preventing the use of alcohol by Native Americans and those likely to organize against the ruling government (Cherrington 1920). In 1681 Louis XIV of France issued a decree prohibiting the sale of intoxicating liquors in New France, which included Michigan, Illinois, Indiana, and Ohio (Douglass 1931). From 1680 to 1685, Native American chiefs of the tribes of Delaware appealed to the Pennsylvania government to prohibit the sale of intoxicating beverages. In Georgia, founder James Oglethorpe directed futile efforts to bring attention to the destructive nature of liquor in his colony, which had a high criminal population (Krout 1925). After the adoption of the Constitution, Alexander Hamilton recommended a high tax on distilled liquors as a means of raising revenue, but this measure was not adopted (Douglass 1931).

Regulation of Alcohol by Communities

On the local level, colonists regulated alcohol to outlaw drunkenness, not to reform social customs (Cherrington 1920). Tavern restrictions closely resembled English methods of alcohol regulation. The goals were to prevent personal excess and public disorder; to protect against Native Americans, especially those under the influence of alcohol; to provide adequate accommodations for travelers in taverns without subjecting them to drunkenness and disorder; to recognize the importance of the brewing and distilling industries for the economy; and to raise revenue by taxing liquor (Krout 1925).

State and local governments felt responsibility toward the drunkard, who was viewed as lacking self-control (Thomann 1887). Strict rules were enacted that governed the behavior of the tavern owner and the patron. Early laws forbade selling or giving wine or distilled spirits to Native Americans, but beer and malt liquors usually escaped the ban. The restrictions were gradually withdrawn to enhance fur traders' profits and increase the availability of land, but they were readopted in the late 1800s as a method of social control over Native Americans (Cherrington 1920).

To encourage prospective innkeepers, the state governments granted a special license conferring a monopoly on the sale of liquor in the licensee's district (Thomann 1887). The authority to license was assumed early by the state legislatures, which delegated the power as they saw fit, usually granting the right of selection to the governor, the county court, or the town board of selectmen (Krout 1925). As population in the colonies grew, it became harder for the governor to select licensees, so they were chosen by the county courts. Colonial justices were not granted full discretionary powers in making selections as were their British counterparts. Statutory mandates required a certificate of good behavior. Licenses issued at this time were not used to raise revenue, so a small clerical fee was the only charge. As trade became more profitable and the establishments more numerous, fees rose. The state legislatures set no limit on the number of taverns.

Colonial statutes imposed strict, specific restrictions on the granting of licenses (Cherrington 1920) that reduced judges' discretionary powers (Krout 1925). Statutes determined the quantity of liquor to be sold at one time, the character of the amusements offered in taverns, and the prices tavern owners could charge for entertainment. The hosts could not serve liquor after 9:00 P.M. or serve drunk patrons. Gambling was not permitted, and no alcohol could be sold on Sundays. Price fixing began as early as 1634 in Massachusetts and was intended to prevent the exorbitant prices that could result from placing a monopoly in the hands of a few sellers.

Later the chief purpose of the license system became generating revenue (Krout 1925). This revenue helped finance a wide range of local services, the largest being defending the frontier and maintaining the military establishment. By 1700 the courts began to grant licenses more liberally. Women began to receive licenses as widows were granted permission to run their husbands' businesses so they would not be dependent on the community.

Role of Religion

The interaction between religion and alcohol also played a key role in the evolution of Prohibition (Cherrington 1920). In 1753 the Methodist Church enacted recommendations of discipline for members who drank. In 1787 the Quakers enacted a resolution that all members refrain from dealing in spirituous liquors. In 1812, at a Presbyterian convention in Philadelphia, members agreed to restrict the use of intoxicating beverages. In 1828 the Methodist General Conference advised members to abandon the sale and manufacture of liquor. The Congregational Church and the Baptist Church also came out with proclamations that drinking alcohol was inconsistent with Christianity. The short-lived Catholic prohibition movement began in the 1840s.

Role of Influential Community Members

By the beginning of the nineteenth century, Americans had grown increasingly concerned with moral standards. Societies aimed at reforming morals began to emerge. Prominent men took it upon themselves to publicly set a standard of moral conduct that all others should follow. In 1789 a group of prominent businessmen in Connecticut pledged to abstain from alcohol (Krout 1925), followed in 1800 by a group of wealthy Virginia farmers. In 1808 the first temperance society was founded in Saratoga County, New York, by a group of wealthy businessmen (Douglass 1931).

In 1813 the first antialcohol society composed of men in high social standing and associated with the Federalist Party, which advocated state power, started in the Mid-Atlantic region and in New England (Krout 1925). The movement later spread to the South and Midwest, although in smaller numbers (Douglass 1931). The antialcohol movement was also encouraged by the increase in crime and poverty after the War of 1812. Many of those in prisons, poorhouses, and workhouses were considered habitual drunkards, and the increase was attributed to the rise in consumption of distilled spirits, which were widely available to those of all income levels. Nearly every town with over a thousand people had its own gin or rum distillery.

Early Political Support for Prohibition

State legislatures began thinking about prohibition in the 1830s. In 1837 Maine became the first state to enact prohibition, under the leadership of Neil Dow (Douglass 1931). This law was later repealed, but from 1851 onward Maine continuously banned alcohol until national prohibition was enacted (table 2.1). Fifteen of forty-eight states never adopted state prohibition. Alaska and Hawaii are excluded from table 2.1 because they became states after national prohibition.

During the mid-1800s the American Temperance Society, a prohibitionist group, grew in influence. Its goals were self-improvement, correcting conduct, and elevating moral standards by intellectual appeals

Table 2.1 State Prohibition: Year of Adoption

Adopting States				Nonadopting States
Maine	1851	Idaho	1915	California
Kansas	1880	South Carolina	1915	Connecticut
North Dakota	1889	Montana	1916	Delaware
Georgia	1907	South Dakota	1916	Illinois
Oklahoma	1907	Michigan	1916	Louisiana
Mississippi	1908	Nebraska	1916	Maryland
North Carolina	1908	Indiana	1917	Massachusetts
Tennessee	1909	Utah	1917	Minnesota
West Virginia	1912	New Hampshire	1917	Missouri
Virginia	1914	New Mexico	1917	New Jersey
Oregon	1914	Texas	1918	New York
Washington	1914	Ohio	1918	Pennsylvania
Colorado	1914	Wyoming	1918	Rhode Island
Arizona	1914	Florida	1918	Vermont
Alabama	1915	Nevada	1918	Wisconsin
Arkansas	1915	Kentucky	1919	
Iowa	1915			

Source: Our analysis of state statutes. Only those states that retained prohibition through implementation of national prohibition are included as adopting states.

(Cherrington 1920). The society was also associated with the antislavery movement. Through the efforts of the American Temperance Society and the Congregational Church, in 1828 there were 1,000 temperance societies with 100,000 members; in 1831 there were 2,200 societies with 170,000 members; and in 1832, 4,000 societies with 500,000 members. Membership in the New England states accounted for one-third of the societies and one-third of the total membership. South of the Mason-Dixon Line and the Ohio River, the societies had only 15,000 total members. Temperance also became a popular intellectual movement in the 1830s. Colleges such as Amherst, Dartmouth, Brown, Middlebury, Yale, Union, Kenyon, and Oberlin all had temperance organizations.

These early antialcohol movements were effective, and by 1855 thirteen states were dry. The first wave toward national prohibition was short-lived, however, with the interruption of the Civil War. Membership in temperance groups declined, and most of the dry states repealed their antialcohol laws. By 1903 only Maine, Kansas, and North Dakota remained dry.

The Women's Suffrage Movement

About 1910 the debate on temperance reemerged as part of a movement toward greater public decency and as a platform for women's groups that were lobbying for the right to vote (Dorr 1929). As part of this movement, nine states became dry again. This new movement was led by three groups: the National Prohibition Party, founded in 1869; the Women's Christian Temperance Union, founded in 1874; and the Anti-Saloon League, founded in 1893. Membership in these associations declined during Prohibition, after women obtained the right to vote in 1920 (Douglass 1931).

Unlike the other two groups, the Anti-Saloon League, which was supported by the Protestant churches in action against the saloon, did not field its own candidates for political office. Rather, it put resources behind existing candidates who opposed alcohol. The league recognized that residents in rural areas were suspicious of rampant immigration and the millions of Catholics coming from eastern and southern Europe. Protestant America worked hard to protect its values through legislation, even if the values were more wishful thinking than reality. These temperance groups wielded great influence over state legislatures, as thirty states enacted prohibition from 1907 through 1919.

National Prohibition

When World War I began in 1914, America was officially neutral, although Americans quickly became anti-German in 1915 with the sinking of the

British passenger ship *Lusitania* by a German torpedo (Van Munching 1997). In 1917 President Wilson asked Congress to declare war. Included in the war bill that Congress enacted was the Food Control Act, supposedly to save grain for the war effort. The act killed the production of beer, wine, and liquor because it forbade using foods to manufacture alcohol. Additionally, the bill granted Wilson the power to limit the alcoholic content of beer. With the assistance of the Anti-Saloon League, in January 1919 Congress ratified the Sheppard Resolution, which proposed national prohibition. The resolution gained quick approval in the state legislatures, and the amendment was ratified by forty-six out of forty-eight states. Rhode Island and Connecticut did not ratify the Eighteenth Amendment. In January 1920 the manufacture, sale, or transportation of intoxicating liquors within, the importation thereof into, or the exportation thereof from the United States and all territory subject to the jurisdiction thereof for beverage purposes was prohibited.

The year-long period between the adoption of the Sheppard Resolution and the implementation of national prohibition gave some liquor manufacturers the opportunity to retool their plants for other uses, such as producing industrial alcohol or soft drinks, and other plants shut down (Fisher 1928). Prohibition, however, enabled organized crime to flourish as ethnic gangs in large cities developed into structured companies built around importing and manufacturing liquor. Owing to widespread demand for alcoholic beverages among citizens, enforcing national prohibition proved impossible. Americans paid highly inflated prices to obtain alcohol because, as expected, Prohibition drove up the cost. In 1916–26 the standard of living rose by less than one-fifth, while the price of alcohol increased three- to sevenfold. The stock market crash of 1929 and high unemployment further emphasized the negative effects of putting brewery workers on the streets.

Pierre du Pont, chairman of the Executive Committee against the Prohibition Amendment, banned drinking at his plant but found it acceptable for his workers to drink after working hours (Fisher 1928). But auto manufacturers thought differently; they felt threatened by the potential danger presented by drinking and driving. Officials of Reo Motor Car Company believed the return of public drinking places would make automobiles a menace on the highways and would depress the sale of the cheaper cars, since the money would be spent at the bar. Alfred P. Slozinak, president of General Motors during Prohibition, supported the idea that prohibition increased national efficiency and thereby improved the individual's purchasing power. W. C. Durant, president of Durant Motors, offered $25,000 to anyone who could develop a plan for making the Eighteenth Amendment effective and criticized businessmen for supporting bootleggers. Ultimately, the automobile industry viewed the saloon as a direct competitor. During Prohibition and perhaps partly as a consequence of it, several industries grew, including automobiles, movies, and radio.

Prohibition Case Law

Several cases concerning Prohibition were brought before the United States Supreme Court. These cases mainly concentrated on the constitutionality of regulating prohibition at the federal level. The Court in general was very supportive of Prohibition and upheld its constitutionality. In *Samuel v. McCurdy*, 267 U.S. 188, 197 (1925), the Court stated that the ultimate legislative object of prohibition is to prevent anyone from drinking intoxicating liquor because of the demoralizing effect of drunkenness upon society.

The Court held that the state has the power to deprive of access to liquor even those members of society who might indulge in its use without injury to themselves in order to remove temptation from those whom its use would demoralize and to avoid the abuses that follow. In *Ducan Townsitle Co. vs. Lane*, 245 U.S. 307 (1917), the Court condemned liquors, finding that

> it must now be regarded as settled that, on account of their well-known noxious qualities and the extraordinary evils shown by experience commonly to be consequent upon their use, a State has power absolutely to prohibit manufacture, gift, purchase, sale or transportation of intoxicating liquors within its borders without violating the guarantee of the 14th Amendment. And considering the notorious difficulties always attendant upon efforts to suppress traffic in liquors, we are unable to say that the challenged inhibition of their possession was arbitrary and unreasonable or without proper relations to the legitimate legislative purpose.

Prohibition Backlash

In the 1920s the backlash against Prohibition grew as the ineffectiveness of the ban on alcohol became apparent. In 1922 Andrew Volstead, who had written the Eighteenth Amendment, was defeated in his bid for reelection to the House of Representatives. Repealing Prohibition became a crucial part of the Democratic platform on which Franklin D. Roosevelt was elected in 1932. Even before he could be sworn in, Congress proposed the Twenty-first Amendment to the states, calling for repeal. The amendment was ratified within a month, and in December 1933 national prohibition was officially voided.

The repeal of the Eighteenth Amendment was aided by the passage of the Nineteenth Amendment, which gave women the right to vote. The link between women's rights and prohibition was dissolved, and those who supported Prohibition lost a large organizing principle. Additionally, the Great Depression and the New Deal legislation made the federal government desperate for new revenue, and taxing liquor became an attractive source.

Post-Prohibition Regulation

Repeal of Prohibition returned liquor control to the states, which began to formulate individual systems of control over the liquor industry.

Rockefeller Commission Report

In 1933 John D. Rockefeller Jr. commissioned a privately funded study of the liquor problem aimed at developing guiding principles for the states. The published study, *Toward Liquor Control,* appeared in October 1933.

The study recommended a state monopoly over retail sale for off-premises consumption of distilled spirits and of wine and beer with more than 3.2 percent alcohol content (Fosdick and Scott 1933). An alternative system, the private-license system, was recommended for states unwilling to create a state liquor monopoly. This system would establish a state licensing board to replace the local authorities that had issued liquor licenses before Prohibition. Under both systems, state authorities were to exert power over a wide range of matters including prices, advertising, design of outlets, and time of sales. The Rockefeller program sought to bring under state control the liquor industry and mass drinking that was uncontrolled during Prohibition.

The alcohol industry supported the Rockefeller program because it promised a stable legal framework for the sale of their products. Consequently producers offered no opposition as the states proceeded to construct alcohol-control systems along the lines laid down by the Rockefeller Commission. By 1936 fifteen states had created state monopolies for the sale of distilled liquors and issued licenses through a state agency for outlets selling lighter liquors. Except for a handful that retained state prohibition, the states adopted license systems, all centralizing control at the state level, although some allowed a local option on what types of licenses should be issued. The number of prohibition states declined, with Kansas repealing prohibition in 1948, Oklahoma in 1957, and Mississippi in 1966.

Rockefeller proposed state-level monopoly control not to discourage public drinking but to control rowdy and dangerous behavior (Fosdick and

Scott 1933). Consequently, arrests for public drunkenness and disorderly conduct continued to decline. Placing responsibility for alcohol control at the state level effectively removed the alcohol issue from the political sphere. Federal and state governments levied special taxes on liquor.

The Rockefeller report noted four weaknesses of public licensing of private sellers (Fosdick and Scott 1933). Although some of these arguments may seem foolish with the hindsight of more than six decades, the reasoning is informative and may explain why some states adopted public monopolies. First, in the authors' view, the primary weakness was in preserving the private profit motive. "A greedy liquor traffic looking only for larger profits will circumvent and evade any system of license defenses which ingenuity can erect" (57). Second, a licensing system is open to political interference. Third, licensing is inconsistent with temperance education. Venders want to stimulate demand, not curb it. Fourth, allowing private sellers encourages investment in alcoholic beverage businesses. These entrepreneurs in turn develop a vested commercial interest in private sales, so they may be expected to oppose any public restriction on alcohol use.

In advocating a state monopoly system, the Rockefeller Commission report stated:

> Under a state monopoly system the liquor would be sold directly by the state through a chain of stores and the profits turned into the state treasury, and that would be the end of it. No individual connected with the retail sales would gain one penny by reason of his sales. . . .In harmony with the underlying principle of the Authority, the salaried employees waiting on the customers in the various stores would be under strict supervision not only to see that there was no encouragement of the sale of liquor, but to make sure that no beverages were sold in violation of the letter *and the spirit* of the law. (Fosdick and Scott 1933, 29; emphasis in the original)

Patterns of State Regulation

In adopting the framework of the Rockefeller Commission's recommendations, each state enacted a unique combination of regulatory policies for the alcoholic beverage industry. State legislatures granted broad discretion to state administrative agencies to ensure the goals of regulation. For the first time, proprietary action in the form of state liquor monopolies developed on a broad scale nationwide.

Shipman (1940, 601) noted that "in retrospect, it seemed that the main share of trouble caused by the sale of alcoholic liquors was occasioned by the public drinking place, an institution which was as much a local social center of dubious character as a dispensary of intoxicating beverages. The firm resolve that the saloon should not return takes concrete legislative form in the separation of 'package' from 'on-premises' sale. 'On-premises' sale is further limited in a number of states to bona fide restaurants and hotels."

Shipman identified three categories of states, each with a different policy emphasis. The first focused on revenue raising. Of the twenty-eight states with licensing systems, twelve fell into this category. Control was placed in the existing state agency for tax administration. States maintained enforcement of law against licensees, but suppressing illegal sales was made a responsibility of local police. Selection of licensees was also often decided locally.

In the second category were states that primarily emphasized control of alcoholic beverage sales. In such cases particular importance was placed on granting licenses, supervising licensees, investigating complaints, holding formal hearings and appeals, and revoking or suspending licenses. Taxes were sometimes collected entirely by another state department.

The third category consisted of the sixteen monopoly states that operated public retail off-site enterprises (liquor stores) and also licensed on-site sellers as well as other firms in the industry, such as those involved in manufacturing and transport. In addition, one state (Wyoming) operated a monopoly for wholesale outlets and another (Delaware) was authorized to operate either a monopoly or a licensing system (Shipman 1940). Some states were authorized to manufacture alcoholic beverages.

In some monopoly states, the state-run liquor stores had to purchase their stock through the monopoly. Others prohibited on-site consumption altogether. Two states, Washington and Iowa, restricted purchasers at state stores by requiring state permits to purchase alcohol (Shipman 1940).

Advocates of a monopoly system cited existing examples of monopolies, including several Canadian provinces and Sweden, and expressed deep reluctance to see the liquor business returned to private hands. Several monopoly states either were close to the Canadian border (Michigan, Ohio, Vermont, New Hampshire, and Washington) or had been dry before national prohibition, with the repeal of Prohibition winning by only small margins (Virginia, West Virginia, North Carolina, and Alabama). As one participant at the symposium on alcohol regulation held at Duke University in 1940 noted, however, these factors may have been coincidental (Shipman 1940).

Public monopoly is not without its shortcomings. A public sector monopoly may be subject to some of the same deficiencies attributed to private sellers of alcohol. As concerns the primary reason against licensing, in a public monopoly one substitutes profiteering by a public monopoly for profiteering by private competitors. Public agencies may also learn to depend on profits from sales. Second, in practice public monopoly extends only to off-site commercial servers. On-site servers—that is, bars—remain private. On-site commercial servers may benefit from public monopoly of off-site sales, since consumers plausibly view liquor stores and bars as substitutes for each other. If alcohol in stores becomes higher priced or inaccessible, drinkers can turn to bars as an alternative source of supply. Therefore bars have an incentive to lobby for protection from liquor store competition in the form of entry barriers, the type of political activity the Rockefeller report criticized.

Structure of Alcoholic Beverage Control Regulation in the Late 1990s
Scope of Regulatory Activity

There are thousands of licensed premises in the United States that legally sell alcoholic beverages in their communities. Licenses issued are of two kinds: on-site and off-site. On-site licenses are for establishments selling liquor by the drink to be consumed there, whereas off-site licenses are issued to those selling it for consumption off the premises. Administrative penalties for illegal alcohol service may be more effective than criminal penalties. Administrative penalties typically punish the firm rather than an individual server, such as by suspending a liquor license or imposing a fine. Criminal penalties restrict individual freedoms through personal fines and jail sentences and therefore require a higher burden of proof, which in turn may entail higher enforcement costs.

As of the late 1990s, state governments regulated off-premises sales by two methods: state control and licensing of private businesses (table 2.2). Sixteen states operated retail sales under state control, where bottled, distilled liquor is sold in state-owned stores. Eleven of these control states also permitted the sale of bottled distilled liquor in privately owned state-licensed stores. In all the control states, the state liquor authority is in the business of wholesaling or retailing alcoholic beverages, holding a monopoly on all or some of them. Thirty-four states and the District of Columbia used license control, where distilled spirits were sold in state-licensed, privately owned stores. Both systems restricted the number of retail and wholesale outlets and their hours of business, regulated franchising, established minimum drinking ages, and restricted advertising of alcoholic

Table 2.2 Control States

Distilled Spirits Sold by ABC Stores Only	Distilled Spirits Sold by ABC Stores and Licensed Stores
Alabama	Iowa
Idaho	Maine
North Carolina	Michigan
Oregon	Montana
Virginia	New Hampshire
	Ohio
	Pennsylvania
	Utah
	Vermont
	Washington
	West Virgina

Note: ABC = alcoholic beverage commission.

beverages. In control states, licenses were issued for privately owned establishments that sell by the drink. In license states, licenses were issued for both on-site and off-site consumption. Based on a review of state statutes, twenty-four states limited the number of off-site and on-site licenses issued.

Three-quarters of the administrative agencies responsible for alcohol licenses were independent departments not connected with another government agency. Licensing was typically carried out by a commission, board, or agency headed by a director who was a political appointee. Licensing agencies also have the power to investigate licensees' citizenship, residence, age, character, reputation, financial stability, and sobriety.

Enforcement

States varied substantially in enforcement of alcohol control regulations. They employed five different methods: alcoholic beverage commission (ABC) agents; local police departments only; special state investigators; state police; and department of revenue agents. Additionally, in all states local police were always authorized to issue citations for illegal alcohol sales. In our review of the state statutes, we found very little change in enforcement methods since the repeal of Prohibition (Mosher 1988).

The most common approach states adopted was direct enforcement of alcohol regulations by ABC agents, especially in private-license states (table 2.3). In these states the ABCs employed their own law enforcement agents, referred to as alcohol law enforcement (ALE). These agents represented the most coordinated approach to alcohol control. The second most frequent approach was using local police departments as the sole enforcers, although some states used additional mechanisms. This approach is advantageous in that local police are always involved in alcohol control to some extent, but it does not provide the same level of coordination with the state ABC as the first approach.

Special state investigators were used only in states with public liquor stores. In these states investigators were appointed to monitor alcohol practices in on-site establishments. The number of investigators varied with state population. In nine states there was a special alcohol enforcement unit within the state police department dedicated to monitoring alcohol regulation. In this approach, state and local police cooperated. Finally, enforcement by the state department of revenue was the least common approach. In these states, obtaining tax revenue was presumably the most important motive for administrative regulation of alcohol sellers. Nevada

Table 2.3 Relation of Alcohol Enforcement to State Alcoholic Beverage Commission, 1998

Local Police Department Only	Department of Revenue	State Police	ABC Enforcement	Special State Investigators
		Control States		
Michigan	Wyoming	Idaho	Alabama	Montana
Oregon		Maine	Ohio	New Hampshire
		Pennsylvania	Vermont	North Carolina
			Virginia	Utah
				Washington
				West Virginia
		Private License States		
Colorado	Louisiana	Alaska	Arizona	
District of Columbia	Maryland	Iowa	Arkansas	
Hawaii	Nevada	Minnesota	California	
Illinois	South Dakota	New Jersey	Connecticut	
Massachusetts		New Mexico	Delaware	
North Dakota			Florida	
Rhode Island			Georgia	
Wisconsin			Indiana	
			Kansas	
			Kentucky	
			Mississippi	
			Missouri	
			Nebraska	
			New York	
			Oklahoma	
			South Carolina	
			Tennessee	
			Texas	

Source: Our analysis of state statutes.

and Louisiana recently adopted enforcement by the department of revenue. This approach falls under the revenue-raising category defined by Shipman in 1940, again attesting to the stability of these arrangements.

Individual state statutes specified administrative penalties for violating an ABC law and defined the formal relations between state and local law enforcement units and state and local ABC units, methods of financing administrative control, the types of establishments regulated, and the kinds of permits issued. Of course a review of the statutes themselves provides no information on how agencies operate in practice, including levels of funding, the extent of the relationship with law enforcement authorities, the number of licenses suspended and revoked, or information the agencies supply to liability insurers about establishments in their jurisdictions.

States employed various investigative strategies to uncover violations by sellers. Among these are decoy programs and passive observation by undercover agents, used to detect selling to minors and serving intoxicated persons. Given budgetary limitations affecting the numbers of investigators on agency staffs, decoys were often deployed only after a complaint. The length of time that owners' licenses may be suspended or revoked for serving alcohol to intoxicated persons varied among states (see U.S. Department of Transportation, various years).

Regulatory Activities and Policies of State Alcoholic Beverage Commissions

Very little has been published on regulatory activities of state ABCs. To learn more about their scope, we surveyed state ABCs in 1996. One topic covered by the survey was state licensing practices. Only twenty-seven states provided data on the percentage of applications they had rejected in the previous year. Of those that responded, the mean rejection rate of those who applied for licenses was only 3.9 percent (table 2.4). It is possible, of course, that some potential licensees who thought they would be rejected never applied.

Rejecting Applications

The top three reasons for rejecting applications were criminal background or convictions, bad location (e.g., too close to a church or school or in a high crime area), or a mistake in filling out or filing the application (box 2.1).

Zoning

States often grant liquor licenses in conjunction with local alcohol control boards, which enforce local zoning ordinances. Over 90 percent of states responding to our Survey of Alcoholic Beverage Commissions (see the ap-

Table 2.4 Licensing Practices

Practice	Percentage
Applications rejected (27 states)	3.9
Local ordinances restricting location of bars (41 states)	90.2
Some counties forbidding commercial establishments (42 states)	52.4
Share information concerning server licensee violations with local police (42 states)	52.4
Regulations requiring sharing of information about violations with insurers (42 states)	33.3
Regulations requiring server training (42 states)	26.2

Source: 1996 Survey of Alcoholic Beverage Commissions.

Note: Standard deviations for all percentages given may be calculated using the following formula:

$$S = \sqrt{\frac{1}{n-1} \sum_{i=1}^{n} (X_i - \overline{X})^2}$$

Box 2.1 Main reasons for the alcoholic beverage commission's rejection of applications.

Criminal background and convictions 19	Unsuitability of location 2
Too close to church/school 7	Prior revocation or suspension on record 2
Did not meet residency requirements 6	Did not qualify 2
Did not file application properly 4	Creation of law enforcement problem 1
Unsuitability of person/reputation 4	Concentration of bars in area too high 1
Misrepresentation of an essential fact 3	Department of Motor Vehicles record 1
Nonpayment of sales taxes 3	Nonprofit entity 1
Evidence of hidden ownership 3	Proximity to residential property 1
Proposed location in a high crime area 3	Failure to take server education test 1
Financial instability 3	Blocking other applicants 1
Unfavorable police or local references 3	Interference with neighborhood 1
Noncompliance with state liquor laws 3	Did not meet club license requirements 1
Bar not in approved location 2	No openings in government quota 1
Municipal denial 2	

Source: 1996 ABC Survey. Numbers are numbers of responses.

pendix) reported that local communities restricted the location of drinking establishments through zoning (see table 2.4). Of the forty-two states responding, twenty-two had "dry" counties, where the sale of alcohol is prohibited. About half regularly shared information about server violations with local police. Fewer required sharing information on violations with insurers. Only about a quarter of boards required server training as a condition of maintaining a license.

Coordination with Other Law Enforcement Agencies

As we noted above, state agencies often work in conjunction with state and local law enforcement personnel to enforce the ABC code. Eighty percent of agencies used undercover agents in their investigations (table 2.5).

Of the complaints investigated by agencies in the seventeen states reporting the information, about 45 percent led to some type of action by the ABC. About half of the reporting agencies followed up on drinking and driving violations to determine if the bar was partly at fault. Slightly more followed up on alcohol-related accidents. Over 60 percent followed up on fights in bars. The agencies followed up most often in the case of illegal alcohol consumption in unlicensed bars and other illegal trade practices such as selling alcohol without paying the required taxes. One interpretation of this behavior is that the state helps to enforce a seller's cartel. Of the twenty-three states that provided this information, ABCs on average issued 0.2 citations annually to each on-site establishment.

The agencies also reported investigating the serving of minors and intoxicated adults, as well as other license violations (box 2.2). The main violations resulting in citation were inadequate checking of patrons' identification, serving intoxicated adults, violation of hours of operation, and entertainment violations.

License Suspensions or Revocations

A liquor license operates as permission to lawfully distribute alcoholic beverages. This privilege can be suspended or revoked for a violation of

Table 2.5 Investigative Practices

Percentage using undercover agents (40 states)	80.0
Percentage of complaints that led to action (17 states)	44.9
Percentage of agencies that follow up on DUI violations to see if establishment selling alcohol was at fault (40 states)	52.5
Percentage of agencies that follow up on accidents caused by intoxicated drivers to see if establishment selling alcohol was at fault (40 states)	55.0
Percentage of agencies that follow up on fights in bars (40 states)	62.5
Percentage of agencies that follow up on other forms of illegal alcohol consumption or trade (40 states)	92.5
Number of citations per on-site commercial establishment (23 states)	0.20

Source: 1996 Survey of Alcoholic Beverage Commissions.

Box 2.2 Main types of conduct investigated by the alcoholic beverage commission.

Illegal transporting or shipping of		Regulation of mail order services	2	
alcohol 15		Criminal violations in licensed places		2
Serving minors 10		Employee consumption 2		
Illegal retail of liquor 9		Drug activity 2		
Service to visibly intoxicated persons 7		Illegal parties 2		
Illegal sale 7		Reports of dancers or lewd		
After-hour operations 5		entertainment 2		
Gambling 5		Illegal advertising 1		
Operating without a license 5		Selling stolen alcohol 1		
Failure to tax 4		All alcohol-related criminal violations		1
Disorderly, noisy, or lewd conduct 4		Public consumption 1		
Importation of alcohol to dry		Motorcycle gangs present 1		
counties 4		History of serious or persistent		
Violation of food qualification		problems 1		
requirement 4		Prostitution 1		
Administrative violations in licensed		Failure to meet minimum purchase		
places 2		requirements for in-state-vendors		1
Making or selling of moonshine 2				
Questionable ownership 2				

Source: 1996 ABC Survey. Numbers are numbers of responses.

the alcoholic beverage code. This action would be carried out in an administrative hearing, where the licensee would have an opportunity to argue against a penalty. There are generally three penalties that may be imposed on a code violator: fines, license suspension, and license revocation. In a few states, jail time may be imposed. As discussed in other chapters, violating the ABC code may result not only in an administrative penalty but in criminal and civil penalties as well.

Of the on-site violations recognized by the agencies, 85.7 percent resulted in a conviction (table 2.6). The penalties for conviction varied, including suspending operations for one day to one year and fines ranging from $15 to $1,000 for first offenses.

On average, in 1994 the agencies suspended 1.2 percent of total commercial licenses. These suspensions lasted an average of 22.8 months; establishments could open again at the end of their suspensions. More severe or frequent violations could result in a temporary or permanent license revocation, canceling the right to sell liquor.

Establishments that were penalized through temporary revocation could reopen at the end of the revocation period but had to apply for a new

Table 2.6 Penalties

Percentage of violations leading to convictions (20 states)	85.7
Number of cases against commercial establishments for selling to minors per bar (21 states)	0.031
Number of license suspensions as percentage of on-site commercial establishments (25 states)	1.2
Average length of license suspension (23 states)	22.8 months
Number of licenses revoked as percentage of on-site commercial establishments (27)	0.31
Average length of temporary revocation (13 states)	17.2 months
Percentage of revocations that are permanent (21 states)	79.7

Source: 1996 ABC Survey.

liquor license. Agencies reported that 0.3 percent of commercial licenses were revoked in the year before the survey, with a mean length of temporary revocation of 17.2 months. Establishments could appeal a revocation; agencies reported that 79.7 percent of license revocations were permanent. Of the twenty-one states reporting this information, state ABCs brought 0.03 revocation cases per commercial establishment for selling alcohol to a minor.

BENEFITS AND COSTS OF ADMINISTRATIVE REGULATION OF SELLERS OF ALCOHOLIC BEVERAGES: CONCEPTS
Rationale for Administrative Regulation

Throughout United States history, much of the rationale for administrative regulation of sellers of alcoholic beverages has combined moral principle and public policy to reduce the social cost of heavy drinking. Additionally, state and local governments, like the federal government, raise revenue by taxing alcoholic beverages.

Regulation of private alcoholic beverage sellers takes several forms, including entry barriers and restriction of business practices such as hours of sale and advertising. Entry of alcohol sellers is limited for three reasons: to keep out the "bad apples" who might be more costly to police; to control seller location (e.g., maintain a distance from churches and schools); and to limit seller density. Imposing barriers to entry confers market power on sellers who are able to gain entry. With fewer sellers, resources devoted to public enforcement may be reduced. Finally, there is some empirical evidence that negative external effects, such as alcohol-related fatalities, rise with bar density (Jones-Webb et al. 1997; Kelleher et al. 1997; Scribner, MacKinnon, and Dwyer 1995; Gruenewald and Ponicki 1995; Giacopassi and Winn 1995; Snow and Landrum 1986; Bonnie 1985; and Rabow and Watts 1982).

The density effect may be explained in the following way. Clustering of retail establishments is common and may lower transaction costs to consumers. A consumer may be willing to travel to a mall with several clothing stores because of the variety of price and style combinations available there. Even though the stores are local competitors, they all benefit from the larger pool of customers. In a sense, a strip of bars is similar. Patrons can skip from one bar to another ("barhopping") to look for friends, sample the ambience, and take advantage of temporary price discounts. With several alternative destinations, it might pay to drive farther to reach the strip, but this choice generates negative externalities as patrons drive home after drinking.

Although regulation may offer some benefits, it also entails some costs. Since licensing restrictions give a degree of local monopoly to the holder of a particular form of license and the license is transferable, these monopoly rents will be capitalized in the market value of these enterprises.

Effective licensing regulation limits entry into the alcoholic beverage market. A licensing program that checks entry and restricts internal expansion and price competition may promote effective cartelization of the industry. Higher prices, restrictions on entry, and limitations on how sellers can compete—such as limits on hours of operation, advertising, and price competition, including prohibitions on "happy hours"—mean losses in consumer and producer welfare. These losses may be at least partly offset by welfare gains from reducing the negative externalities that come from heavy drinking. Most drinkers drink responsibly, and they are made worse off by paying higher prices per drink and having to drive farther to obtain alcohol as well as by other inconveniences. Added to this is the cost of operating a public agency with responsibility for administering and enforcing the alcohol control laws.

Administrative penalties for alcohol violations may be less burdensome than criminal penalties. First of all, no moral judgment is made in the case of an administrative violation. An establishment may be fined or have restrictions imposed on its alcohol license, but penalties are not imposed on an individual level as with criminal penalties. Accordingly, the burden of proof required for administrative violations is lower than for criminal violations. Because of the different standards of proof required, it is easier to go after an establishment's license than to seek criminal penalties against an individual server.

Public Interest Theory

One favorable view of alcohol regulation is public interest theory. According to this theory, regulation serves the public interest and is intended to enhance efficiency or reduce externalities. In this sector, one would argue that control statutes and taxation are needed to deal with externalities associated with drinking. Even if responsible drinkers are inconvenienced by less availability and higher taxes, the community as a whole is better off because some are discouraged from drinking (Beauchamp 1980).

Alternative Theories of Regulation: Markets for Regulatory Interventions and Regulatory Capture

A much less sanguine view, embodied in the interest group theory of regulation, suggests that however well intentioned the original rationale for regulating alcohol, eventually, if not initially, regulation falls under the control of the industry that government seeks to regulate (Stigler 1971; Peltzman 1976; Becker 1983). In his seminal article on regulation, George Stigler (1971) argued that regulation generally is acquired by the industry and is designed for its benefit.

The critics of regulating entry, pricing, and other practices of firms argue that in a pluralistic political system outcomes are determined by competition among alternative interests. In this context the ability to secure political control and reap the benefits is highly concentrated in commercial sellers of alcoholic beverages. In contrast to the citizenry in general, which has many interests and concerns (education, roads, public health, parks, etc.), only the sellers have the focused interest to lobby political officials. Unlike firms, consumers with an interest in a particular type of legislation are often dispersed and hence not well organized.

Political arguments can be couched in public-spirited language. Indeed, entry barriers may reduce consumption of alcoholic beverages, an issue to be discussed in greater detail below, but they also confer a de facto franchise on those sellers fortunate enough to have gained entry. Individual commercial servers of alcohol benefit financially from the controlled growth of new firms and for this reason may support government control. Every industry that has enough political power to utilize the state will seek to control entry. In essence, many interest groups compete for influence with the regulator, and how far regulation serves particular interest groups will depend on their relative influence. Groups that are more efficient at exerting political pressure are ultimately expected to receive a larger share of the economic rents allocated by the regulator.

The theory of economic interest groups posits that cohesive interest groups seeking legislation beneficial to themselves will be more politically effective in securing benefits for their members. But because each firm in the regulated industry shares in the benefit of the interest group's activity regardless of the amount invested in it, there is a potential free-rider problem. A firm that does not contribute to the special-interest group still can enjoy the fruits of its labor.

For this reason, industries that have low information and organization costs, making it easier to detect shirking by individual firms, and that have high stakes in the outcome should be more successful than consumer interest groups in obtaining regulation. The industry must be prepared to pay for regulation favorable to its interests, in the form of either votes or (perhaps more likely) resources (Stigler 1971). Aside from the industry constituents for regulation, another interest group is the bureaucracy administering the regulations. The bureaucracy has an interest in preserving and augmenting its power and therefore lobbies for legislation likely to expand its resources. Civil servants generally stand to gain by increasing the size and activity of the regulatory agency. The probability that beneficial policies for licensees will be implemented is higher in states without cohesive opposition to licensing; such opposition represents a political cost of supplying the legislation. As the strength of the group adverse to the legislation grows, enacting such legislation becomes more costly to politicians.

Public Health and Regulation

Legislative measures are likely to be represented, especially by the alcohol industry, as another example of government interference with private decisions of individuals (Beauchamp 1980). But in some cases, as with alcohol, poor decision making by individuals can have great costs to society in mortality, morbidity, and need for health care. Limiting consumption is the main way of regulating alcohol policy. In controlling alcohol consumption and related problems, however, society has available only limited and partially effective tools.

Does Interest Group or Regulatory Capture Theory Apply to the Alcoholic Beverage Cartel?

A major conceptual problem with the view that regulation serves the regulated is that it cannot explain some of the basic facts of alcoholic beverage control. In particular, the private sector could not plausibly have benefited from state or national prohibition. Such outright bans might have succeeded if the constituency supporting absolute bans on alcohol sales had been so strong as to raise to prohibitive levels the seller constituency's cost for opposing such legislation. Further, it is difficult to see how private liquor stores could benefit from the public monopoly, because such a monopoly precludes their entry. On the other hand, bars might benefit from a public liquor store monopoly in that monopoly leads to output restriction and hence greater demand for alcohol at bars. Citizen groups opposing alcohol consumption have been strong throughout the history of this country. In recent years Mothers against Drunk Driving (MADD) has become a major political force arguing for laws aimed at reducing excessive consumption leading to driving under the influence of alcohol. The success of MADD, as well as previous citizen antialcohol efforts, suggests that the cost of citizens' organizing around this focused issue must not be that high.

Some of the issues raised here about regulation of alcoholic beverage sales also apply to other sectors. For example, the tobacco industry has opposed excise taxes on its product. Price controls, unless accompanied by other restrictive practices such as government-run entry barriers, seem counter to the regulated industry's interests. As Peltzman (1993) noted, regulatory innovation occurs in cycles. At times there arise political pressures for controls that run counter to regulated industries. At other times there is stronger sentiment for laissez-faire or controls that favor the regulated industry.

Ultimately, whether the benefit outweighs the cost cannot be decided on theoretical grounds. The proof lies in the empirical evidence to be presented in this and later chapters.

EMPIRICAL EVIDENCE ON BENEFITS VERSUS COSTS OF ADMINISTRATIVE REGULATION: PREVIOUS STUDIES
Tests of Theories of Regulation

Administrative law may influence the amount of drinking by limiting the number of drinking establishments, by setting standards for management practices, and by establishing guidelines for ownership (Mosher 1984; Nelson 1990). ABC agencies are accountable for reviewing and approving liquor licenses and collecting taxes (Saltz 1993). However, resources often are not available to ABCs to promote prevention, such as responsible beverage service, or to enforce laws. In response to political pressures to do something about the social problem of drinking and driving, criminal statutes are often enacted to enforce administrative provisions (Saltz 1987).

A study of twenty-five ABC boards in California questioned the effectiveness of the licensing process (Rabow, Watts, and Hernandez 1993), finding that although ABC investigators were influenced by public protests, such objections did not overcome their propensity to license applicants. This study found high approval rates for all types of applications, particularly those without community protest. The authors concluded that the ABC was influenced greatly by the industry it is supposed to regulate, lending some credence to economic interest theory as a way to explain patterns of administrative regulation in this industry.

To our knowledge, Smith (1982) is the only article that has rigorously analyzed state regulation of liquor licenses based on the economic interest group theory described above. She argued that religious groups seeking restrictions for reasons other than private profit are natural allies of private establishments that have a vested interest in restricting the number of licenses to promote their own financial gain. Thus, when these groups are strong, states are likely to implement restrictive entry regulation and other government-imposed restrictive practices. However, a strong restaurant and tourist industry is a natural opponent of limiting licenses.

Smith estimated regressions for the probability of resale price maintenance, prohibitions against price advertising, other restrictions on advertising, bans on grocery stores' selling liquor, and limits on the number of liquor licenses set by the state regulatory authority. Explanatory variables were the percentage of a state's total number of packaged liquor retail stores located in cities with over 100,000 population; the percentage of a state's total church membership affiliated with Protestant churches; a binary variable that was one when administration of liquor control policy was vested in a government agency or board staffed with full-time members and zero if administration was vested in an independent board staffed with part-time commissioners paid a per diem fee; and annual payroll derived from hotels, motels, and tourist industries as a percentage of state personal income.

The variable for concentration of liquor stores was included to test the hypothesis that greater concentration of sellers reduces the transaction costs of organizing for self-interest. Also, several Protestant denominations have historically opposed or discouraged drinking on religious grounds. A higher percentage of Protestants in the state may lead to greater restrictions. Full-time regulators have a greater vested interest in lobbying for policies that expand their roles. For the reasons argued above, the tourist industry should impose restrictions, since difficulty in obtaining a liquor license makes it less profitable.

Smith's analysis was restricted to the thirty-four private-license states. With such a small sample, the study lacked statistical power. The variable for seller concentration generally had positive coefficients in her regression analysis, a result consistent with economic interest group theory, but only one coefficient was statistically significant at the 20 percent level or better. In contrast, the variable for Protestant church membership performed better. In the analysis of limits on the number of licenses, the coefficient was positive and statistically significant at the 5 percent level, implying that when this religious group is dominant, restriction is more common. In general, the variable for a full-time alcohol control board had a positive effect on restrictions, as the author anticipated, but it did not reach statistical significance at conventional levels. She found no consistent pattern for tourism.

Smith also analyzed interstate variation in state taxes on distilled spirits. She found that tax rates were lower in states where the industry was more highly concentrated, a result consistent with her theory. She also found that taxes on distilled spirits were higher where Protestants were more numerous and where state and local taxes were higher as a percentage of state income. The board and tourism variables had no statistically significant effects. In the area of excise taxes, Smith found that interests of industry and religious groups were not aligned. The former presumably wanted to keep taxes on its product low, whereas opponents of alcohol would be expected to favor high taxes as a method for curbing use.

Smith concluded that licensing policies are enacted subject to the constraints posed by interest group forces. She argued that the results indicated a systematic relation between constituent concerns and outcomes. A more accurate conclusion would be that these results are suggestive but not conclusive, especially since lack of statistical power made her empirical tests highly imprecise.

Effects of Availability on Alcohol Consumption

Several studies have assessed the impact of availability on alcohol consumption using regression analysis. Seeley (1960) found an early link between easy alcohol availability, low alcohol price, and increased deaths from liver cirrhosis. Expanding on this earlier work, Popham, Schmidt, and deLint (1978) did not uncover any link between consumption and cirrhosis mortality but did find that such mortality is significantly associated with apparent per capita consumption and is an inverse function of relative price. Using state time-series cross-section data, Wilkinson (1987) found that availability had a small but statistically significant positive effect on demand. He also found that allowing outlets to close after 2:00 A.M. had a negligible effect on alcohol demand but that restrictions on advertising reduced consumption by 7 percent. Godfrey (1988), using data from the United Kingdom that attempted to resolve conflicting evidence from earlier studies in that country (McGuinness 1980; Duffy 1983), obtained mixed results. She recognized that availability of outlets may be endogenous to consumption; some of her specification tests rejected exogeneity of outlets. Gruenewald, Ponicki, and Holder (1993) conducted the same type of research with United States data and determined that, independent of the effects of price and controlling for the endogeneity of sales and availability, the physical availability of alcohol is directly related to sales of spirits and wine.

Effects of Availability on Social Costs of Drinking

Some evidence from the experience during national prohibition in the United States is highly suggestive that controlling alcohol availability reduces alcohol consumption and its social costs. During Prohibition, alcohol-related deaths fell. According to Fisher (1927), there were 2.9 such deaths per 100,000 persons in 1915 compared with 2.4 in 1927. Cirrhosis mortality fell by almost 50 percent (Warburton 1932; Clark 1976). Violent crime rose, however, particularly in cities where bootleggers and beer runners became more active.

The conventional wisdom is that heavy consumption of alcohol and drugs increases violence. Consequently, bans on use should reduce violence. An alternative view, however, is that such bans create black markets that in turn increase violence as a mechanism for resolving commercial disputes. Miron (1999) tested the hypothesis that prohibiting drugs and alcohol raises the homicide rate. Using time-series data for nearly one hundred years and controlling for other potential determinants of homicides (age composition of the population, incarceration rate, economic conditions, gun availability, and the death penalty), he found evidence that in fact homicides increased when such substances were banned. Even without controlling for the other factors, it is evident that the United States homicide rate rose markedly during Prohibition.

There is a link between high density of alcohol stores and more alcohol-related problems owing to the easy accessibility of alcohol. A number of journalistic accounts maintain an association between crime and the availability of liquor. For example, the *Raleigh News and Observer* reported that Charlotte-Mecklenburg (North Carolina) police said they found a geographic link between crime and stores selling alcohol. Most robberies, thefts, assaults, and drug and prostitution arrests occur within five hundred feet of stores selling alcohol (Eisley 1998). The same article reported that community leaders in Raleigh and Durham (North Carolina) have complained for years that stores peddling alcohol are contributing to the deterioration of their communities and endangering children. The stores offer cheap malt liquor, fortified wine, and disguised crack pipes that promote violence and decay.

In 1993 in Chicago, Mayor Richard Daley declared that the city had far too many liquor licenses (Novak 1998a). Since then the city has reduced their number and banned new bars and liquor stores in some high crime areas. According to the article's author, "Taverns and liquor stores have borne the brunt of the crackdown, while the number of 'incidental' licenses—those issued to restaurants, theaters, and stadiums—has risen 8 percent since 1991" (Novak 1998b, 4A). In developing the program, the director of the Mayor's Liquor Control Commission said he was responding to community complaints of people waking up in the morning and finding liquor bottles on their lawns.

Drunk driving may be more frequent in areas with high concentrations of alcohol outlets. The connection between alcohol availability and accident rates has been analyzed previously with mixed results. Colon, Cutter, and Jones (1982) found that the on-premises availability of alcohol was significantly and inversely associated with motor vehicle fatalities. Contrary to accepted ideas and the findings we report in chapter 9, this result implied that when on-premises outlets are fewer and more geographically dispersed, the likelihood of drinking and driving is increased.

Using data from 213 California communities, Watts and Rabow (1983) found that outlet densities measured in California communities were significantly related to public drunkenness arrests, drunk driving arrests, and cirrhosis mortality. Scribner, MacKinnon, and Dwyer (1994) presented evidence linking alcohol availability directly to motor vehicle crashes in Los Angeles County. This study measured the density of four types of alcohol outlets—restaurants, bars, liquor stores, and minimarkets—and the rates of two types of alcohol-related motor vehicle crashes involving injury and property damage. It found that alcohol availability is geographically associated with increased alcohol-related crashes and that this association is robust to inclusion of other variables explaining variations in crash rates.

Two-thirds of fatal motor vehicle accidents occur in rural areas (Kelleher et al. 1997). The largest urban areas have the lowest death rates, which could be attributed to the greater availability of public transportation, affecting the number of people who drive, the slower pace of traffic, and the shorter distances between home and drinking establishments and between crash sites and emergency medical services.

In an analysis of time-series cross-sectional data from thirty-eight states over twelve years, Gruenewald and Ponicki (1995) evaluated the effect of changes in alcohol sales and the physical availability of alcohol on single-vehicle nighttime fatal crashes. The study showed that the rates of such crashes were most strongly related to sales of beer and less to sales of distilled beverages and wine. When beverages were combined in the analysis, the availability of alcohol was not related to measurable changes in fatal crash rates. Reducing availability so as to decrease alcohol sales and problems did not appear to increase traffic-related crashes and drunk driving incidents through greater driving exposure. Other studies using a time-series cross-sectional design found evidence that reducing availability led to fewer crashes.

In a study of alcohol-related traffic injuries and distance to alcohol in Kentucky, a state with both dry and wet counties, Giacopassi and Winn (1995) found that the distance variable was significantly and negatively related to the rate of alcohol-related crashes. However, distance did not appear to be a substantial determinant of accident rates in dry counties.

High density of alcohol outlets may also be related to other ill effects of alcohol use within a community. Several researchers have found a relation between the per capita number of on-premises liquor outlets and various alcohol-related problems, including cirrhosis and alcoholism (McGuinness 1980; Colon 1981; Parker, Wolz, and Harford 1978).

Although some of the results suggest that restricting availability lowers both heavy alcohol use and the social costs attributable it, Saffer, Grossman, and Chaloupka (1998), who reviewed the literature on alcohol use, expressed some reservations about concluding that a firm link had been established between availability and use. Instead, the researchers said that there is "not enough evidence to conclude that restricting availability can permanently reduce alcohol consumption and related costs" (47).

Effects of Alcohol Regulation on Price

An early empirical investigation comparing prices of liquor in control versus private-license states found that prices were higher in the latter (Simon 1966), implying that the state monopolies did not fully exploit their market power. The same study found that control states obtained greater revenues from off-site sales in spite of their lower prices.

Four alternative explanations were offered. First, control states gain profit by exploiting their monopoly power through joint buying. This explanation was dismissed, however, because the buying agreement guaranteed purchasers only the lowest price offered by wholesalers in private-license states. Second, sellers in the control states may realize scale economies through operating fewer stores. Third, there were differences in accounting practices, such as treatment of interest on inventories. Fourth, private-license states may keep out inefficient firms by restricting entry.

Other studies have focused on the effect of retail price maintenance agreements on retail liquor prices. These include single-state studies (Ferguson 1982; Luksetich 1975) and multistate studies (Ornstein and Hanssens 1987; Simon and Simon 1996). This research supports the notion that retail price maintenance and retail price-posting regulation raise prices. These types of regulation began to be removed in the 1970s, however, and regulations that continued to be operative lost their effectiveness.

Effects of Alcohol Advertising Bans

Administrative statutes often include restrictions on alcohol price advertising (table 2.7). This was true in twenty-four states in 1998. Also, advertising control may be imposed by both the alcohol industry and the media. For example, until 1996 manufacturers of hard liquor voluntarily declined to advertise on the radio and television. Today, with few exceptions, the

Table 2.7 Characteristics of Administrative Alcohol Control Statutes, 1998

State Has Restrictions on Price Advertising	State Does Not Allow Wine and Beer Sales in Grocery or Drug Stores
Alabama	Delaware
Georgia	Maryland
Hawaii	Mississippi
Idaho	Oklahoma
Indiana	
Iowa	
Kansas	
Kentucky	
Maryland	
Montana	
New Hampshire	
New Jersey	
North Carolina	
Ohio	
Oklahoma	
Pennsylvania	
Rhode Island	
South Carolina	
Tennessee	
Texas	
Utah	
Virginia	
Washington	
West Virginia	

Source: Our analysis of state statutes.

broadcast media have refused to air advertising for these products. In the case *44 Liquormart v. Rhode Island,* 517 U.S. 484 (1996), the United States Supreme Court ruled that a ban on print price advertising violates the First Amendment guarantee of freedom of speech.

Ornstein and Hanssens (1985) examined the effect that outdoor advertising bans and bans on price advertising had on alcohol consumption in the United States from 1974 to 1978. They found no effect on consumption owing to outdoor advertising and discovered that price advertising increased beer consumption. Saffer (1991) examined the effects of bans on broadcast advertising on alcohol abuse in seventeen countries. He found that bans on the advertising of all alcoholic beverages have a significant effect in reducing alcohol abuse.

Atkin, Neuendorf, and McDermott (1983) found that exposure to advertisements for wine, beer, and liquor had a moderate positive correlation with heavy drinking and with drinking and driving among young people aged twelve to twenty-two. In a similar study, Atkin, Hocking, and Block (1984) surveyed teenagers about their exposure to television and magazine advertising for beer, wine, and liquor. This study reported significant relations between advertising exposure and drinking behavior, particularly for liquor and beer.

Nelson (1999) examined effects of broadcast advertising and print advertising on alcohol consumption, using an aggregate time series of quarterly data for 1947–94. The results of the analysis indicated that advertising has little or no effect on demand for alcoholic beverages. He concluded that the empirical evidence supports the notion that regardless of media, advertising mainly influences brand shares. Overall, it appears that evidence on how advertising and advertising bans affect alcohol use is mixed.

EMPIRICAL EVIDENCE ON BENEFITS VERSUS COSTS OF ADMINISTRATIVE REGULATION: NEW EMPIRICAL EVIDENCE
Control of Entry

In order for restrictions on alcohol availability to provide a benefit by reducing the social costs of heavy drinking, administrative regulation of sellers must curb availability. Regulation of this type (entry regulation) is by no means guaranteed to reduce the number of suppliers (Breyer 1982). As we emphasized above, administrative restrictions carry a welfare cost. To determine the effects of particular administrative policies on the number of sellers, both on-site and off-site, we conducted our own empirical analyses.

Data

We used data on all states from the 1997 edition of *SelectPhone* to assess the impact of alcohol regulation on the number of sellers per county, both on-site (SIC code 5813) and off-site (SIC code 5921).

The dependent variable was the number of sellers in the county. Rather than analyze a continuous variable, we defined several mutually exclusive categories: under ten; ten to ninety-nine; and one hundred or more. Most counties had either fewer than ten or more than ninety-nine off-site or on-site establishments. There tended to be more on-site than off-site sellers per county.

Hypotheses and Empirical Specification

The key explanatory variables related to regulatory practices in the state were whether or not the state controlled off-site sales; whether or not it permitted beer and wine to be sold in drugstores and grocery stores; whether or not there were limits on advertising of alcoholic beverages (see table 2.7); and whether or not the state ABC maintained enforcement powers rather than delegating this power to another agency (see table 2.3). Except for the final variable, the more restrictive practice was assigned the value one. For ABC enforcement, the binary variable was one if the state ABC did not have direct enforcement power.

We hypothesized that more restrictive regulatory practices would reduce the number of sellers in the county. Conceptually, the effect of state control on the number of on-site sellers is more complex. On the one hand, restricting entry of liquor stores should increase demand for bars. In some states, however, public sector control of off-site stores is accompanied by entry restrictions for on-site establishments. We accounted for on-site restrictions by including an explanatory variable in the on-site analysis. But it is also possible that existing on-site sellers find a more receptive audience among regulators in control states. If so, off-site control may result in restrictions on entry in the on-site sector.

Placing enforcement powers with the state ABC should result in more enforcement at the local level, since local police have many tasks besides enforcing alcohol-related statutes. Greater enforcement has an ambiguous effect on entry. To the extent that public enforcement is a substitute for private monitoring, a private seller's input costs decrease, leading to increased entry. However, enforcement may increase in the aggregate, and a high level of enforcement may provide a hostile environment, thus curbing demand, especially for bars.

To control for other factors, we also included explanatory variables for county population, per capita income, climate using the average annual temperature (from the area resource file), percentage male, percentage black, percentage Hispanic, percentage married, binary variables identifying counties in urban and standard metropolitan statistical areas (SMSAs), and religious mix—percentages Catholic, Jewish, Mormon, Baptist, and other Protestant, with those having no religious affiliation as the omitted reference group.

Estimation

We estimated the equations with ordered logit. To gauge the importance of each explanatory variable, we computed the change in the probability of being in each of the three categories given a unit change in the explanatory variable ("marginal effects"). We present only the marginal effect for the top category, "one hundred or more firms in the county." Since there are only three mutually exclusive categories, when the marginal effect was positive for the top category it was almost always negative and similar in absolute value for the bottom category.

Results

As expected, the number of liquor stores was lower in control states, and the coefficient was highly significant at conventional levels (table 2.8). Permitting beer and wine to be sold in drugstores and grocery stores and imposing advertising bans also significantly reduced entry of licensed liquor stores. Additionally, locating alcohol enforcement outside the state ABC ($p = 0.002$) reduced the number of such off-site establishments. This result seems counterintuitive at first glance, but it may be explained if alcohol enforcement is directed mainly toward on-site establishments.

Although our primary goal was to analyze the effect of administrative regulation on entry, other findings are of interest, in part because plausible results lend general credibility to the empirical analysis. Many of the other coefficients are plausible. There were more liquor stores in counties with higher population, higher per capita income, more males relative to females, and fewer Mormons, and in urban areas and SMSAs relative to rural areas. There were fewer such establishments where there were more blacks relative to whites and other nonwhites and more married persons, and in warmer climates.

In general, results for the regulatory variables differed in the analysis of on-site commercial servers. State control had a positive effect, implying that the number of bars was higher in states with control over liquor stores, although this result was not significant. Recall that liquor stores were less

Table 2.8 Analysis of Entry of On-Site and Off-Site Establishments

Explanatory Variables	Off-Site			On-Site		
	Coeff.	Std. Err.	M. E.	Coeff.	Std. Err.	M. E.
Monopoly	-0.56[a]	0.16	-0.0005	0.011	0.15	0.0001
Grocery stores allowed to sell beer and wine	-0.64[b]	0.27	-0.0006	0.13	0.24	0.0011
Limits on liquor store advertising	-0.81[a]	0.15	-0.0008	-0.17	0.13	-0.0014
Alcohol enforcement outside state ABC	-0.56[a]	0.18	-0.0005	0.47[a]	0.15	0.0039
ABC follows up on bad situations	-0.0085	0.049	0.0000	-0.10[b]	0.043	-0.0008
Nonresponding ABC	-0.61	0.82	-0.0006	-0.24	0.62	-0.0020
Population of county (thousands)	0.095[a]	0.0052	0.0001	0.098[a]	0.0049	0.0008
Per capita income	1.55[a]	0.16	0.0015	0.36[b]	0.16	0.0033
Climate	-0.034[a]	0.01	0.0000	-0.0046	0.011	0.0000
Male (%)	0.059[b]	0.029	0.0001	0.017	0.026	0.0001
Black (%)	-0.027[a]	0.0091	0.0000	-0.040[a]	0.0080	-0.0003
Hispanic (%)	-0.0018	0.065	0.0000	-0.015[a]	0.0056	-0.0001
SMSA (= 1)	0.67[a]	0.14	0.0006	0.56[a]	0.14	0.0046
Urban (= 1)	1.93[a]	0.28	0.0018	1.78[a]	0.19	0.015
Married (%)	-0.13[a]	0.018	-0.0001	-0.11[a]	0.014	-0.0009
Catholic (%)	0.0036	0.0088	0.0000	0.026[a]	0.0077	0.0002
Baptist (%)	-0.013	0.0090	0.0000	-0.026[a]	0.0083	-0.0002
Other Protestant (%)	-0.011	0.011	0.0000	-0.011	0.0099	-0.0001
Mormon (%)	-0.038[a]	0.12	0.0000	-0.0098	0.0092	-0.0001
Jewish (%)	-0.0073	0.048	0.0000	-0.11[a]	0.040	-0.0009
	N = 2,428			N = 2,450		

[a]Statistically significant at 1 percent level.
[b]Statistically significant at 5 percent level.
Coeff. = coefficient; Std. Err. = standard error; M. E. = marginal effect.
Table reports nonstandardized regression coefficients.

numerous in states that operated such stores. Advertising bans had a negative effect ($p = .19$). As expected, placing enforcement outside the state ABC increased the number of bars, whereas having an active ABC, which followed up on illegal behavior by patrons, significantly decreased it. This may have been because active intervention by the public regulatory agency lowered patron demand or because such agencies were more stringent in granting licenses.

Among the other explanatory variables, the number of bars rose with higher population, higher per capita income, being in an urban area or an SMSA, and being in an area with a higher proportion of Catholics. Counties with more blacks, Hispanics, married persons, Jewish people, and Baptists had fewer bars.

On balance, the regression analysis suggests that state alcoholic beverage regulation affected exit and entry patterns, but differently for on-site and off-site establishments. Perhaps the most interesting result was for regulatory structure—in particular, alcohol enforcement located within the state ABC. In states where entry and enforcement were more directly linked, there were more liquor stores and, correspondingly, fewer bars. To the extent that alcohol enforcement is mainly oriented to bars, this result is reasonable. The public ownership of off-site stores resulted in fewer off-site sellers but had no effect on the number of on-site establishments. This finding implies that on-site establishments should be indifferent to whether the state controls off-site establishments.

Effects of Administrative Regulation on Commercial Servers

Using data from the Survey of Commercial Servers, we assessed the effect of ABC policies and other factors on how owners and managers perceived the probability of being cited by the ABC for three types of infractions. The infractions were serving minors, serving obviously intoxicated adults, and rowdiness. We also analyzed the probability that the liquor authority had taken action against the commercial server or its employees in the past year.

The dependent variables in the analysis of perceived probability of citation were ordered responses to questions about the likelihood of receiving a citation if certain infractions were to occur. We analyzed three infractions: serving minors, serving obviously intoxicated adults, and rowdiness. The respondents picked one of five ordered categories ranging from "not at all likely" to "very likely." Realistically, a citation would never be categorized as "very likely." It is plausible that the ordered responses were systematically related to the underlying probability. Thus in our analysis we treated the ordered responses as if they were probabilities of being cited.

The ABC policies analyzed were a count of specific policies the ABC followed; full-time equivalent employees of the ABC per thousand bars in the state; whether there was a public monopoly for off-site establishments; whether alcohol enforcement was outside the ABC (i.e., department of revenue, local police, special state investigators, or state police); and whether the ABC in the state responded to our survey. When there was no response, the values of the other policy variables were set to zero.

The count of specific policies were ABC followed up on DUI violations to see if establishment selling alcohol was at fault; ABC followed up on accidents caused by intoxicated drivers to see if establishment selling alcohol was at fault; ABC followed up on fights in bars; and ABC followed up on illegal alcohol consumption or trade practices. We hypothesized that perceived probability would be higher when ABCs followed up on more of the situations mentioned above, when they had more resources, and when alcohol enforcement was outside the ABC. We expected states that controlled off-site establishments to be more stringent, but given the results discussed earlier of exit and entry of on-site sellers, this variable may also have no effect. The binary variable for nonresponding ABCs was included to determine whether the eight nonresponding states were perceived as more or less stringent by the bars they regulated.

We included other variables that might affect the perceived probability of a citation. Four basic establishment characteristics included were incorporation status, whether the establishment was part of a chain, age of the establishment, and fraction of the establishment's revenue coming from food. We included measures of the establishment's clientele, measured as fraction of customers aged twenty-five to forty; customers aged forty and over; students; blue-collar workers; regular customers; men; customers who come alone; customers who come by car; and customers who come in groups. We also included population density.

Two of the policies were statistically significant at the 5 percent level or better in almost every case (table 2.9). As we anticipated, the number of specific policies the state ABC followed had a positive effect on the perceived probability of being cited by the ABC in all three regressions.

The binary variable for alcohol enforcement outside the ABC had a negative effect in all three regressions and was statistically significant at the 1 percent level in two of them: serving minors and serving obviously intoxicated adults. The measure of richness of staffing of the administrative agencies—full-time equivalent ABC employees per thousand bars in the

Table 2.9 Perceived Probability of Citation by Alcoholic Beverage Commissions

Explanatory Variables	Serving Minors			Serving Obviously Intoxicated Adults			Rowdiness		
	Coeff.	Std. Err.	M. E.	Coeff.	Std. Err.	M. E.	Coeff.	Std. Err.	M. E.
ABC policies									
Number of follow-up situations	0.15[b]	0.071	0.038	0.23[a]	0.062	0.051	0.24[a]	0.066	0.040
Full-time equivalent ABC employees per thousand bars	0.047	0.032	0.012	0.026	0.025	0.0059	0.0086	0.027	0.0015
Monopoly	0.17	0.24	0.043	0.25	0.21	0.056	0.14	0.21	0.023
Alcohol enforcement outside ABC	−0.57[a]	0.19	−0.14	−0.51[a]	0.18	−0.11	−0.22	0.18	−0.037
Nonresponding ABC	0.61[a]	0.23	0.15	0.46[b]	0.21	0.10	0.22	0.22	0.037
Establishment characteristics									
Incorporated	0.51[a]	0.17	0.12	0.31	0.16	0.069	0.37[b]	0.16	0.062
Part of chain	0.28	0.43	0.069	−0.42	0.40	−0.094	0.054	0.38	0.0091
Age of establishment	0.0043	0.0046	0.0011	−0.0083	0.0042	−0.0019	−0.0071	0.0043	−0.0012
Fraction of sales from food	0.051	0.44	−0.013	0.40	0.41	0.088	0.23	0.41	0.039
Clientele characteristics									
Fraction of									
Customers aged 25–40	−0.40	0.69	−0.099	−0.99	0.64	−0.22	0.081	0.64	0.014
Customers aged 40+	−0.12	0.67	−0.029	−0.0071	0.63	−0.0016	1.56	0.63	0.26
Students	0.27	0.89	0.067	−0.76	0.79	−0.17	0.77	0.78	0.13
Blue-collar workers	0.30	0.31	0.075	0.63[b]	0.30	0.14	0.56	0.30	0.094
Regular customers	−0.50	0.37	−0.012	−0.74[b]	0.35	−0.17	−0.56	0.35	−0.094
Men	−0.16	0.58	−0.039	0.43	0.54	0.096	0.52	0.55	0.089
Customers who come alone	0.69	0.54	0.017	0.58	0.52	0.13	0.23	0.53	0.038
Customers who come in groups	0.55	0.62	0.013	0.72	0.58	0.16	−0.84	0.59	−0.14
Customers who come by car	−0.34	0.29	−0.084	−0.30	0.26	−0.067	−0.23	0.25	−0.040
Population density	−0.0016	0.0018	−0.0004	−0.0003	0.0016	−0.0001	−0.0010	0.0014	−0.0002
	N = 606			N = 601			N = 595		

[a]Statistically significant at 1 percent level.
[b]Statistically significant at 5 percent level.
Coeff. = coefficient; Std. Err. = standard error; M. E. = marginal effect.
Table reports nonstandardized regression coefficients.

state—had positive effects on the three dependent variables, implying that richer staffing increased the bars' perceived probability of getting caught for infractions and being cited by the agency. Although the coefficients exceeded their respective standard errors, none of them were statistically significant at conventional levels. Thus, even though the results suggest that additional resources translate into a greater threat of citation from the standpoint of the bars, the lack of statistical significance warrants some caution in interpreting these findings. The variable for public monopoly had a positive effect, but the coefficient was imprecisely estimated. For two of the three dependent variables, the perceived probability of citation by the ABC was higher for the nonresponding ABCs. These results were statistically significant at the 5 percent level or higher.

Taken as a whole, these results are encouraging, indicating considerable correspondence between policies as stated by the state ABCs and the perceptions of threat of citation reported by the parties they regulate. The more active states gave the bars a greater incentive to be careful in their serving practices.

As above, we controlled for other factors that might affect the perceived probability of being cited, and results for some of these variables merit discussion in their own right. Other variables affecting perceived probability of citation by the ABC were being incorporated ($+$), blue-collar workers ($+$), and regular customers of bars ($-$). Perhaps bars with more working-class clients were more likely to be scrutinized by ABC agencies. Bars with a high proportion of regular patrons may have succeeded in weeding out the troublemakers. We are unable to interpret the finding on incorporation status.

A parallel question asked owners or managers to estimate the probability of being cited by the alcohol law enforcement agency (ALE). We assessed the effect of state ALE policies and other factors on the probability of being cited for serving minors or obviously intoxicated adults.

Holding other factors constant, commercial servers in control states believed they were more likely to be cited by the ALE in their locality than were bars in states that licensed private bars (table 2.10). Parameter estimates on this variable were statistically significant at the 5 percent level or better. The marginal effects were computed as the probability of being in the highest category, that is, being very likely to be cited. The marginal effects of being a control state on the probability of falling into the highest category were substantial: 0.13 for serving minors and 0.16 for serving obviously intoxicated adults. This means, for example, that the perceived probability of being "very likely" to be cited for serving minors was 0.13

Table 2.10 Perceived Probability of Citation by Alcohol Law Enforcement Agencies

Explanatory Variables	Serving Minors			Serving Obviously Intoxicated Individuals		
	Coeff.	Std. Err.	M. E.	Coeff.	Std. Err.	M. E.
ALE policies						
Monopoly	0.56[b]	0.23	0.13	0.70[a]	0.19	0.16
ALE						
with local police	−0.47	0.42	−0.11	−1.01[a]	0.36	−0.23
with department of revenue	−0.14	0.64	−0.033	−1.19[b]	0.56	−0.28
with state police	0.063	0.42	0.014	−0.34	0.35	−0.078
with ABC with help from local police	0.056	0.42	0.013	−0.28	0.35	−0.064
Establishment characteristics						
Incorporated	0.57[a]	0.18	0.13	0.53[a]	0.16	0.12
Part of a chain	−0.10	0.42	−0.024	−0.48	0.39	−0.11
Age of establishment	0.0033	0.0046	0.0008	−0.0046	0.0041	−0.0011
Fraction of sales from food	−0.18	0.45	−0.041	0.27	0.40	0.064
Clientele characteristics						
Fration of						
Customers aged 25–40	−0.31	0.77	−0.072	−0.67	0.67	−0.16
Customers aged 40+	−0.64	0.75	−0.15	−0.039	0.65	−0.0090
Students	−0.0070	0.96	−0.0016	−0.21	0.83	−0.048
Blue-collar workers	−0.064	0.33	−0.015	0.34	0.30	0.080
Regular customers	−0.34	0.38	−0.078	−0.80[b]	0.35	−0.19
Men	−0.36	0.59	−0.084	0.77	0.54	0.18
Customers who come alone	0.51	0.59	0.12	1.10[b]	0.53	0.26
Customers who come in groups	−0.44	0.66	−0.10	0.81	0.60	0.19
Customers who come by car	−0.59	0.33	−0.14	−0.25	0.26	−0.058
Population density	−0.0018	0.0019	−0.0004	−0.0004	0.0014	−0.0001
	N = 621			N = 610		

[a]Statistically significant at 1 percent level.
[b]Statistically significant at 5 percent level.
Coeff. = coefficient; Std. Err. = standard error; M. E. = marginal effect.
Table reports nonstandardized regression coefficients.

higher in monopoly than in private-license states, holding the other factors in the analysis constant.

In the analysis of the perceived probability for adults, we found that when the ALE was run by the local police or by the state department of revenue, rather than by the ABC, the perceived probability of being cited was much lower. We obtained no statistically significant differences on ALE organization for the perceived probability of being cited for serving minors.

Incorporated establishments assessed the probability of citation as higher. A larger fraction of patrons who came to the bar by car reduced the perceived probability of a citation for serving minors at an almost significant level ($p = 0.074$). For adults, establishments with a larger fraction of regular customers believed they had a lower threat of citation. Conversely, when patrons came alone the perceived threat was higher. Overall, this analysis supports the view that the ABC-ALE organizational scheme has systematic effects on how establishments perceive these regulatory agencies.

Fewer that 10 percent of the bars reported that a liquor authority had taken disciplinary action against them or their employees during the year before the survey. The most important reasons for citation by the ABC were serving minors, gambling, and indecent exposure or lewd conduct (box 2.3). Very few bars were cited for serving an obviously intoxicated adult. With such a low percentage, our ability to characterize sources of variation in the propensity to take disciplinary action was limited.

Box 2.3 Activities prompting most recent action by the alcoholic beverage commission.

Serving minors	9	Fake IDs	1
Gambling	5	Solicitation of club memberships	1
Minor sting operations	4	Health code violation	1
Indecent exposure/lewd conduct	4	Unpaid taxes	1
Unclean beer taps	2	Having reduced drink prices after 9:00 P.M.	1
Patrons drinking after hours	2	Vagrants soliciting for alcohol	1
Employees drinking after hours	2	Falsely accusing patron of being a minor	1
Drinking by entertainers	2	Neighbor complaint	1
Employees drinking on the job	2	Serving alcohol on election day	1
Reentry by patron kicked out of bar	1	Bouncer accused of roughing up patron	1
Serving an intoxicated person	2		

Source: 1996 Survey of Commercial Servers. Numbers are number of responses.

Table 2.11 Liquor Authority Took Disciplinary Action against Commercial Server or Its Employees in Past Year

Explanatory Variables	Coeff.	Std. Err.	M. E.
ABC policies			
Number of follow-up situations	0.33[b]	0.15	0.011
Full-time equivalent ABC employees per thousand bars	0.044	0.047	0.0015
Monopoly	−0.21	0.48	−0.0070
Alcohol enforcement outside ABC	0.62	0.41	0.021
Nonresponding ABC	0.46	0.50	0.015
Establishment characteristics			
Incorporated	1.04[a]	0.39	0.035
Part of chain	0.35	0.72	0.012
Age of establishment	−0.0021	0.0097	−0.0001
Fraction of sales from food	−1.35	1.07	−0.045
Clientele characteristics			
Fraction of			
Customers aged 25–40	0.66	1.34	0.022
Customers aged 40+	−2.01	1.51	−0.067
Students	3.69[b]	1.62	0.12
Blue-collar workers	−0.32	0.70	−0.011
Regular customers	0.026	0.79	0.0009
Men	4.48[a]	1.35	0.15
Customers who come alone	0.20	1.15	0.0068
Customers who come in groups	−1.72	1.48	−0.057
Customers who come by car	0.66	0.68	0.022
Population density	−0.0034	0.0057	−0.0001
Constant	−7.93[a]	2.07	−0.26
	$N = 650$		

[a]Statistically significant at 1 percent level.
[b]Statistically significant at 5 percent level.
Coeff. = coefficient; Std. Err. = standard error; M. E. = marginal effect.
Table reports nonstandardized regression coefficients.

We conducted empirical analysis of determinants of whether an alcoholic beverage regulatory agency actually had taken disciplinary action against the bar during the year before our Survey of Commercial Servers. Again, the most notable result was for the count of ABC policies (table 2.11). The coefficient was positive and statistically significant at the 5 percent level. Bars in states where alcohol enforcement was outside the ABC were more likely to have had a disciplinary action against them, but the result was not statistically significant at conventional levels. This result contradicts our findings from the analysis of perceived probability of citation reported above. As in that analysis, incorporated establishments were more likely to have been cited by the ABC. Bars oriented toward students and men were also more likely to have been cited. Overall, this second analysis provides partial confirmation that the bars regulated perceive ABC policies in the ways the ABCs intend. In chapter 7 we will assess whether and how far higher perceived risk translates into safer serving practices.

Finally, the survey asked owners to name the ways the ABC had affected the bar's business practices. We classified the responses into three categories: increased precaution level, effect on demand, and other. Most of the responses were in the first category (box 2.4). Many respondents said that they "follow their [regulators'] rules."

CONCLUSION

Administrative regulation of commercial sellers of alcohol has a long history. The original impetus for regulation was first moral, but second economic—that is, reduction of losses associated with high rates of consumption of alcoholic beverages. Administrative regulation of sellers of alcoholic beverages is not costless. Running public agencies is one cost, but we must also consider the welfare losses that reduced consumption imposes on the majority of the public who are moderate drinkers, both because they pay higher prices and in the extra time needed to obtain a commodity they value. Benefits of such regulation are reduced external costs and lower rates of family disruption attributable to heavy drinking. A major policy concern is whether the benefits of such regulation exceed the costs.

Regulating commercial sellers of alcohol appears to be effective. Some key ABC policies were systematically correlated with the perceived probability of citation and with actual citations. Since the data for our empirical analysis of ABC policies and of perceived probability of citation and actual citations came from entirely different and independent sources, there is strong evidence that the regulatory policies have at least the potential for being effective.

Clearly, states differed in their regulatory policies. Some were more active in monitoring behavior than others. We also learned that active ABCs that followed up on reports of bad behavior were more effective than were less active agencies, gauged in terms of perceived probability of citation. The more active ABCs followed up on DUI violations to determine if the establishment selling alcohol was at fault; on accidents caused by intoxicated drivers to determine if the establishment selling alcohol was at fault; on fights in bars; and on illegal alcohol consumption and other trade practices. Although regulation affected perceived probability of citation, for the policies to be an effective deterrent the perception must affect servers'

Box 2.4 Ways the alcoholic beverage commission has affected your business practice: opinions of commercial establishment owners and managers.

Increased Precaution Level			
We follow their rules	51	Agency is entirely political	3
Undercover agents	7	Monitor for drinking and driving	2
Come in and check all the time	6	They are always around	2
Spot checks 3–4 times a year	5	Make owners more responsible	2
Provide regulations and laws	5	Make us more careful	2
Have become more strict over the years	5	Always under the threat of them closing us down	2
They check IDs	4	Affect all the rules	1
Harass us at least once a month	4	They try to set me up	1
Provide education	3	They have made it safer	1
Same as police	3	Come in and check because they are sneaky	1
Restrict our hours of operation	3	Ineffective—85 percent of their arrests are dropped	1
Supply server training	3		
Effect on Demand			
Can suspend our license	4	Changed legal limit of intoxication	1
Customers afraid to stay very long	4	Had to raise prices	1
In charge of issuing licenses	4	Fined our customers for drinking after hours	1
Can fine us	3	We send them a lot of money every month, which made us raise our prices	1
Customers worried about DUI	2	Tighter controls on alcohol and gambling	1
Scared they will find someone with fake ID	2	Have to hire security	1
Patrons afraid to come in	2	No drink specials	1
Bureaucratically buried us	1	Territorial limitations affects type of liquor sold to customers	1
Suspended our license	1		
Affects prices	1		
Other			
Not at all	6	Don't have an ABC	1
Not too much	3	Not sure	1
Lobby against higher increased liabilities	1	Am strict on IDs so they don't bother me	1

Source: 1996 Survey of Commercial Servers. Numbers are number of responses.

actual behavior. That is, those establishments that perceive themselves as at particular risk of receiving a citation must engage in better server practices. We defer the task of establishing the latter relation to chapters 7 and 8.

Some accounts suggest a link among alcohol availability, consumption, and the social costs related to drinking too much. Although some empirical evidence supports a causal relation, as Saffer, Grossman, and Chaloupka

(1998) concluded, the evidence is far from conclusive. Some forms of alcohol regulation, such as advertising bans, have been found to be effective, although the Supreme Court has recently found such bans unconstitutional. As we noted above, the empirical evidence does not show that advertising increases aggregate demand for alcoholic beverages. Overall, the evidence for the effects of advertising on consumption is weaker than the evidence for availability effects.

A risk of administrative regulation is that it may lower the competitiveness of the market by reducing entry and limiting the business practices the regulated firms can engage in. An example of the anticompetitive effects of regulating business practices in another context is blue laws, which ban commercial enterprise on Sundays. Such laws may be favored on religious grounds, but they are also favored by businesses that would like to close on Sundays for business reasons if they knew their competitors would be closed as well. In fact, we found that certain regulatory practices were associated with reduced numbers of on-site and off-site sellers. The policies of administrative agencies result from the interplay of vested interests, both those for and those against alcohol regulation. Our analysis focused on the policies of the agencies and their effects on commercial servers of alcohol rather than on the forces leading these public agencies to adopt the policies they did. For this reason we did not make an original contribution to understanding the regulatory regime of politics of choice.

Administrative regulation of commercial sellers of alcohol does not operate in isolation. Rather, it acts in conjunction with criminal and tort law. Criminal enforcement is undertaken by some of the ABCs but is largely left to police enforcement, which is the subject of the next chapter.

3

Criminal Liability for Illegal Alcohol Service

Driving under the influence of alcohol, being a minor in possession of alcohol, and public drunkenness are all examples of alcohol-related crimes that impose substantial costs on society. Servers of alcohol also commit alcohol-related crimes when they serve a minor or an obviously intoxicated person. There are many strategies for controlling and preventing alcohol-related crimes, based on understanding their impact on society and why offenders commit them. In this chapter we examine enforcement and punishment strategies designed to reduce alcohol-related crimes and resulting injuries.

Alcohol-related offenses, such as serving obviously intoxicated adults or minors, drunk driving, and other acts committed under the influence of alcohol (such as assault and trespassing), are usually classified as misdemeanors. These laws represent ex ante regulation of socially undesirable acts. That is, the regulation applies before harm is committed on grounds that such acts often represent a danger to others. Another example of such ex ante regulation is gun control (Cook and Leitzel 1996). Some alcohol-related criminal acts result in felony charges, such as voluntary manslaughter when a drunk driver causes a fatal accident. Such ex post regulation is designed to provide a disincentive for engaging in such careless behavior.

We also examine criminal server punishments for these acts and survey empirical evidence from past research on the effectiveness of criminal enforcement and punishments as deterrents of drunk driving and other alcohol-related harms. We present new empirical evidence on criminal enforcement from our Survey of Police Departments and the effects of variation in police enforcement on server perception of the enforcement threat, using data from our Survey of Commercial Servers.

TYPES OF ACTS COVERED UNDER CRIMINAL LAW

Many types of socially unacceptable behavior are made criminal under our legal system: various forms of coercive behavior such as rape, murder, and robbery; forced transfers such as price fixing; value-maximizing voluntary exchanges such as prostitution and selling narcotics; and other acts that might be difficult to enforce under tort, such as leaving the scene of an accident. The role of criminal law is particularly important in victimless crimes, where it would be impossible to punish certain bad behavior using tort law.

Criminal law may also reflect society's moral values (Andenaes 1974). For example, the passage of a strict alcohol service law may indicate widespread moral commitment to control in the community, and implementation of the law further consolidates commitment to compliance. The law also serves an educational and moralizing function that fosters a widespread change in moral outlook and promotes habitual law-abidingness. This can be demonstrated by a long-term reduction in road fatalities attributable to attitude changes that might not immediately follow new legislation (such as speed limit restrictions).

GOALS OF CRIMINAL LAW

Criminal law has four main goals: deterrence, retribution, rehabilitation, and incapacitation. Deterrence and rehabilitation aim to reduce the number of future crimes, whereas retribution and incapacitation punish the offender for crimes that have already taken place.

Deterrence

Criminal law identifies prohibited acts and prescribes the legal penalties associated them. Deterrence deals with preventing undesirable behavior through the use or threat of legal sanctions. Deterrence achieves its effect because punishing a criminal discourages other potential offenders from committing the same crime, thus enhancing public safety.

The concept of deterrence is based on the premise that individuals modify their behavior in response to incentives. Criminal punishment should be considered a negative incentive, and criminal penalties should prevent future crimes by at least some of those sanctioned and by others not sanctioned. Because crime imposes costs on society, and because deterring crime uses resources, there is an optimal amount of crime and a corresponding optimal amount of deterrence (Cooter and Ulen 1988). The optimal amount of crime is determined as the point at which the marginal benefit of crime reduction equals the marginal cost of deterrence.

Retribution

By developing formal systems for achieving retribution, societies reduce demands for retribution outside the law. Given that empirical evidence on the actual effects of criminal laws on deterrence is generally lacking, retribution is often an important motive for enacting criminal laws.

Rehabilitation

Criminal penalties often include requirements that the offender undergo certain amounts of instruction, either in the risks of the criminal activity to self or others or through more general training designed to improve the person's market productivity and hence influence choices in the future. The penalty may also include some type of mandatory therapy and education specific to the offense committed. Rehabilitation for the server who engages in illegal alcohol service may involve attending a server education course or other required alcohol education, and such treatments for the drunk driver could include safe driving courses and alcohol abuse treatment.

Incapacitation

"Putting the criminal away"—imprisonment—is also a goal of criminal law. For illegal alcohol service by individuals, jail terms are generally not long enough for criminal law to serve this function. Additionally, they are often not imposed on first-time offenders. Ordering the bar to be closed, however, will achieve the goal of incapacitation and is generally the method used in this context.

THE ECONOMICS OF CRIME AND OPTIMAL CRIMINAL SANCTIONS
Criminal Activity: Irrational or Rational?

To some, crime appears to be among the least rational of activities. Economic theory dictates that crimes that do not involve financial gain to the perpetrator are irrational. To the extent that criminals do not fit within the norms of society, it is necessary to incapacitate those likely to commit crimes. This can be accomplished by imprisoning offenders or by lesser means such as the impounding a motor vehicle, taking away a driver's license, or for violent crimes, impounding the weapon.

An alternative view is that committing a crime, like other human behavior, involves a rational calculation of cost versus the benefit the would-be criminal derives from the crime (Becker 1968). In this view, the "market" for criminal activities parallels a market for legal ones. In the criminal market, offenses are undertaken for gain that may be financial or nonfinancial.

The distinction between irrational and rational actors has important implications for alcohol control policy. If people make rational choices, then imposing heavy penalties and increasing criminal enforcement will deter those who might otherwise become involved in an illegal activity. Irrational behavior may reflect responses to social norms ("I get drunk because everyone is doing it"), present-oriented behavior, or inability to forecast the consequences of one's behavior because of mental illness. Irrational behavior may result from an underlying addiction, but some economists have hypothesized that such behavior may also reflect a rational choice (Becker and Murphy 1988).

Various attempts have been made to modify the assumption of rationality. In one framework, there are three bounds that represent departures from the rationality assumption underlying economic models (Jolls, Sunstein, and Thaler 1998). The first, "bounded rationality," an idea introduced by Herbert Simon (1982), refers to the limits on human cognitive abilities. This might apply to the complexities of drivers' precautions, both in computing the correct strategy, given the actions of other drivers, and in knowing all criminal and tort law applicable to daily life. In contrast to drivers, bartenders have fewer actions to monitor, and the applicable law is relatively specialized and narrow. For this reason, bounded rationality seems more applicable to drivers than to alcohol servers.

The second is "bounded willpower." Humans may take actions that may conflict with their own long-term interests—for example, smokers and heavy drinkers who say they want to quit but do not or overweight persons who contemplate going on a diet. Limiting hours of alcohol sales is a rather blunt method for dealing with bounded willpower.

Third, there is "bounded self-interest." In many contexts, people care about being treated fairly and want to treat others fairly, even if they are in a position to extract financial gain. Bounded self-interest relates to the goals of law, retribution, and justice. The law is not about deterrence only.

The economic approach to crime and punishment described here assumes rationality. Rather than debating assumptions, the "proof of the pudding" lies in the empirical evidence. The model implies that those facing losses from crime will be deterred from engaging in it. If the empirical evidence suggests that increases in enforcement of laws and in punishments do not discourage criminal behavior, then this gives reason to question the relevance of the economic framework.

The Market for Criminal Activities: Conceptual Framework

The "criminal system" involves several participants. Crime rates reflect incentives facing the criminal and incentives facing courts and police, including promotion of the public safety. In deciding whether to commit a crime, a person balances the benefit to be derived from the act, both pecuniary and nonpecuniary, against the cost, which includes the cost of various inputs to the act, such as time and equipment, and also expected criminal punishment.

Individuals are assumed to be utility-maximizing agents. The cost of a crime to the individual is the product of the probability of being apprehended on committing the crime, the probability of conviction if apprehended, and the monetary fine or sentence if convicted. One might add to this the stigma of being labeled a criminal as well as other motives, such as effects on employment in the legitimate sector and higher premiums for automobile or liquor liability insurance.

On the benefit side is the product of the probability that the crime will succeed and the benefit if it does. In the context of our study, the benefit would include retaining customers who engage in heavy drinking and possibly an increase in tips for the server and business for the establishment. The probability that the "crime" will succeed may be 1.0. But some who choose to engage in illegal alcohol service may end up with rowdy, obnoxious customers and regret their conduct in the end. Persons for whom the expected benefit exceeds the expected cost will elect to engage in the criminal behavior.

An insightful way to view the criminal justice system is as a mechanism for allowing individuals to borrow against their future utility (Lott 1990; Grogger 1991). A criminal benefits from the crime now but pays for that benefit if later caught and imprisoned. An alcohol server may benefit from the criminal act of illegal service by receiving higher tips or gaining a loyal customer base.

The other part of the market pertains to those charged with carrying out the laws. Here it is useful to distinguish between normative and positive issues. Normative issues deal with optimal levels of enforcement and penalties. These are conceptually distinct from how courts, police, and lawyers behave in practice. Such parties are also utility maximizers. Given that time and other resources are limited, they will choose to concentrate on crimes with the largest payoff net of costs to their organizations.

The optimal level of criminal sanctions depends in part on the loss to society associated with the criminal act. Higher social loss should carry a higher expected punishment. Such loss must be balanced against the cost of mitigating this loss. The potential criminal is motivated by the expected loss, defined as the product of apprehension and conviction probabilities and the penalty on being apprehended and convicted. Thus it is necessary to determine the most efficient combination of the three instruments that will yield the socially optimal loss for committing the crime. The volume of offenses committed by the population is influenced by the allocation of private and public resources to law enforcement and other methods of crime prevention (Ehrlich 1998).

Changes in the law that alter either the probability that the perpetrator of a crime will be punished or the magnitude of the resulting punishment should affect the attractiveness of the criminal act and how frequently such crimes occur. The efficient combination depends on the relative price of apprehension, prosecution and trial, and punishment. In general, the least expensive way to encourage compliance is to employ the highest possible sanction and, given this sanction, the lowest probability of detection. If the sanction succeeds as a deterrent, there are potential savings not only in carrying out the sanctions (arrest, imprisonment, etc.) but in resources devoted to enforcement as well (Polinsky and Shavell 1999). The solution to this question involves trading off costs and benefits to criminals, victims, and the enforcement system. Since imprisonment is costly, the use of fines should generally be encouraged, subject to the constraint that the nonaffluent may not have the funds to pay monetary penalties (see, e.g., Levitt 1997). Risk preferences of would-be criminals should be considered in determining the expected penalty. Otherwise, when penalties are set at an optimal level, risk-loving individuals may still commit crimes (Lott 1990).

Economics and crime also interact in court procedures used to determine guilt or innocence and in sentencing. One of the wrongs American courts try to avoid is convicting an innocent person. The fear of unjust imprisonment may cause the courts to reduce the optimal penalty below what would normally reflect the true cost of crime (Lott 1990). In the absence of such errors, for optimal cost allocation, the state should set penalties for criminal offenses to reflect the full costs these wrongful acts impose on society.

The conduct of alcohol servers who commit criminal acts plausibly conforms to these theories. Servers who do not fear detection because of inadequate police resources may choose to provide illegal service to enhance their tips or to increase business for their employer. Servers will also assess the risk of detection and punishment, including a potential loss of the liquor license for the bar and personal fines or jail time for the server.

EMPIRICAL TESTS OF CRIME AS A RATIONAL CHOICE

Several studies have attempted to examine whether engaging in crime is a rational choice, as is engaging in legal activities. The general deterrence hypothesis is premised on the notion that actions of the criminal justice system (e.g., arrests) affect the decisions of individuals who have no contact with the system as well as those apprehended and punished by it. Such research also tests whether policies that make criminal behavior relatively less attractive succeed in this objective. One insight of these studies is that concentrating enforcement and penalties for one type of criminal offense may cause criminals to substitute pursuits that are also criminal but are less tightly regulated. More resources devoted to punishing alcohol-related offenses may lead people to engage in other socially undesirable acts, including use of other controlled substances.

Perhaps the best-known empirical study to test the economic approach to crime and punishment is Ehrlich (1975). Based on empirical analysis, this study concluded that a high expected penalty for murder is a deterrent to individuals who might consider killing someone. Particularly given the policy implication that capital punishment effectively deters homicides, this paper has elicited much criticism and reanalysis (see, e.g., Bowers and Pierce 1975 and Ehrlich's response [1975], as well as more recent studies cited below). A more general implication is that more severe sanctions may reduce the crime rate by deterring potential offenders even if they have little effect on actual offenders (Ehrlich 1998).

Andreoni (1995) reanalyzed Ehrlich's (1975) model, allowing for the possibility that higher penalties may reduce arrest rates indirectly by reducing the probability of conviction. The underlying idea is that when sentencing policies are relatively stringent, judges and juries make decisions that mitigate their impact. Considering this indirect effect, sentencing policies had no influence on twelve categories of crime rates ranging in severity from property crimes to homicide.

A previous arrest may influence the decision maker's perception of the probability of another arrest (Shapiro and Votey 1984). The first arrest is likely to inform a person about the operations of the criminal justice system, including the true chance of an arrest and the associated consequences. On the other hand, those who break the law and are not caught may lower their estimates of the probability of an arrest. Those who are caught may be singled out by the police because of their own carelessness or recklessness, which may result from too low an assessment of the risk of arrest. Thus, those arrested may reflect a segment of the population who underestimate the probability of arrest (Shapiro and Votey 1984). Additionally, police are said to have discretion because they can choose not to arrest someone who qualifies under the law (Reiss 1984; Mastrofski, Snipes, and Ritti 1994). Even though all police decisions are subject to review, in reality the overwhelming majority are not reviewed. This discretion available to individual law enforcement officers helps explain why some people are arrested while others are not or are simply warned.

There is a literature on the effects of enforcement of handgun ("right-to-carry") laws on violent crime and whether such laws induce substitution into property crime (Cook and Leitzel 1996; Lott and Mustard 1997; Black and Nagin 1998). The last word on this controversy has probably not yet been written. Recent results obtained using extreme bound analysis, a technique developed by Leamer (1983) designed to deal with model uncertainty, suggest that concealed handgun laws deter violent crime. Using this test with existing data, however, it is unclear whether such laws cause a substitution into other types of crime such as property crimes (Bartley and Cohen 1998).

Much of this research has used aggregate data. By contrast, Tauchen, Witte, and Griesinger (1994) used panel data from a 10 percent sample of males born in 1945 who resided in Philadelphia between their tenth and eighteenth birthdays. They created two panel data sets and specified two dependent variables—whether the individual had been arrested during the past year and an index of criminal offenses that reflected both the seriousness and the frequency of arrests. The principal measure of general deterrence was the police budget (in real dollars) per Federal Bureau of Investigation index offense. Alternatively, the authors used measures of police employment and total criminal justice system employment. The hypothesis that people respond to the threat brought about by committing greater resources to police was strongly supported by the empirical analysis. The elasticity for the expected number of years with no arrests with respect to police resources was 0.47. Tests for endogeneity of the police variable failed to reject the null hypothesis of exogeneity. Although the results are interesting, as the authors note, they are based on a single cohort in a single city. Further, even though they studied a panel data set, police policies did not change during the observational period. As with the other studies reviewed in this section, the research provides general support for the view that potential criminals know what crime can cost offenders.

A more direct test would involve objective or subjective measures of the probability of arrest rather than police resources. Police engage in a tremendous range of tasks. Crime rates may be unchanged because aggregate police resources do not necessarily affect the probability of arrest (see, e.g., Benson, Kim, and Rasmussen 1994).

Brumm and Cloninger (1996) provided some evidence on the relation between arrest probability and police resources, using data from fifty-eight cities in thirty-two states. Because average punishment risk levels as perceived by potential murderers were not directly observed by the researchers, this was treated as an endogenous latent variable. The authors found that the homicide rate was significantly and negatively correlated with the perceived risk of punishment and significantly and positively related to police presence. The former result provides empirical support for the deterrence hypothesis. The latter finding implies that greater police resources have a positive effect on the arrest rate for homicides. Later in this chapter we present results from our own test of the relation between police resources in the bar's locality and the bar owner's or manager's perception of the risk of arrest for violating a local alcohol ordinance.

Most analysis of criminal deterrence has focused on the effect of criminal enforcement on crime rates. Viscusi (1986) analyzed the criminal deterrence hypothesis by assessing whether financial rewards were greater for those crimes for which the probability of being arrested for committing the crime, the probability of conviction after arrest, and prison terms were all relatively high. The probabilities and prison terms were perceptions elicited from a sample of persons at relatively high risk of committing criminal offenses. In a normally functioning "market" for crime, one would expect the financial rewards to rise with the cost of doing business—in this context arrest, conviction, and punishment. Viscusi found that returns did rise with increases in such cost. In fact, risk premiums for arrest, conviction, and prison accounted for between one-half and two-thirds of all crime income. Higher levels of enforcement and punishment are entry barriers to criminal pursuits, which supports the criminal deterrence hypothesis.

Philipson and Posner (1996) argued that there may be a natural rate of crime analogous to the natural rate of unemployment. This means that a decrease in public protection would be offset by an increase in private protection by individuals. In addition, businesses and other enterprises employ armies of security guards and invest heavily in other measures of self-protection. This relationship has important implications for the efficacy of public measures to control crime and leads to new insights into why public interventions tend to have limited deterrent effects. Philipson and Posner presented empirical evidence in support of their natural rate of crime hypothesis using data concerning burglar alarms. In the context of our study, a natural rate of crime would imply that reduced enforcement by police would increase the number of private security guards commercial servers employ.

For drinking and driving, matters are conceptually more complicated. If police protection was reduced, the propensity to drive after drinking might increase because the probability of getting caught is reduced. Yet other drivers might become more reluctant to drive when there are a lot of drinkers on the road. This in turn should reduce the number of motor vehicle fatalities. Although it may seem plausible that fatalities would rise on balance, this cannot be logically deduced. At a minimum, less driving would reduce the increase in fatalities that would have otherwise occurred. We examine these issues empirically in our own analyses in chapters 7 and 9.

Overall the empirical analysis provides some support for the hypothesis that criminal laws deter criminal behavior, but there are exceptions to this generalization. Evidence on other crimes may apply to alcohol, but the general literature in this field provides only a hint. More direct tests of the type we present in later chapters are needed.

BEHAVIOR OF LAW ENFORCEMENT AGENCIES AND THE COURTS
Incentives, Constraints, and Optimizing Behavior

To motivate all relevant parties requires balancing costs and benefits to criminals, victims, and the enforcement system (Friedman 1987). Law enforcement agencies are virtual monopolists in the jurisdictions they serve. Since they are accountable to a political constituency, not a market, their objective function cannot be to maximize the value of the firm. Rather, they may attach a value to successfully prosecuting particular kinds of cases. Given a fixed budget constraint (certainly true in any given year), such agencies decide how to allocate resources to enforcement and prosecution based on comparisons of marginal benefit that reflect the utility weights and the marginal cost of pursuing the case type. A particular case may yield substantial utility, but if the marginal cost of pursuing that case is even higher, resources will be allocated elsewhere. In the context of server violations, lack of enforcement may well reflect a lack of public support, especially in view of the alternative uses of resources.

Some judges are elected and therefore are directly accountable to a political constituency. Others are appointed. In both cases they may be motivated by prestige, by doing good, and by power. Judges face the resource constraints of the court and of scarce prison capacity. In this "market," convicting drunk drivers and illegal servers must compete with other priorities.

Appropriate sentences vary proportionately with the magnitude of the crime's harm (Waldfogel 1993). However, deterrence and incapacitation motivate the imposition of sentencing schemes that are only partly based on harms. Criminal sentences are justified by how well they discourage crime, either directly or indirectly, and allocate sentencing resources so as to prevent the greatest amount of criminal harm.

Prosecutors in the United States have great discretion not to prosecute, and when they do proceed they have broad power to determine which charges to file (Schulhofer 1988). After filing, they have virtually unlimited discretion about whether to offer a plea bargain. Judges also have great discretion in selecting a sentence from a wide range of options. This power of choice in the criminal justice system can lead to disparate treatment of offenders and even to abuse of authority (Schulhofer 1988).

Mandatory Sentencing

Mandatory penalties shift power from judges to prosecutors, meet with widespread circumvention, produce dislocations in case processing, and too often result in penalties that everyone involved believes are unduly harsh (Tonry 1996). The primary and strongest argument for mandatory penalties is that their enactment and enforcement deter would-be offenders and thereby reduce crime rates and spare potential victims from suffering (Tonry 1996).

The effectiveness of mandatory penalties can be evaluated using two sources—government advisory committees or national commissions and evaluations of the deterrent effects of newly enacted mandatory penalties. In 1993 the National Academy of Sciences Panel on Understanding and Control of Violent Behavior compared average prison sentences per violent crime from 1975 to 1989 and found that violent crime increased the prison population very little (Tonry 1996). In Britain the Home Office, an agency similar to the U.S. Department of Justice, also expressed skepticism about the deterrent effects of penalties. "Deterrence is a principle with much immediate appeal, . . . but much crime is committed on impulse, and it is committed by offenders who live from moment to moment; their crimes are as impulsive as the rest of their feckless, sad, or pathetic lives. It is unrealistic to construct sentencing arrangements on the assumption that most offenders will weigh up the possibilities in advance and base their conduct on rational calculation" (Tonry 1996). A Canadian government study commission reached similar conclusions in an analysis of mandatory sentencing laws. The commission found that deterrence cannot be used with empirical justification to guide sentencing (Tonry 1996).

In Massachusetts, studies were conducted on the crime-prevention effects of a statute requiring a one-year minimum sentence for people convicted of possessing an unregistered firearm (Tonry 1996). The studies concluded that mandatory penalties either had no deterrent effect on the use of a firearm in violent crimes (Tonry 1996; Beha 1977; Rossman et al. 1979; Carlson 1982) or had a small, short-term effect that quickly disappeared (Tonry 1996). Similar studies of mandatory sentencing for use of a firearm examined populations in Detroit (Loftin, Heumann, and McDowall 1983), in Tampa, Jacksonville, and Miami (Loftin and McDowall 1984), and in Philadelphia (McDowall, Loftin, and Wiersema 1992). These studies concluded that the mandatory sentencing laws have no preventive effect (Tonry 1996).

CRIMINAL LAW AND INCENTIVES OF COMMERCIAL ALCOHOL SERVERS
Enforcement of Criminal Penalties against Servers

In the nineteenth century alcohol servers faced criminal penalties for serving obviously intoxicated customers or known drunkards. This was not because such heavy drinkers were viewed as endangering themselves, but rather because they were seen as a danger to their families owing to the suffering wives and children endure through their relationship with a heavy drinker. For example, a drunkard was likely to lose his job and thus eventually would pass along the costs of maintaining his family to others.

Today, commercial sellers of alcoholic beverages may face criminal punishments for serving minors and obviously intoxicated persons, including fines, alcohol license revocation, and even jail time for owners, managers, wait staff, and bartenders. These sanctions not only penalize the individual but also aim to punish the business financially for bad server behavior. They provide incentives for commercial sellers to follow the rules of legal alcohol service. A seller, however, may evaluate a perceived low risk of detection and a correspondingly high profit when deciding whether to engage in illegal service. Additionally, financial penalties may be small in proportion to the low risk of detection and potential profits to be made.

Serving an intoxicated person is a criminal offense in all states except Florida, New Jersey, Vermont, and Wyoming. Penalties for server offenses range from personal fines or jail time to administrative license suspension for the establishment. Criminal penalties for serving minors and intoxicated persons differ among states (Colman, Krell, and Mosher 1985; U.S. Department of Transportation, various years). Penalties (jail, fine) for serving minors and intoxicated persons differ according to whether this violation is considered a misdemeanor or a more serious offense and for first or repeat offenses. Individual state statutes are again a source of information on criminal liability—but a limited one, because statutes do not reveal the extent of enforcement. Enforcing criminal penalties against the intoxicated drinker, such as for driving while intoxicated, helps to increase consumers' acceptance of server intervention (Saltz 1989).

To detect server offenses, police may undertake stakeouts. Michigan began a program of placing undercover police officers in bars and taverns to monitor service to obviously intoxicated persons (Levy and Miller 1995) and issue citations to those who served them. The data indicated that before the program, 18 percent of intoxicated patrons were refused service. After the program was implemented, service was refused to over 40 percent (Levy and Miller 1995). When comparing the costs of drunk driving to the costs of the program, the benefits of the program far outweighed the costs.

Enforcement of Laws against Serving Minors

The arrest rates for people under twenty-one for liquor law violations vary widely from state to state. In some states police officers make enforcement of the drinking age a priority, while in other states the law is barely enforced. For example, in Louisiana there were 12 arrests per 100,000 total population for underage drinking. By contrast, in South Dakota, the mean value was 561 arrests per 100,000. The same study documented that common methods of purchase include false identification, buying from stores known to sell to underage people, and purchasing liquor from young clerks. On average, only 2 of every 1,000 occasions of youth drinking resulted in an arrest, and only 5 of every 100,000 youth drinking occasions resulted in an ABC action against an alcohol outlet (Wagenaar and Wolfson 1994).

For youth drinking enforcement, states with high numbers of officers relative to population had low rates of arrest for youth drinking (Wagenaar 1994). This is generally the opposite of the expectation that having more officers available would increase the odds of attention's being focused on youth drinking enforcement, unless youths drank less because they were aware of more officers. High ratios of officers to population were related to high rates of arrest for other crimes, leaving little time available for attention to youth drinking (Wagenaar and Wolfson 1994). Wagenaar also found that states with more arrests for minor crimes tended to have fewer arrests for underage drinking. According to this study, penalties were too lenient to deter providers of alcohol from serving alcohol to minors. As a result, tens of thousands of minors were arrested each year for possession or consumption of alcohol, but very few commercial alcohol outlets that sold to minors or adults who provided alcohol to minors were cited.

Survey of Police Departments: Purposes and Description

During the summer of 1996, students and staff of Duke University interviewed local police department officials by telephone in the Survey of Police Departments (see the appendix for further details). The surveyed departments were in the same areas as the participating bars and restaurants in our Survey of Commercial Servers. In total, 103 interviews were conducted. Police were questioned about information on local criminal laws that pertained to alcohol servers and establishments, frequency of alcohol violations and convictions, types of penalties imposed for alcohol offenses, and police resources dedicated to such offenses. For bars in standard metropolitan statistical areas (SMSAs), we were able to match responses from the Survey of Police Departments with responses to our Survey of Commercial Servers. For bars in nonmetropolitan areas, we obtained some location-specific information from the survey firm, which allowed a match better than at the state level. Since we promised confidentiality, we were not told the identity of the bars surveyed.

Police Activity and the Allocation of Police Resources

We found that the police tend to be passive in citing and arresting people for alcohol-related offenses. The effectiveness of criminal sanctions depends critically on how fully laws are enforced. Communities make a variety of demands on police departments, only one of which is the control of excessive alcohol use and its effects. Allocating police to this task depends on the level of competing demands and on budget constraints.

Our Survey of Police Departments revealed considerable variation in police staffing per thousand population in the communities served (table 3.1). The standard deviation was almost twice the mean. The range in number of officers per thousand persons in the patrol area was from a minimum

Table 3.1 Police Practices

	Mean	Std. Dev.	Min.	Max.
Number of officers per thousand people in patrol area (96)	2.9	5.3	0.5	48.0
Citations per officer from routine Saturday night patrol (81)	1.0	1.3	0.0	10.0
Arrests per officer from routine Saturday night patrol (90)	0.5	0.6	0.0	3.5
Budget ($) per capita population (83)	167.2	355.3	0.19	3,200.0
Percentage with special team focused on drinking establishments (97)	27.8			
Percentage with special personnel in district attorney's office (95)	13.7			

Source: 1996 Survey of Police Departments.
Note: Numbers in parentheses are number of departments responding to item.

Table 3.2 Enforcement

	Mean	Std. Dev.	Min.	Max.
Complaints per number of bars on typical Saturday night (93)	0.30	0.44	0.0	2.75
Citations per number of bars on a typical Saturday night (81)	0.18	0.65	0.0	5.56
Arrests per number of bars on a typical Saturday night (86)	0.13	0.6	0.0	2.08
Percentage of complaints prompted by fights (92)	44.3			
Percentage of complaints prompted by other disorderly conduct (90)	35.2			
Percentage of complaints prompted by other conduct (27)	20.7			
Main other complaints				
Loud noise (13)	16.7			
Underage drinking (10)	12.8			
Domestic violence (9)	11.5			
Illegal use or sale of drugs (7)	9.0			
Refusal fo leave or trespass (6)	7.7			
DUI/DWI (6)	7.7			

Source: 1996 Survey of Police Departments.
Note: Numbers in parentheses are number of departments responding to item.

of 0.5 to a maximum of 48.0. In part the variation reflects the inadequacy of the population denominator. For example, in an area with many businesses and few residents, the ratio may be high.

There was substantial variation among departments in other measures as well. On average there was 1.0 citation per office from routine Saturday night patrol around bars, but this ratio varied from 0.0 to 10.0, probably owing in part to interarea variation in population characteristics. There was 0.5 arrest per officer from routine Saturday night patrol around bars. There was less geographic variation for arrests than for citations. On average, $167 (1996 dollars) was spent per capita on police, but this amount varied from practically zero (probably in a jurisdiction without local budgeting) to over $3,000. A minority of departments had special teams focusing on drinking establishments or special personnel that dealt specifically with alcohol-related issues in the district attorney's office.

There was also considerable variation in the number of complaints to the police from bars, of citations, and of arrests per bar on a typical Saturday night (table 3.2). Nearly half of the complaints to police were prompted by fights. Another third were prompted by other types of disor-

Box 3.1 Types of complaints investigated by police at bars.

Loud noise	Hit-and-run car accidents
Underage drinking	Property damage
Domestic violence	Assault
Illegal sale/use of narcotics	Parking problems
Refusal to leave/trespass	Disturbance over fake ID
DUI	Transients
Disorderly conduct	Prostitution
Public intoxication	Large out-of-hand parties
Theft/robbery	Public nuisance
Public lewdness/indecent exposure	Consumption in parking lots
Fights	Injured person

Source: 1996 Survey of Police Departments.

derly conduct. Other complaints included loud noise, underage drinking, and domestic violence, but these were far less frequent.

A full list of complaints, ranked in descending order of frequency, is shown in box 3.1. We recorded and present complaints exactly as the police characterized them. Fights and assaults appear as separate items farther down the list.

RELATION BETWEEN OBJECTIVE MEASURES OF POLICE DEPARTMENT RESOURCES AND RISK PERCEPTIONS OF OWNERS OR MANAGERS OF BARS

We studied the relation between two measures of resource allocation—full-time equivalent employees in police departments per thousand population within the patrolling area (or precinct) and the police budget per capita population—and the perceived probability of being cited by the local police for various infractions, as reported by owners or managers responding to our Survey of Commercial Servers. (See chapter 2 and the appendix for a description of this survey.)

The Survey of Commercial Servers asked about the perceived probability of being cited for serving minors, serving obviously intoxicated adults, overcrowding, and rowdiness. Respondents were asked to rank the probability of a citation on a five-point scale, with one being "very likely" and five being "not at all likely." Other explanatory variables were included in the analysis to control for influences other than resource allocation. Since the dependent variable consisted of five mutually exclusive order categories, we used ordered logit analysis.

The coefficients on the police staffing variable were uniformly positive (table 3.3), suggesting that higher staffing raised the perceived probability of being cited by the police. However, only in the equation for serving of intoxicated adults was the coefficient statistically significant at even the 10 percent level, again implying that establishments' management believed there would be consequences for infractions.

By contrast, the coefficients on the budget variable were positive and statistically significant at the 5 percent level in the regressions for rowdiness and serving intoxicated adults and at the 10 percent level in the overcrowding regression and were positive in all regressions. Clearly there is a link between the resource allocation measures and servers' perceptions of the probability of being cited.

In contrast, the paucity of significant results from the clientele and establishment characteristic variables indicates that they do not generally affect perception of the likelihood of being cited. Those results that were statistically significant at conventional levels are plausible. Bars with a large student population reported that they would be more likely to be cited for overcrowding, while older establishments reported less chance of a citation for this. Establishments with more regular customers were less likely to be cited for serving already intoxicated adults. Establishments with a high percentage of regulars should be familiar with their customers and their drinking patterns.

The marginal effects show the magnitude of response to a change in an explanatory variable. Since we used ordered logit analysis, there is a marginal effect for each of the categories. In the tables we show the marginal effect for the highest category, "very likely" that the bar would be cited if it engaged in the practice mentioned. For example, for the budget per capita in the equation for serving an obviously intoxicated adult, a $1,000 increase in per capita budget would increase by 0.14 the perceived probability of its being "very likely" that a citation would be issued.

Our Survey of Commercial Servers asked owners and managers of bars similar questions about other types of law and regulation. In chapters 7 and 8 we will use these measures of servers' perceptions to study the impact of administrative, criminal, and tort threats on servers' behavior.

We also analyzed effects of resource variables and other factors on responses to two questions from our Survey of Commercial Servers: whether local police regularly patrol around the establishment in the evening, and whether police ever come into the bar and check patrons' identifications. The vast majority of respondents (88.6 percent) said that local police patrolled around their establishments, but most (62.1 percent) said the police never entered (table 3.4). When they came in, it was often as a result of a

Table 3.3 Perceived Probability of Citation: Local Police

Explanatory Variables	Serving Minors			Serving Obviously Intoxicated Individuals			Overcrowding			Rowdiness		
	Coeff.	Std. Err.	M. E.	Coeff.	Std. Err.	M. E.	Coeff.	Std. Err.	M. E.	Coeff.	Std. Err.	M. E.
Budget per capita (thousand $)	1.10	1.46	0.23	0.66[b]	0.33	0.14	0.46	0.27	0.038	0.74[b]	0.31	0.15
Full-time equivalent employees per thousand population in jurisdiction	0.11	0.10	0.023	0.11	0.064	0.024	0.082	0.056	0.0067	0.085	0.069	0.017
Establishment characteristics												
Chain	0.22	0.64	0.045	−0.32	0.49	−0.068	0.086	0.47	0.0070	−0.44	0.53	−0.088
Age of establishment	0.0054	0.0064	0.0011	−0.0058	0.0049	−0.0012	−0.014[a]	0.0052	−0.0011	0.0007	0.0047	0.0001
Incorporated	0.68[a]	0.25	0.14	0.22	0.20	0.047	0.24	0.21	0.020	0.18	0.20	0.036
Fraction of sales from food	0.24	0.60	0.050	0.28	0.48	0.059	0.42	0.49	0.035	0.66	0.49	0.13
Clientele characteristics												
Fraction of												
Customers aged 25–40	−1.23	1.04	−0.26	−0.46	0.87	−0.097	−0.31	0.84	−0.026	−0.81	0.79	−0.16
Customers aged 40+	−0.63	1.00	−0.13	0.60	0.84	0.13	0.29	0.81	0.024	1.08	0.76	0.21
Students	0.17	1.32	0.035	0.45	1.01	0.096	2.60[b]	1.04	0.21	1.20	0.94	0.24
Blue-collar workers	0.14	0.45	0.029	0.22	0.38	0.046	0.12	0.39	0.0097	0.10	0.38	0.020
Regular customers	0.41	0.52	0.087	−0.89[b]	0.44	−0.19	−0.14	0.48	−0.011	−0.62	0.46	−0.12
Men	0.46	0.85	0.096	0.22	0.68	0.047	1.13	0.69	0.092	0.39	0.73	0.078
Customers who come alone	−0.62	0.76	−0.13	−0.11	0.63	−0.023	−0.088	0.65	−0.0072	−0.39	0.63	−0.076
Customers who come in groups	−1.21	0.84	−0.26	−0.84	0.74	−0.18	−0.18	0.73	−0.014	−0.67	0.75	−0.13
Customers who come by car	−0.32	0.42	−0.068	−0.33	0.30	−0.070	0.038	0.35	0.0031	−0.30	0.29	−0.060
Population density	−0.0091	0.0087	−0.0019	0.0021	0.0070	0.0004	0.0079	0.0080	0.0006	0.0009	0.0072	0.0002
	N = 380			*N* = 377			*N* = 375			*N* = 374		

Source: 1996 Survey of Commercial Servers.
[a]Statistically significant at 1 percent level.
[b]Statistically significant at 5 percent level.
Coeff. = coefficient; Std. Err. = standard error; M. E. = marginal effect.
Table reports nonstandardized regression coefficients.

Table 3.4 Policies of Local Police and Alcohol Law Enforcement

Question	% Yes	% Missing
Local police patrol around establishment	88.6	0.7
Local police never entered establishment in past year	62.1	4.6
ALE never entered establishment in past year	27.4	16.9
Local police called as result of fight during past year (345 establishments with fights only)	73.6	0.6

Source: 1996 Survey of Commercial Servers.

fight, indicating that police respond to reported problems but do not frequently enter bars looking for violations.

We used logit analysis to study determinants of regular local police patrols in the evening and police ever coming into a bar to check patrons' identifications. Although both parameter estimates were positive, only one of the two resource allocation variables had positive and statistically significant effects on the likelihood of police patrols (table 3.5). Bars in communities with high police budgets were significantly more likely to report that police came into their establishments to check identifications. The probability that this would occur rose by about 0.015 per $100 increase in the per capita budget for local law enforcement. Police staffing had no effect on this measure. Police were significantly less likely to check for identification in bars that had a high fraction of sales from food, older customers, and regular customers. They were significantly more likely to check identification at bars where more customers came in groups, probably because these bars cater to a younger clientele.

The Survey of Commercial Servers included an open-ended question about the ways local police and alcohol law enforcement agents, where employed, have affected the respondent's business practices (boxes 3.2 and 3.3). We classified responses into three general categories: increased precaution level, effect on demand, and other. Most of the responses were in the first category and included: "they come in the parking lot and watch," "enforce drunk driving laws," and "patrol the area." Under affect demand, some respondents said that the police "harass customers" and that "their presence outside keeps people from coming in." A minority of owners or managers had praise for the local police.

CONCLUSION

In a survey of policymakers, 61.4 percent admitted that Mothers Against Drunk Driving (MADD) had influenced their opinions about drunk dri-

Table 3.5 Measures of Police Activity: Commercial Server Owner or Manager Experience

Explanatory Variables	Local Police Regularly Patrol in Evening			Police Have Ever Entered Bar to Check Patrons' Identifications		
	Coeff.	Std. Err.	M. E.	Coeff.	Std. Err.	M. E.
Budget per capita (thousand $)	0.43	0.98	0.029	0.65[b]	0.33	0.15
Full-time equivalent employees per thousand population in jurisdiction	0.24	0.30	0.016	−0.0040	0.074	−0.0009
Establishment characteristics						
Chain	0.33	1.10	0.022	−0.0069	0.52	−0.0016
Age of establishment	0.0049	0.010	0.0003	0.0094	0.0059	0.0021
Incorporated	0.90[b]	0.39	0.061	0.30	0.24	0.068
Fraction of sales from food	−1.14	0.86	−0.077	−2.19[a]	0.61	−0.49
Clientele characteristics						
Fraction of						
Customers aged 25–40	−0.33	1.62	−0.022	−1.25	0.97	−0.28
Customers aged 40+	−1.29	1.53	−0.087	−1.85	0.96	−0.42
Students	1.90	2.39	0.13	0.045	1.17	0.010
Blue-collar workers	0.96	0.67	0.065	0.23	0.46	0.051
Regular customers	−0.67	0.91	−0.046	−0.99	0.54	−0.22
Men	−0.46	1.32	−0.031	−0.71	0.86	−0.16
Customers who come alone	0.33	1.16	0.022	0.81	0.79	0.18
Customers who come in groups	0.21	1.28	0.014	1.87[b]	0.87	0.42
Customers who come by car	−0.84	0.79	−0.057	−0.13	0.38	−0.030
Population density	0.018	0.017	0.0012	0.0075	0.0083	0.0017
	$N = 385$			$N = 385$		

Source: 1996 Survey of Commercial Servers.
[a]Statistically significant at 1 percent level.
[b]Statistically significant at 5 percent level.
Coeff. = coefficient; Std. Err. = standard error; M. E. = marginal effect.

Box 3.2 Ways alcohol law enforcement has affected business practices: opinions of commercial establishment owners and managers.

Increased Precaution Level

Increased care level 16	Higher taxes 2
Laws are enforced 16	Monitor for everything you do 2
We follow all their rules 14	Monitor drinks per person 2
Same as the police 12	Have road checks 2
Alert for undercover agents 8	Not serving drunks 1
ALE comes in to monitor 7	Everyone has to have an ID 1
They affect all the rules we have to follow 6	We've lowered the percentage on our Breathalyzer 1
ALE monitors from outside 5	Watch for potential DUI 1
Do not serve minors 4	Have minor decoys 1
Same as ABC 4	Can't remove alcohol from premises 1
Customers more aware of checkpoints 4	Do not admit any minors 1
Investigate serving minors 3	Investigate serving drunk people 1
More careful because I know they are out there 3	Limit advertising 1
Perform inspections 3	Signs have to be posted 1
ALE provides educational materials 2	Investigate employee drinking 1

Effect on Demand

Business has slowed 7	Fewer repeat customers 1
People are afraid of being arrested for DUI when they see ALE outside 6	No carry-out after midnight 1
People scared to drive after 10:00 P.M. because of DUI when they are around—business decreases 5	Closed us down 1
	Nonalcoholic sales are up, but general business has gone down 1
Scare customers away 5	Regulate last call 1
People don't drink as much 5	Customers do not stay as late 1
Customers more conscious of how much they are drinking 5	Regulate last call 1
	People do not return after they have been caught for drunk driving 1
Easier to get DUI 4	Lowered revenue 1
Has killed late-night business 4	Cut back hours of operation 1
Intimidate customers 2	Makes it damn tough to sell a beer 1
Out to get our customers 2	Influences customer's decision to drive 1
More off sale and less bar retail 1	We now give rides 1
Make it more expensive to train servers 1	

Other

Have no effect 8	Not much 1
Has influenced business quite a bit 4	We respect each other and work together 1
Don't know 3	Has helped business 1
Don't have ALE here 2	Have no respect for us 1
They don't bother me because I card minors 1	Patrons have no responsibilities as soon as they start drinking 1
They are good to deal with 1	Have been very helpful 1
Have no effect—I have to pay them all the time 1	

Source: 1996 Survey of Commercial Servers. Numbers are number of responses.

Box 3.3 Ways local police have affected business practices: opinions of commercial establishment owners and managers.

Increased Precaution Level

They come in the parking lot and watch   22

Enforce drunk driving laws   21

Patrol the area   15

Decoys or sting and undercover operations   0

Road blocks   7

Drive by frequently every night   6

Check for minors   5

Here all the time   5

Help with rowdy customers   5

Check up on my closing time   5

Provide positive support   5

Police educate our servers   4

Pull over cusotmers on highway for DUI   4

Police monitor our patrons   4

Come inside and visit   4

We follow policies correctly   3

Hang out at bar at closing time   3

Entrapment   3

Park outside and walk through bar   3

Pain in the butt   3

Bar checks once in a while   2

Park in shadows/alleys and wait for people   2

Enforce alcohol laws   2

Conduct inspections   2

Make us aware of laws and regulations   2

Follow our customers home   2

We now monitor our customers   2

Watch out bar more than they patrol for drunk driving   2

Warn us about loud music   1

They hang out to control drugs   1

Target my bar and look for minors   1

Provide rides   1

They are not doing their job   1

We are friendly with them   1

At bar every day   1

People are more careful   1

Being noisy all the time   1

They hang out across the street, make our customers paranoid   1

Tickets are a revenue generator for the city   1

Find reasons to pull people over for drunk driving   1

Make us more aware of how we should conduct our business   1

Enforce ABC laws   1

Check for obviously intoxicated persons   1

Hawk people   1

We have cut back on underage customers   1

Effect on Demand

Harass customers   9

Their presence outside keeps people from coming in   5

Cuts down on drinking because people are afraid to drive   4

Slowed business   4

Make our customers nervous   2

Strict on drunk driving, scares customers   2

Those who have been arrested for DUI don't come back   1

Had to stop dancing because police would follow patrons   1

Chase down customers who have been drinking, scare them to death   1

Since BAC has been lowered, business has dropped   1

Afraid of drinking because afraid to be pulled over   1

People drink more at home   1

Have told me they will destroy my business   1

Other

None   4

I do nothing wrong, so they don't bother me   2

Source: 1996 Survey of Commercial Servers. Numbers are number of responses.

ving and alcohol abuse (Kinkade, Leone, and Welsh 1995). Thus, with continuing public awareness and the lobbying efforts of MADD and other community groups, we can expect alcohol laws to become even stricter. However, increasing the strictness of drunk driving laws may place a heavier burden on an already overburdened criminal justice system.

The goals of criminal law are well defined. Criminal behavior may be usefully analyzed as a form of constrained utility maximizing. Law enforcers and courts are other agents in this market, as are potential victims. The interplay of these agents leads to observed rates of crime, arrest, and conviction rates and of levels of resources—both public and private—allocated to crime prevention. One implication of the conceptual framework is that the amount devoted to a particular type of crime depends on the marginal value of loss prevention as well as resources available to law enforcement agents.

In this general sense, criminal laws most directly aimed at deterring excessive use of alcohol and mitigating its social cost are no different from laws that address other purposes. The distinction is plausibly empirical. Given variation in both preferences and resources among areas and time periods, both enforcement and rates of criminal activity may be expected to differ.

The task of assessing whether criminal laws are effective deterrents in the context of alcohol control is left for later chapters. The new empirical results of this chapter are in describing the allocation of police resources and in determining whether variation in the probability of citation was reflected in owners' and managers' perceptions that they would be cited if they were to violate a law, such as by serving an obviously intoxicated adult or by serving a minor irrespective of blood alcohol content.

On police activity and allocation of police resources, departments seemed very passive overall in citing and arresting people for alcohol-related offenses. There was substantial variation in resources, such as staffing, among jurisdictions we surveyed. In general we found a correspondence between measures of resources devoted to law enforcement and commercial servers' perceived probability of being cited by criminal law enforcement agencies.

This result is important for at least two reasons. First, it shows that respondents to our Survey of Commercial Servers took our questions seriously. But second, and more important, to the extent that commercial servers of alcohol actually perceive a threat, and that perceptions are sensitive to variations in public law enforcement inputs, there is at least the possibility that criminal law may deter. By looking inside the "black box" of commercial servers' decision making, we may have learned more than had our analysis been exclusively limited to statistical analysis of resources, laws, and regulations and their effects.

Finally, before becoming too optimistic about the deterrent potential of criminal law, it is noteworthy that although bar owners often saw their presence as an annoyance, police were helpful in responding to disturbances in the bar. Probably owing to limited resources, they did not issue many citations for alcohol violations on an average weekend night. Recognizing this, bar owners and managers were not particularly fearful of being cited for illegal serving practices, although the perceived probability of being cited was higher than actual establishment experience. Based on these results, it appears that, unless police resources are plentiful, the police do not provide an effective means of controlling alcohol consumption and do not deter bad server behavior, which would in turn reduce drunk driving.

4

Tort Liability and the Drunk Driver

Drunk driving and roadway safety are intricately related: a large share of motor vehicle collisions involve alcohol. In the United States, the probability of being injured in a motor vehicle accident, surviving, and incurring some economic loss was twenty-six per thousand total population in 1989 (Hensler et al. 1991). In the United Kingdom in 1976, the probability was two per thousand total population that a person would suffer incapacity for two weeks or more because of a road accident (Harris et al. 1984). In all industrialized countries, motor vehicle fatalities are a major cause of death and long-term disability, especially of younger persons.

In this chapter we discuss the societal impact of drunk driving in greater detail and present the characteristics of a typical drunk driver. We will also discuss the drunk driver's liability for property damages and personal injuries caused by drunk driving accidents. In contrast to most of the chapters in this book, this one does not contain new empirical evidence; rather, we summarize existing literature on the topic. In chapter 5 we will discuss liability of third parties who may be held responsible for the drunk driver's intoxication.

CONSEQUENCES OF DRUNK DRIVING

Among persons who died in fatal crashes in 1990, about 35 percent of those aged twenty-one to twenty-four had a blood alcohol content level (BAC) over 0.10, the current threshold level in most states for driving under the influence (DUI).[1] Of those aged twenty-five to forty-four, about 30 percent had a BAC this high (U.S. Department of Health and Human Services

---

1. Some states have a lower minimum BAC of 0.08.

1998). In a study of motor vehicle death rates in nineteen developed countries, Smart and Mann (1991) found that one variable, per capita alcohol consumption, explained 70 percent of the differences in motor vehicle death rates between countries, while a recent article in the German magazine *Stern* stated that in Germany drunken drivers make eighty million trips a year (Von Weyer 1997).

Drinking any amount of alcohol poses some risk to those who drive afterward and also to other drivers who are on the road with the drinker. It has been estimated that each 0.02 increase in BAC nearly doubles the driver's risk of being involved in fatal crash (Zador 1991). This risk increases more rapidly with each drink for drivers under age twenty-one. Fatal crash involvement per mile driven increases ninefold at BACs of 0.05 to 0.09 (Hingson 1996). Even though high-level drinking provides a higher risk of alcohol-related harm per driver, moderate consumption of alcohol, defined as drinking alcohol on four to six days out of twenty-eight, may also be consequential because so many more people drink at this level (Gruenewald, Treno, and Mitchell 1996). In this sense, concentrating exclusively on the heavy drinker will not completely solve the problem of drunk driving.

Using a very innovative method, Levitt and Porter (1999) have estimated the effect of alcohol on driver risk using only statistics from the Fatal Accident Reporting System (FARS) for 1983–93. Drivers who were identified by police as having been drinking (but not necessarily legally intoxicated) were eight times as likely to cause a fatal motor vehicle accident as those for whom no alcohol involvement was reported. Drivers above the blood alcohol level of 0.10 were at least fourteen times as likely to cause fatal crashes. Drinking was generally far more important than other predictors of accidents such as male gender, youth, and a bad driving record. Peak hours for drinking and driving were between 1:00 A.M. and 3:00 A.M., when as many as 25 percent of drivers were estimated to have been drinking. The proportion of drinking drivers appears to have declined over the decade, but the relative risk of a crash, given that the driver had been drinking, was stable.

Viewed from still another perspective, drunk driving places a huge burden on prisons and the court system. The proportion of prisoners who are incarcerated for drunk driving is rising. Before states established mandatory sentencing laws, only 5.5 percent of county jail admissions were DUI offenders (Blank 1994). With the enactment of mandatory sentencing, by the mid-1990s DUI admissions accounted for almost 40 percent of those entering prisons across the country. Prosecutors spent five times as much time prosecuting drunk drivers as a decade earlier (Blank 1994). In 1995 more than 1.4 million people were arrested for driving while intoxicated, 10 percent of all arrests made that year (Hingson 1996).

One "solution" to jail overcrowding might be to relax the DUI laws, including mandatory sentencing. Insofar as such laws do not deter, perhaps they should be relaxed.[2] But given the external cost of drunk driving, there would a strong rationale for substituting more effective preventive measures instead of relaxing the DUI laws.

Identifying Drunk Drivers
The Adult Drunk Driver

To prevent drunk driving, it is helpful to identify the characteristics of those most likely to drink and drive. The percentage of Americans who self-report episodes of drinking and driving within the past month has fallen since 1984 from slightly over 4 percent of the population to about 2 percent (fig. 4.1). Although underage consumption of alcohol is a major public policy problem, most drunk drivers are adults. From studies of individual drinkers and drivers, considerable information is known about problem drinkers and their driving propensities. First, drunk drivers are more likely to be male (Gruenewald, Treno, and Mitchell 1996). Second, younger adults are more likely to drive when intoxicated. In one study of persons driving under the influence of alcohol, the probability of driving while intoxicated at age twenty-one was 7 percent. At age fifty it was 2 percent (Gruenewald, Treno, and Mitchell 1996).

Risky Driving Behaviors

Those who drive drunk also typically exhibit risky and hostile driving behavior. Donovan, Marlatt, and Salzberg (1983) found four characteristics of drivers at high risk for drunk driving: emotional instability; impulsiveness and thrill seeking; hostility; and depression and low perceived personal control. MacDonald (1989) noted great similarity between the psychosocial characteristics of those arrested for DUI and those with poor driving records, namely high frequency of accidents and violations. High-risk drivers and DUI offenders have lower rates of seat belt use than non-drinking drivers (Wilson 1992). Mean collision frequencies were higher for DUI offenders than for the controls on both property damage and injury damage, as well as for total collisions (Wilson 1992; Deery and Love 1996).

---

2. Given the motivation of retribution, some would still argue that strict DUI laws should be maintained.

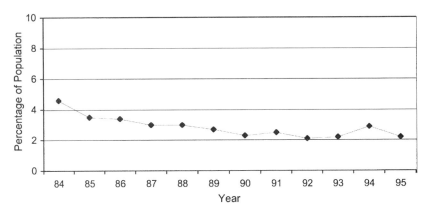

Fig. 4.1 Percentage of the United States population who drink and drive. Source: Unpublished data from annual Behavioral Risk Factor Survey.

DUI offenders were also consistently more deviant on behavioral and personality measures (Wilson 1992).

Drunk driving offenders commit more moving violations and more violations involving negligence (e.g., failing to avoid an accident) (Wilson 1992). About 9 percent of nondrinking drivers had at least one traffic violation in a year compared with 15 percent of unimpaired (BAC < 0.05) and 23 percent of impaired (BAC > 0.05) drinking drivers (Wilson and Jonah 1985). Even small amounts of alcohol (BAC < 0.05) adversely affect driving skill, reaction time, and motor control (Carpenter 1962; Moskowitz and Robinson 1988). Although the numbers of traffic violations are high for drunk drivers, important differences in risk perceptions have been found between impaired and nondrinking drivers. For example, nondrinking drivers perceived a higher probability of being arrested if they drove under the influence than did unimpaired and impaired drinking drivers. Of course, drinking drivers could have better knowledge of arrest probabilities from their own experience (Wilson and Jonah 1985). As we discussed more fully in chapter 3, the probability of a legally intoxicated driver's being arrested for DUI is very low, which may encourage drinking drivers to exercise less caution.

Drinking Behaviors and Effects

In the same study, Wilson found that impaired drivers drank more in total and drank greater amounts per occasion than nondrinking and unimpaired drivers. Another predictor of impairment was an affirmative answer to the following statement: "At a party, I usually drink the same amount whether I am driving or not." People who drove while impaired were either less willing or less able to curb their drinking when they drove (Wilson and Jonah 1985). Other evidence indicates that drivers at risk for drunk driving believe they have an increased capacity for alcohol. High-risk drivers estimated that they could consume more drinks before their driving ability was impaired (Wilson 1992). Those with a prior DUI offense estimated that they could have drunk even more before reaching a level of impairment (Wilson 1992).

Alcohol affects both driving skill and driving style among young adult drivers. Deery and Love (1996) found that, with a 0.05 blood alcohol content, subjects took longer to detect hazards and responded to them more abruptly. In the same study, these effects were particularly profound for DUI offenders. Regardless of drunk driving patterns, participants saw hazards arising from the driver's own actions as less dangerous than those arising from the actions of other road users. DUI offenders and impaired drivers tended to be more externally controlled, resentful, verbally hostile, and impulsive. They were also more likely to be identified by law enforcement officers because of their high-risk driving. They may have been more prone to fail to respond to hazards caused by other road users because they did not fully perceive the increased risk from those dangerous situations, when intoxicated and even when sober.

Criminal History

Individuals with prior convictions are more likely to be arrested and convicted of drunk driving than those without arrest records (Shapiro and Votey 1984). In a study by Argeriou, McCarty, and Blacker (1985), over three-quarters of DUI offenders had a history of court arraignments, and more than a quarter had previously been arrested for DUI. Among those with prior DUI arrests, 68 percent also had prior criminal arrests,and 63 percent had prior criminal arrests. Prior arrest was more common among male DUI offenders than among females: 53 percent of the men and 32 percent of the women had prior arrests for criminal offenses. The most frequent reasons for prior arrests were traffic offenses (59 percent), public order offenses (34 percent), and property offenses (29 percent).

Recidivism

Repeat offenders represent a substantial part of the drunk driving problem in the United States. It has been estimated that one-third of all drunk drivers are recidivists (Ross and Cleary 1996). These drivers typically have a heavy drinking style. The probability of offending again increases with each additional DUI experience, perhaps because repeat offenders have experienced a relatively low likelihood of being caught or are alcoholics (Ross and Cleary 1996). Of course the repeat offenders were eventually apprehended, but there is an implication that many people arrested for DUI continue this behavior and are not caught again. Yu and Williford (1995) reported that the highest recidivism rates were among those whose first alcohol tickets were dismissed or who were prosecuted but not convicted.

The conclusions above generalize to a variety of countries. For example, in a study conducted in Sweden, Shapiro and Votey (1984) found that repeat offenders estimated a much lower probability of getting caught than the general population. Whether this reflects differences in perceptions or in the utility of drinking and driving was not determined.

The repeat drunk drivers may have been correct in their perception. Shapiro and Votey found that multiple offenders were less likely to be arrested than those with no prior arrests or only one. Alcoholics in particular frequently drove after drinking. Heavier drinkers, who on average drank on twelve days out of twenty-eight and consumed six drinks on each occasion, drove after drinking with a probability of 0.88 and drove while intoxicated with a probability of 0.61. The same study reported that even though high-level drinkers had a higher individual risk of alcohol problems, moderate and low-level drinkers constituted the majority of problem drivers simply because there are so many more of them. Thus the author cautioned that preventing heavier drinking per se may only negligibly reduce the risk of alcohol-related motor vehicle accidents because there are relatively few heavy drinkers on the road.

Gruenewald, Treno, and Mitchell (1996) found no relation between alcoholic beverage preferences and the likelihood of driving after drinking. However, in this study relative frequency of drinking at bars or restaurants was significantly related to driving after drinking. There was a positive relation between the frequency of drinking at bars and restaurants and the propensity to drive after drinking. Another study did find a relation between the type of beverage preferred and the probability of being arrested for DUI. Buntain-Ricklefs and others (1995) found that the risk of DUI was two times as great for those who reported drinking beer as for those who drank liquor.

There are also notable increases in risk for drunk driving among those who started to use drugs and alcohol at an early age and those who have a family history of alcoholism (Gruenewald, Treno, and Mitchell 1996). In a study comparing characteristics of bad drivers with and without a DUI charge, having a problem with alcohol or drugs in high school increased the risk of DUI threefold for alcohol and twofold for drugs (Buntain-Ricklefs et al. 1995). DUI offenders had more family members with drinking problems and drank significantly larger amounts. They also had a higher incidence of injuries (Buntain-Ricklefs et al. 1995).

Ross and Cleary (1996) reported that DUI offenders tended to drive older cars, which presumably have less safety equipment and are more prone to accidents than those driven by those never cited for DUI.[3] The higher mean age of motor vehicles may reflect the lower income of such drivers or their more frequent loss of vehicles in crashes or by impoundment.

The Minor Drunk Driver

Some of the data on alcohol consumption by persons under age twenty-one are indeed alarming. For example, according to Wagenaar and Wolfson (1994), 6 percent of ten- to eleven-year-olds are current users of alcohol; the rate increases to 25 percent by age twelve to fourteen and to 55 percent by age fifteen to seventeen. Among high school seniors, 35 percent reported regularly being intoxicated. Motor vehicle crashes are the leading cause of death for teenagers, with one-third to one-half involving alcohol. Minors, who may or may not be intoxicated, also face deciding whether to ride with a drunk driver. In a study by Grube and Voas (1996), as many as 40 percent of American adolescents had driven after drinking, and 62 percent admitted that they had ridden with an intoxicated driver. Young drinking drivers were at higher risk than adult drinking drivers for fatal accidents at all levels of blood alcohol concentration. Believing that DUI was dangerous and that friends would disapprove of it reduced the incidence both of drinking and driving and of riding with underage drinking drivers. Teenagers who perceived alternatives to riding with a drunk driver drank less and rode with a drunk driver less often. The expectation of being caught and punished reduced the frequency of riding with a drunk driver, but not of DUI. Drinking increased incidents of DUI, but not the frequency of riding with a drunk driver. Study participants who frequently drove at night reported higher rates of DUI, and younger respondents reported more occasions of riding with a drunk driver.

Underage drunk drivers typically were not averse to risk taking and fre-

3. The offenders drove cars that were on average three years older (10.6 years old in Minnesota, 11.2 in Iowa) than cars driven by the rest of the population (7.6 years old in Minnesota, 8.5 in Iowa). Repeat DUI offenders tended to drive even older cars, which were about thirteen years old in Minnesota and more than sixteen years old in Iowa (Ross and Cleary 1996).

quently engaged in other risky behavior as well. Often, minor drunk drivers in the Grube and Voas survey did not see such behavior as unsafe. The respondents who self-reported more instances of drinking and of not using seat belts or of risky driving were less likely to believe the DUI was dangerous. Those who engaged in both drinking and risky driving perceived less risk of being caught by police. Higher levels of education, however, increased the perceived probability of arrest. Respondents who drank more frequently reported it was harder to find alternatives to DUI and riding with a drunk driver. In this study drinking increased with age and was higher among males, European Americans and Latinos, and those who reported more nighttime and total driving.

USING TORT LIABILITY TO CONTROL DRUNK DRIVERS

Ideally, imposing tort liability on a drunk driver should lead those at risk for drunk driving to choose safe rather than risky driving practices. In practice, however, there are many reasons these conditions do not hold. The care level must be well defined and adhered to by the courts. Courts must make accurate determinations of damages. Injury victims must initiate claims for all damages. Drivers' care levels must be responsive to the financial incentives furnished by the imposition of liability. In the context of automobile accidents, liability insurance potentially blunts financial incentives that tort might otherwise offer (see box 4.1 for a general summary of the types of insurance discussed in this chapter). As seen below, the extent to which liability insurance affects drivers' motivations is partly related to the extent to which insurers base premiums on their accidents and violations.

Imposing tort liability on a drunk driver may also compensate victims. Tort tends to undercompensate loss incurred by motor vehicle accident victims, however, especially for serious injuries (Houchens 1985). Payments for the same injury tend to be less for auto accident claims than for other tort claims, such as for medical malpractice (Bovbjerg et al. 1991).

Box 4.1 Types of Insurance.

First or Third Party	*Examples*
First party:	Health disability
Party insures self against loss	Automobile collision
	No-fault insurance
Third party:	Automobile liability
Party insures self against loss to others	Dram shop
	Corporate liability

Delays in resolving claims are common but are less than for some other forms of tort, such as medical malpractice (All-Industry Research Advisory Council 1989; Sloan, Bovbjerg, and Githens 1991). Also, other things being equal, awards in tort cases are larger when it can be demonstrated that the defendant had been drinking at the time the accident occurred (Wittman 1986).

Providing corrective justice is still another goal of tort (see, e.g., Calabresi 1970). In this context also, tort is far from perfect. For one thing, the vast majority of claims filed are settled out of court, thereby avoiding full disclosure of fault (All-Industry Research Advisory Council 1989). Unlike other types of tort, such as medical injuries, it appears that a high proportion of negligently injured victims do in fact initiate claims (compare Dewees, Duff, and Trebilcock 1996 for motor vehicle accidents with Weiler 1991 for medical malpractice).

Several tactics based on both insurance and tort law principles have been proposed as means to reduce drunk driving. These include reducing the burden of proof against the drunk driver in civil cases, allowing punitive damages, imposing extra insurance fees on those convicted of drunk driving, and expanding liability for third parties who are responsible for the drunk driver's intoxication.

TORT VERSUS OTHER FORMS OF REGULATION

Historically, most of the effort to control traffic accidents has been concentrated on changing drivers' behavior through police surveillance and prosecution (see, e.g., Dewees, Duff, and Trebilcock 1996). Thus, at least comparatively speaking, imposing tort liability on unsafe drivers is a secondary line of defense. Given the high frequency of motor vehicle accidents, however, tort claims involving drivers of motor vehicles are among the most common types (Bovbjerg et al. 1991).

Under other types of regulatory regimes, such as administrative and criminal law, the victim has no financial incentive to supply information about the injury and the circumstances in which it occurred. Of course, there may also be nonfinancial motives for reporting injury irrespective of the regulatory regime. Uniquely under tort, however, the victim stands to recover loss attributable to the injury. The incentive to file a tort claim is in direct proportion to the magnitude of such loss.

The major reasons for imposing tort liability on both the driver and the server are to deter unsafe driving and to compensate injury victims. Most public policy has been oriented toward criminal and administrative sanctions, some of which are nonmonetary penalties. Sanctions imposed by tort are more appropriate when injurers' assets are not low relative to the harm caused, injurers' knowledge about risk is superior to that of the regulatory or other social authority, and victims must be induced to supply information to the state about harm because the state's independently acquired information would be poor (Shavell 1987, chap. 12). In the context of motor vehicle safety, these conditions are not totally favorable to tort, suggesting that it is desirable to combine tort with other strategies for promoting safe driving.

In particular, the first condition is not likely to be satisfied. The deterrent effect of tort liability depends on how fully potential tort-feasors are made to bear the cost of the injuries they cause. Injurers are at risk only up to the value of their assets. The cost of many motor vehicle collisions far exceeds the wealth of most drivers (Miller, Luchter, and Brinkman 1989). For this reason, that most drivers have limited liability has led to speculation that the affluent tend to be more careful than the poor (Shavell 1987; Beard 1990). Since many drivers who cause motor vehicle accidents cannot pay the full loss, states have implemented compulsory liability insurance, but the minimum amount drivers must carry is low. Also, imposing additional tort liability on bar owners and servers increases the likelihood that victims will recover their losses, particularly when the drunk driver has bought alcohol from a large chain or corporation.

The rationale for tort is stronger on the second and third conditions. Motor vehicle safety involves literally thousands of decisions by drinkers and interactions among drivers that it is far beyond the state's ability to monitor alone. Thus it is important to provide an additional incentive for drivers to be careful. Imposing tort liability on careless driving provides this incentive. In the bilateral version of the model of accidents, both injurers and victims can take precautions and in this way lower the probability that an accident will occur. Each potential party to an accident considers the precaution level of others in making his or her own decision about care. In equilibrium, no party has an motivation to alter his or her behavior (Shavell 1987, chap. 2).

Comparison between Tort and Criminal Liability

In the case of alcohol abuse, including drinking and driving, the injurer's ability to compensate a victim may fall short of the victim's loss. To adequately punish the injurer, criminal liability, including incarceration, may also be imposed. If apprehended, the driver will have difficulty escaping criminal punishment, since one cannot insure against the hazard of a criminal conviction.

In criminal law, illegal conduct is defined by statute or common law; such law, unlike tort, applies even in the absence of a victim. For example, criminal law would apply to drivers with a blood alcohol content above the statutory threshold. Under tort, this would not suffice to determine liability. For analytical purposes, the effect of criminal liability on driver precautions is the same as the effect of the negligence standard in tort.

Individual Drivers' Incentives for Preventing Accidents

Optimal deterrence is achieved if individuals adopt all measures to avoid accidents, since the costs of accident avoidance, such as inconvenience and the increased travel time required by being more careful, are less than the expected costs of an accident. If all crashes were single-vehicle accidents there would be less of a need to impose liability on the driver, who would bear all accident costs stemming from personal injury. Harm to others' property would still be a possibility for such accidents, however. Alternatively, if drivers would costlessly and effectively contract among themselves before the accident and enforce contract provisions after the accident occurred, a socially optimal amount of care might be exercised without imposing liability (see, e.g., Dewees, Duff, and Trebilcock 1996).

Realistically, however, such conditions do not hold. Most accidents involve people besides the driver and the car's other occupants. Given the number of potential injured parties, ex ante contracting is not a possibility. Also realistically, there may be limits to individuals' ability or willingness to act in their own self-interest (chapter 1), at least as others would see it.

The probability of an accident and the magnitude of loss can be reduced at a cost, either by reducing the frequency of risky behavior or by undertaking costly precautions at the start. An insight of economic analysis first discussed by Brown (1973) is that drivers can "produce" safety by combining various inputs such as good brakes and tires, eyeglasses if needed, and individual characteristics associated with alertness. But safety depends not only on the individual driver's actions but also on the actions of others.

Drivers' probability of being in an accident depends on both their own care level and the level selected by other drivers (Diamond 1974; Brown 1973). In such circumstances, if no liability is imposed, the injurer has no incentive to take precautions to avoid accidents. Victims, seeking to avoid harm to self, will make the most efficient use of inputs under their control. Drivers may be induced to invest in an efficient amount of care if they are made to bear such external costs. Some form of public intervention is needed to induce drivers to take an efficient level of precaution. This may be accomplished by imposing liability when the injurer and the victim are different people. But sometimes, as with the drunk driver involved in a single-car accident, the injurer and the injured are the same. In this case the optimal level of precaution should be achieved without legal intervention (Posner 1986, chap. 6).

The simplest liability rule is the negligence rule in tort, whereby the victim cannot collect from the injurer unless there is a finding that the injurer failed to take due care, that is, was negligent. Payment under tort presumes an accident is accompanied by loss to the victim.

A negligence rule (tort) system should encourage drivers to invest the proper amount if courts correctly set the due care standard at the socially optimal level and compel tort-feasors to bear the full cost of the injuries. The socially optimal level of care minimizes the social cost of accidents and includes both the cost of precautions and the cost of the injury itself. A broader concept of social cost includes the administrative costs of liability insurance and of operating the legal system.

The strong prediction that imposing liability for negligence induces parties to undertake the efficient level of precaution implies that there would be no negligence. Also, with universal adherence to the due care standard, the probability of being sued would be zero, and hence there would be no demand for liability insurance. These predictions are clearly at variance with reality.

One way to rescue the analysis is to assume that courts make mistakes in enforcing the due care standard. If courts do not enforce it, precautions will fall short of the socially optimal level. As discussed below, in certain circumstances liability insurance may blunt the incentives to take precautions that tort would otherwise offer to potential insurers.

An alternative rule, and one that was in effect for much of United States history, is negligence with the defense of contributory negligence. Under this rule, the injurer is liable only if the victim did not contribute at all to his own injuries. If the victim is found to be at all negligent, the injurer is not liable. Under certain restrictive assumptions, this rule will also lead to an efficient combination of precautions (see, e.g., Brown 1998).

EFFECTS OF LIABILITY INSURANCE

The risks a driver takes may be influenced by the availability of liability insurance. The purpose of insurance is to spread risk by means of risk pooling. Lacking government intervention, insurance is demanded by risk-averse individuals. With some exceptions, such as payment for punitive damages and willful negligence, individuals can insure against losses imposed by tort. Government policy directly affects the demand for insurance in two ways—by tax subsidies of premiums, most notably for employer-provided health insurance, and by making minimum purchases compulsory, as with workers' compensation and automobile liability insurance.

Given widespread risk aversion, the possibility that drivers may be liable under tort for much, if not all, of their wealth provides a motive for purchasing liability insurance. If insurers cannot perfectly observe precaution levels of individual policyholders, they cannot adequately link premiums to precaution levels. As a result, a problem of moral hazard arises. The purpose of tort liability is to make people more careful. The effect of moral hazard is to offset, at least in part, the incentive for safety that tort provides.

One response to moral hazard is for people to purchase incomplete coverage. Then injurers bear a higher proportion of the loss from accidents and therefore have a greater incentive to drive safely. Recognizing that moral hazard is likely to occur once individuals are covered, insurers tend to include an implicit moral hazard surcharge in the premium. With perfect observability by insurers, risk-averse persons would demand full coverage (Shavell 1982).

The driver's precaution level before a mishap cannot be directly observed by insurers. There are far too many drivers to permit direct inspection, and in any case drivers' precautions may vary from day to day. Rather, insurers observe accidents and violations of law. Based on these events, they can and do adjust premiums to varying degrees on the assumption that recorded instances of bad driving reflect a general tendency toward bad driving. Insurers may take a violation- and accident-free record as reflecting overall careful driving and subsequently lower premiums for those with exemplary records. The practice of basing premiums on good or bad records is called "experience rating" or "merit rating."

Perfect observability is not likely to occur in the "real world." Although on average a history of motor vehicle collisions is predictive of future accidents, there is considerable variation in future accident rates. Few who violate traffic laws are actually arrested. It is a reasonable presumption that many, if not most, people who have driven drunk have not been arrested (Jacobs 1989).

With liability insurance and the observations of insurers, the cost of the accident no longer depends on the victim's loss or the tort-feasor's wealth, whichever is less; rather, the proportion of the victim's loss borne by the injurer is the part not covered by liability insurance in conjunction with the present value of the rise in premiums resulting from the accident. Even if premiums are raised to reflect the change in the actuarial value of future loss, the increase when a driver has been found liable under tort may be appreciably less than the compensation paid to the injury victim, especially for costly accidents (Lemaire 1985).

Insurance regulation may preclude insurers from using all the information they have available to them in setting premiums. Jurisdictions differ in how far premiums are experience rated or based on other risk categories that reflect expected loss. Insurance regulation affects the extent of experience rating or other risk classification systems (Bruce 1984; Lemaire 1985; Sloan and Githens 1994). In many states, insurers are required to offer insurance to high-risk drivers at premiums well below market levels (Schwartz 1998). States differ in their requirements about surcharging for accidents and violations, and conversely, in their creation of risk pools to guarantee access to insurance for all drivers, often at premiums below the actuarial value of the loss. Reducing premium differentials based on expected loss or forming risk pools to guarantee insurability at an actuarially unfair premium reflects a societal belief that driving is a "right."

As discussed above, that many negligent drivers do not have sufficient wealth to fully compensate injury victims has led to state statutes requiring mandatory minimum liability coverage. If purchasing liability insurance were purely voluntary, those with wealth below the level of loss likely to result from an accident ("potentially judgment-proof injurers") would have little incentive to purchase insurance. Injurers clearly have little motivation to pay for coverage that exceeds their assets, since such excess is of no personal benefit except possibly for altruistic reasons (Pitchford 1998).

Making drivers buy liability insurance plausibly makes them less careful or freer to pursue risky activities. An insured driver may be less inclined to avoid instances of harm that are covered by the liability policy (Schwartz 1998). The extent of moral hazard, however, depends both on the minimum liability limits imposed and on the sensitivity of premiums to the individual's driving record. Moral hazard arises in this context because, although the outcome of failure to take care can be directly observed by the insurer, neither the insured's actions nor states of nature, such as deer crossing the road or a patch of ice that may cause an accident, are seen.

Mandatory liability insurance with little or no experience rating should reduce the driver's motivation to be careful. Conversely, substantial experience rating, especially when a driver may also be surcharged for traffic violations, may increase precautions against accidents. With compulsory coverage and mandatory premium surcharges for violations and chargeable accidents, drivers who have little wealth and might otherwise not purchase automobile liability insurance coverage are made to pay for being careless through higher premiums. Even without experience rating, high mandatory premiums may affect the amount of driving and the composition of drivers. Youths who are accident-prone may drive less.

Accidents may be prevented not only by taking precautions in performing an activity such as driving or drinking alcohol but also by curbing its frequency. One may decide how much to drive as well as whether to drive carefully. There is no liability rule that simultaneously offers the right incentives for the parties to take the efficient precaution level and to select the appropriate amount of activity (Shavell 1980, 1987). This provides a rationale for more than one policy instrument for achieving socially optimal outcomes.

ALTERNATIVE LIABILITY RULES

Traditionally, the common-law rule of contributory negligence applied to automobile accidents as it did to most other tort claims. Liability was made to depend on the defendant's causing the accident, a victim's incurring damage, and the defendant's failing to take care. Under contributory negligence, an injurer is not liable if it can be proved that the victim was also somewhat negligent.

Two major changes in liability pertinent to an analysis of tort and automobile accidents have occurred in the United States and in other countries: partial substitution of first-party liability for the traditional common-law rule that held injurers responsible for the cost of accidents they cause, and comparative negligence. Under a first-party rule, the victim of injury bears the cost of accidents, irrespective of fault. Typically, the victim's cost is covered by some type of first-party insurance such as health or disability insurance or no-fault automobile insurance.

Under comparative negligence, the victim's compensation is reduced in proportion to the percentage of fault attributed to the plaintiff's actions. As of 1992, forty-four states in the United States, as well as Austria, Canada, France, Germany, Japan, New Zealand, the Philippines, Poland, Portugal, Russia, Spain, Switzerland, and the United Kingdom had some form of comparative negligence (Chung 1998). The rationale for comparative negligence is fairness: it seems unjust that a defendant who was more than 50 percent at fault should be let off because the plaintiff was also slightly at fault for the accident.

Analytically, these changes in tort rules provide variation for studying the effects of tort on automobile accident rates and driver precaution levels. If, by contrast, only the common-law rule prevailed, there would be no variation in rules to enable empirical investigation of tort's effects.

EVIDENCE THAT TORT DETERS CARELESS DRIVING
From Theory to Empirical Testing

Given that a major objective of tort liability is deterrence, the most important general empirical question is whether imposing tort liability actually succeeds in this regard. Another way of posing the question in the context of motor vehicle safety is whether removing the threat of tort liability either by substituting first-party for third-party liability or by compelling drivers to purchase liability insurance with premiums that are not experienced rated will remove drivers' incentive to be careful. Regarding commercial servers of alcohol, for whom imposing liability is a more recent trend, the question can be posed in terms of whether dram shop liability increases servers' level of care when dealing with customers.

One view, which seems to have widespread popular support, holds that tort liability is unlikely to be a major incentive (see, e.g., Schwartz 1994, 1997 for a discussion of controversies about the role of tort and its effects). Proponents of this view hold that driving is a very complex undertaking, with each driver making literally thousands of decisions and having many near collisions. Thus introducing third-party insurance will not affect safety, and a shift in liability rules, such as a change from contributory to comparative negligence, should not matter either. But as Trebilcock (1989) argued, this view is illogical. The implication is that not only are civil sanctions futile, but so are criminal and administrative sanctions.

Empirical analysis has employed two types of dependent variables: (1) outcomes measured by motor vehicle fatality rates and, much less frequently, by numbers of motor vehicle collisions and accident victims, and (2) precaution taking as measured by self-reports of careless behavior such as binge drinking (consuming five or more alcoholic beverages on one occasion). Although self-reports of careless behavior are subject to measurement error, motor vehicle fatalities provide a very partial indication of the underlying accident rate. The vast majority of collisions do not result in deaths. Key explanatory variables relate to implementation of no-fault laws, the switch from contributory to comparative negligence or to hybrids of both rules, the extent to which liability premiums are based on prior accident and citation history, and implementation of dram shop liability.

No-Fault Insurance

In several states and in several other countries (Australia, Canada [Quebec], Israel, Sweden, New Zealand), first-party liability has replaced third-party liability in part or in full (Joost 1992, chap. 2). In the United States no-fault was enacted in the 1960s, mainly in response to rapidly rising automobile liability premiums. At the time only two states, New York and Michigan, enacted plans that provide a serious alternative to tort liability as a system of accident compensation.

Under the traditional third-party rule, injurers who fail to take adequate care are made to bear the cost of the injury they cause. Under first-party liability, potential victims each bear the cost of their own injury but may purchase (or be compelled to purchase) insurance as protection against such loss, which is "no-fault" insurance. Under first-party liability, there is no scrutiny of negligence as under third-party liability.

Determining negligence may be one reason for the high cost of dispute resolution under tort. Eliminating the negligence standard may reduce the incentives potential injurers have to avoid causing injuries. The effect that the change from third-party to first-party liability has on deterrence depends on the fraction of claims barred from tort and the sensitivity of first-party insurance premiums to changes in the precaution level. Since a primary purpose of no-fault is to eliminate costly determinations of fault, it seems unlikely that no-fault premiums reflect precaution to any important extent. In the United States, some states permit premium surcharges for no-fault auto insurance based on driving records (Sloan and Githens 1994).

Results from empirical studies of no-fault automobile insurance laws are mixed, but the trend appears to be toward concluding that no-fault reduces road safety. Yet some commentators remain unconvinced that it discourages precaution and recommend it as a cornerstone of a reform strategy (see Dewees, Duff, and Trebilcock 1996).

Landes (1982) found that implementing no-fault increased the rate of motor vehicle fatalities, but Kochanowski and Young (1985) and Zador and Lund (1986) found no effect with the same dependent variable. In an analysis of New Zealand's experience, Brown (1985) found an increase neither in the amount of driving nor in the accident rate after adoption of no-fault in that country in 1974. However, his analysis did not control for other determinants of motoring and accidents. Gaudry (1987) analyzed the influence of no-fault in Quebec. The total number of accidents and accident victims increased substantially after implementation of no-fault. These results were confirmed with Devlin's (1990) regression analysis. The number of drivers also increased, for two reasons. First, premiums decreased overall, making insurance more affordable. Second, premiums decreased for high-risk drivers. All drivers were compelled to purchase insurance at premiums that did not reflect the driver's record, at the same time that victims' option of filing tort claims was eliminated. A highly experienced rated, compulsory no-fault plan might have had the opposite effect.

Sloan, Reilly, and Schenzler (1994b) included two explanatory variables for no-fault insurance in their time-series cross-section analysis of motor vehicle fatality rates with states and years as the observational units: a variable for the fraction of accidents involving bodily injury for which a tort claim could not be filed, which took a zero value in states without no-fault, and a binary variable for states that did not bar tort claims for bodily injuries caused by a motor vehicle but did require that drivers purchase minimum amounts of first-party insurance. They found that raising the fraction of claims barred from tort liability from 0 to 0.25 increased fatalities by 18 percent. Requiring individuals to purchase first-party insurance without limiting the ability to sue also increased fatalities, but by a smaller amount than did no-fault automobile insurance that reduced victims' ability to sue. In Sloan, Reilly, and Schenzler's 1995 analysis of binge drinking, no-fault had a negative impact on the probability of such behavior, but the coefficient was statistically significant at only the 10 percent level and the implied marginal effect was very small.

Comparative Negligence

The traditional common-law rule has been to allow contributory negligence by a victim as an affirmative defense. Under contributory negligence, an injurer is not liable if it can be proved that the victim also was negligent. In this context the victim might also have drunk alcohol or have been speeding and therefore not have been in a position to avoid the accident.

An alternative rule, comparative negligence, is to make the injurer liable but reduce the victim's compensation to the degree that the latter's failure to exercise care helped cause the accident. Based on our review of state statutes, some form of comparative negligence was employed in forty-five states in 1998. Modified comparative negligence, which essentially operates like contributory negligence, may be used to prevent recovery when the percentage of fault attributable to the plaintiff's actions is sufficiently high. A theoretical result is that switching from contributory to comparative negligence does not affect care levels. Under each rule, potential injurers and victims have incentives to set care at socially optimal levels (Shavell 1987).

In recent years in the United States (Curran 1992) and in other countries (see, e.g., Brown 1985; Rea 1987), there has been a shift toward comparative negligence. The old all-or-nothing rule had become haphazard in its application and riddled by various exceptions such as last clear chance and fault difference in kind, not merely in degree. The last clear chance applies to situations where the driver could have avoided the accident but failed to do so. In this case the driver would be liable under a contributory negligence regime. In this sense the switch, at least in the United States, was really part of an evolutionary process (Fleming 1988). The main opposition to comparative negligence came from the trial bar and from insurers and their clients, who held that a change to comparative negligence would lead to a substantial increase in liability insurance premiums by affecting the tactical balance in settlement negotiations (Fleming 1988).

Considering that most potential tort-feasors purchase or are compelled to purchase insurance complicates the analysis. For injurers, a major effect reflects the increased premium following an at-fault accident. Under contributory negligence, the injurer escapes liability when the victim is partly at fault and thus does not pay the surcharge. Under comparative negligence, however, the premium surcharge may be imposed even if the victim is partly to blame. The higher probability of a successful suit under comparative negligence followed by a higher premium may make drivers more cautious.

In practice, the relation between share of fault attributable to injurer versus victim and victim compensation is not as close as the articulated negligence doctrines imply (see, e.g., Wittman 1986; White 1989; Kessler 1995). For example, Wittman (1986) found that juries often decide cases in a way that shares liability for damages, even under the contributory negligence rule, presumably because they regard sharing as fair. The vast majority of legal disputes are settled out of court (Cooter and Rubinfeld 1989), and settlement amounts are based partly on expectations of proof. Not surprisingly, awards tend to be higher under comparative negligence (Low and Smith 1995). Nevertheless, examination of incentives as the law operates under comparative versus contributory negligence suggests that incentives to take care are weaker under comparative negligence (White 1989; Kessler 1995).

Flanigan and coauthors (1989) investigated whether automobile insurance premiums for policies covering bodily injury and property damage were higher in states that used a comparative negligence rule. They found that premiums were highest under pure comparative negligence, followed by no-fault and then by modified comparative negligence, which maintains contributory negligence for cases involving high percentages of defendant fault. Premiums were lowest under contributory negligence. These results suggest that drivers' incentives to avoid accidents are lower in states with comparative negligence, since insurance premiums plausibly are higher where more is paid for losses caused by accidents.

Virtually no empirical study has directly examined the effect on deterrence of changing from contributory to comparative negligence. Sloan, Reilly, and Schenzler (1995) found more binge drinking in states with comparative negligence, but the same researchers found no effect on motor vehicle fatalities (Sloan, Reilly, and Schenzler 1994b). In spite of their attempt to control for many other influences, the result for binge drinking may reflect factors not accounted for by their regression analysis.

Effects of Compulsory Liability Insurance for Motor Vehicle Owners and of Surcharges on Premiums

There is a paucity of empirical evidence on the effects of compelling drivers to purchase liability insurance and of adding premium surcharges based on a policyholder's accident or violation record. Analysis of motor vehicle fatalities by Sloan, Reilly, and Schenzler (1994b) showed that making a minimum level of liability insurance compulsory increased motor vehicle fatalities, suggesting moral hazard when drivers are forced to buy such insurance, but that such deaths declined appreciably as substantial premium penalties on compulsory liability insurance were imposed for convictions for driving under the influence of alcohol, having a chargeable accident, or both. In an analysis of binge drinking, Sloan, Reilly, and Schenzler (1995) found that compulsory liability insurance, with premium surcharges for careless behavior, deterred such behavior.

CONCLUSION

The main rationale for tort liability is its use as a deterrent. Overall, past empirical evidence suggests that imposing tort liability on drivers, especially when coupled with compulsory experience-rated liability insurance, improves roadway safety. In chapter 9 we present new empirical evidence on how tort, criminal liability, and administrative regulation affect motor vehicle fatalities, excess alcohol consumption, and self-reported drinking and driving. This analysis improves on past work in two respects: it specifies potential deterrents in more detail, and it extends through a more recent period, the mid-1990s.

5

Imposing Tort Liability on Commercial Servers

RATIONALE FOR DRAM SHOP LIABILITY

That much heavy drinking and subsequent drunk driving begins in bars and restaurants constitutes the foundation for imposing tort liability on establishments serving alcohol. There is a multipart rationale for placing liability on a third-party server rather than on first-party offenders such as drunks and minors, beginning with the understanding that individuals in such situations lack the capacity to make appropriate compliance decisions (Shavell 1987; Kraakman 1998). Also, there are fewer third parties to regulate. Bar owners and managers may be relatively efficient monitors of alcohol service practices of their bartenders and wait staff. Additionally, commercial sellers of alcohol may be in a better financial position to compensate drunk driving victims than are individual drivers. Commercial sellers of alcohol include liquor stores, bars, restaurants, and others. In addition to assets, these establishments may also carry liability insurance.

Much of our study's empirical analysis focuses on bars, and for this reason so does our discussion in this chapter. In a few jurisdictions, third-party liability has been extended to social hosts. Here the rationale again is the relative ability of hosts to monitor their guests' drinking before driving.

As we have already explained, a high percentage of motor vehicle accidents can be attributed to driving under the influence of alcohol. Drunk drivers obtain much of their alcohol from commercial servers. In reality, however, far too many transactions occur between alcohol servers and patrons for public administrative and criminal law agencies to monitor, especially in view of competing priorities within each jurisdiction. In contrast, servers and bar owners may be in a position to control overall alcohol consumption and thus help to eliminate excessive consumption and prevent intoxicated customers from causing injury.

CHAPTER OVERVIEW

This chapter begins with a capsule description of the difference between common law and statutory liability. We then give a history of dram shop liability in the United States, including constitutional tests of dram shop laws. In the next section, we describe the current status of dram shop laws. The rest of the chapter is an empirical analysis of the effects of dram shop liability. We begin with a review of results from previous studies, followed by a report of results from the two focus groups we conducted of owners or managers of bars and from our national Survey of Commercial Servers. Results from servers' perceptions of the probability of being named as a defendant in a dram shop suit will be used in later chapters where we report our results on how this perceived probability affects servers' and employees' behavior.

WHERE DO DRUNK DRIVERS OBTAIN THEIR ALCOHOL?

To develop effective policies for preventing drunk driving, one must know where drunk drivers obtain their alcohol. Several surveys provide evidence on their sources of supply.

Many drunk drivers get their alcohol from establishments that sell it for consumption on the premises, such as bars and restaurants. O'Donnell's 1985 review of eleven studies concluded that such premises were the drinking place of choice for 40 to 63 percent of drivers arrested for DUI, 43 to 64 percent of drivers with blood alcohol content exceeding legal limits for driving (0.10) who participated in roadside surveys, and 26 percent of drivers involved in alcohol-related crashes. Wieczorek, Miller, and Nochanjski's 1989 survey of arrested drunk drivers who were referred to DUI school in Buffalo, New York, found that 69 percent reported drinking in bars before arrest. By contrast, only 10 percent of respondents reported drinking at home, 20 percent in someone else's home, and only 5 percent in restaurants. Bar drinkers reported more alcohol use before their arrest and higher consumption per occasion than did home drinkers.

Other evidence indicates that many patrons have elevated blood alcohol content on leaving a bar and are impaired as drivers (Meier, Brigham, Handel 1984; Russ and Geller 1987; Van Houten, Nau, and Jonah 1985; unpublished sources listed in McKnight 1991). A survey of 223 persons convicted of DUI in California revealed that 59 percent drank alcohol in licensed establishments before being arrested for drunk driving (Christy

1989). Of those who had been drinking in licensed establishments, 26 percent were arrested on Friday nights and 19 percent on Saturday nights, mostly after midnight. A survey of over eight thousand individuals convicted of DUI in Mississippi found that respondents most frequently drank at home, followed by bar or lounge and friend's home; however, the question was intended to assess drinking rather than drinking and driving (Snow and Anderson 1987). A survey of locations of pre-DUI arrest alcohol purchases in two California counties revealed that only 2 percent of offenders had purchased alcohol from convenience stores or bar outlets before arrest (Fontaine 1992).

An Australian study, based on Breathalyzer readings from people leaving bars the authors labeled as "high risk" and "low risk," found that patrons from high-risk bars were far more likely to have high blood alcohol content when they left (Stockwell et al. 1992). High risk versus low risk was defined in terms of number of traffic accidents known to have involved drunk drivers from the bar and number of DUI offenses from traffic accidents involving its patrons in the year before the survey. Also, more patrons of the high-risk bars that refused to participate in the study appeared to be intoxicated. These results indicate that there is appreciable variation in frequency of drinking and driving after leaving the bar among bars facing the same criminal and civil laws and that differences persist over time.

Interestingly, there is a link between frequenting bars and using tobacco products. According to one source, over a third of those who smoke two packs of cigarettes a day have also had drinking problems (Hwang 1999). Thus bargoers are particularly receptive to tobacco promotions. Recognizing that tobacco advertising will be limited in the future, tobacco companies are turning to promotions based in bars. Externalities from smoking differ from those associated with heavy consumption of alcohol, but the costs to society of tobacco use are considerable.

TYPES OF LIABILITY
Rationale and Goals of Dram Shop Liability

Through third-party tort liability, servers of alcohol may be held liable for injuries stemming from accidents caused by an obviously intoxicated adult patron or a minor patron. The rationale for this "dram shop liability" is that the threat of a lawsuit will cause dispensers of alcohol to carefully monitor their customers while simultaneously transferring the social costs arising from alcohol abuse to the alcoholic beverage industry. Third-party liability imposes a duty to the drinker on commercial servers, who now must make sure that the intoxicated patron does not harm himself or innocent third parties. Dewees, Duff, and Trebilcock (1996, 40) mentioned a less noble purpose of dram shop liability, stating that the "search for deep pockets has allowed even careless drivers to recover against tavern owners who serve them alcohol, public authorities responsible for designing and maintaining highways, repair shops, and of course manufacturers."

From a financial perspective, dram shop liability is more feasible than other forms of liability, since injured parties may be more likely to recover costs of their injuries from a bar or restaurant than from an individual drunk driver. Whereas a drunk driver may be insolvent, a bar or restaurant may have more funds to compensate the injured victim and may carry dram shop insurance with higher liability amounts than the combined insurance and assets of a drunk driver.

Before national prohibition, although the accident rate per mile driven was high, accidents were infrequent because few miles were driven. The primary goal of tort laws that imposed liability on a commercial server was to keep individuals from overindulging in alcohol. Since the late 1970s, the dual rationale for adopting dram shop liability laws has been overall deterrence and compensating victims of alcohol-induced traffic accidents rather than addressing the immoral implications of heavy drinking (Mosher 1988).

Dram shop law has three main goals: to protect the health, safety, and welfare of the general public by regulating liquor sales and service; to provide compensation for victims; and to regulate and discipline those who violate dram shop acts by serving or selling alcohol to an intoxicated person or a minor (Mosher 1988). Dram shop actions are not limited to drunk driving accidents. Claims have also arisen from bar fights, off-site sales to minors and intoxicated persons, unsafe conditions in the bar, suicides, homicides, and self-inflicted ethanol poisoning (Mosher 1988 and 1997 supplement). Irrespective of the type of injury, a key issue facing both legislatures and judges is whether the consumption or the serving of alcohol is the proximate cause of injury.

Whatever socially beneficial effect these laws may have in encouraging commercial servers of alcoholic beverages to monitor the behavior of their patrons, servers have opposed liability laws on at least two grounds. The first objection is moral: that (adult) drinkers should be held accountable for their own actions and that servers should not be placed in the role of police officers (Jacobs 1989). Second, servers take issue with the presumption that they are efficient monitors. The following quotation from Jacobs (1989) appears to be typical: "How much care can and should we expect from bartenders, waiters, and waitresses, many of whom are young people not long in the liquor business? Can we expect that they be able to determine what it means to be 'intoxicated,' and identify customers who have reached this state? The determination is by no means simple" (140).

As we discussed in the previous chapter, those injured by a drunk driver may recover compensation for their injuries through compulsory insurance or through a negligence claim brought against the driver. In a negligence claim, the injured party alleges that the driver behaved carelessly, thus causing the accident.

Statutory Liability

Under dram shop statutes, plaintiffs who are injured by an intoxicated adult or minor may also sue those who sold or served alcohol to the injurer. Cases brought under a dram shop statute do not require proof of negligence. Instead, proving a violation of the statute—that is, an illegal sale or illegal service of alcohol to an intoxicated adult or a minor—suffices to win a case.

There is great variety among the dram shop statutes, partly because of their age, since some of them date back to the nineteenth century. Among these old statutes are those that provide for causes of action against dram shops that serve habitual drunkards. Other states have statutes that limit liability to extreme cases involving willfully and knowingly serving a minor or an obviously intoxicated person.

Today, in most states, a plaintiff in a dram shop action is required to prove only that there was (1) service of an alcoholic beverage by (2) the defendant, who is potentially liable, to (3) a minor or an obviously intoxicated person, and that (4) the service of the alcohol was the proximate cause of (5) injuries to the plaintiff for which the dram shop statute was designed to compensate.

Common Law

In states that allow common-law claims (table 5.1), cases alleging negligence, which are not based on a specific dram shop statute, may now be brought against a commercial server of alcoholic beverages. The specifics of the common-law claims are laid out through case law that is handed down by the courts of each state.

Evolution of Dram Shop Liability as an Instrument for Controlling Drinking and Driving
History of Dram Shop Liability

Under traditional common-law rules, servers or suppliers of alcoholic beverages were not liable for injuries resulting from another person's con-

Table 5.1 Dram Shop Liability for Serving an Adult and Serving a Minor, 1998

State	Recognized Dram Shop Liability	Has Statutory Dram Shop Liability Only	Has Common Law Dram Shop Liability Only	Has Both Statutory and Common Law Dram Shop Liability
Alabama	✓	✓		
Alaska	✓	✓		
Arizona	✓			✓
Arkansas				
California	✓	✓		
Colorado	✓	✓		
Connecticut	✓			✓
Delaware				
District of Columbia	✓		✓	
Florida	✓	✓		
Georgia	✓	✓		
Hawaii	✓		✓	
Idaho	✓	✓		
Illinois	✓	✓		
Indiana	✓			✓
Iowa	✓			✓
Kansas				
Kentucky	✓	✓		
Louisiana	✓		✓	
Maine	✓			✓
Maryland				
Massachusetts	✓	✓		
Michigan	✓	✓		
Minnesota	✓			✓
Mississippi	✓			✓

Missouri	✓	✓		
Montana	✓	✓		
Nebraska				
Nevada				
New Hampshire	✓			✓
New Jersey	✓	✓		✓
New Mexico	✓			✓
New York	✓			✓
North Carolina	✓			✓
North Dakota	✓			✓
Ohio	✓			
Oklahoma	✓		✓	✓
Oregon	✓			✓
Pennsylvania	✓			
Rhode Island	✓	✓		
South Carolina	✓		✓	
South Dakota	✓	✓	✓	
Tennessee	✓	✓		
Texas	✓			✓
Utah	✓			✓
Vermont	✓	✓		
Virginia				
Washington	✓		✓	
West Virginia	✓		✓	
Wisconsin	✓	✓		
Wyoming	✓			✓

Source: Our analysis of state statutes.

sumption of alcohol. This view was predicated on the theory that the drinking rather than the serving of alcohol was the proximate cause of intoxication. Under the common law, even if a vendor breached a duty to those injured by an intoxicated person, the vendor was not legally liable because he was not considered the proximate cause of the injuries. According to this early common-law view, the chain of legal causation between the negligent serving of an alcoholic beverage and the injury was severed by the customer's voluntary act in drinking the alcohol (see *Fleckner v. Dionne*, 94 Cal. App. 2d 246 [Dist. Ct. App., 1949]; *King v. Henkie*, 80 Ala. 505 [1886]).

Departing from the traditional common law, states began to enact dram shop acts or statutes before national prohibition. Wisconsin passed the first dram shop statute in 1849, requiring each tavern owner to post bond to support all poor people, widows, and orphans injured by a patron's excessive drinking and to pay the expenses of all civil and criminal prosecutions attributable to the sale of alcohol. Recovery under this statute was limited to the amount of the bond. In 1853 Indiana passed the prototype of the present-day dram shop statute, which stated: "Any wife, child, parent, guardian, employer or other person who shall be injured in person, or property, or means of support, by any intoxicated person, or in consequence of the intoxication, habitual or otherwise, of any person, shall have the right of action in his or her own name against any person, and his sureties, on the bond aforesaid, who shall, by retailing spirituous liquor, have caused the intoxication of such person for any and all damages sustained and for exemplary damages" (Ind., Act of March 4, 1853, sec-tion 10).

The temperance movement was primarily responsible for the passage of dram shop statutes, and by the mid-1870s eleven states had enacted them, including Connecticut, Illinois, Indiana, Iowa, Kansas, Maine, Michigan, New Hampshire, New York, Ohio, and Wisconsin. With the repeal of Prohibition, states stopped enacting such laws; no state passed a dram shop statute between 1935 and 1978. After World War II state legislatures, facing pressure from bars and taverns, repealed their dram shop statutes. Since the 1970s, however, several states have enacted such laws, and in other states dram shop liability has been introduced through modern common law (see table 5.1). In 1978 California became the first state to adopt a dram shop statute in the post-Prohibition era.

In a departure from the traditional common-law rule outlined above, victims injured by an intoxicated person also began to bring dram shop suits through modern common-law liability, set forth in the case law of individual states. One of the first known cases of imposing common-law liability comes from South Carolina in 1847, where a judge held a shopkeeper liable for illegally selling a gallon jug and bottle of whiskey to Bob, a slave, who was supposed to deliver the liquor to his master. Instead, Bob drank the liquor and later died from overindulgence and exposure. The judge ordered payment of $650 to the slaveowner, finding that dispensing the alcoholic beverage to the slave was in fact a proximate cause of his subsequent death (*Harrison v. Berkley,* 32 S.C.L. [1 Strob.] 525, 47 Am. Dec. 578 [1847]).

After Prohibition ended, a few states imposed common-law liability, including Arizona and Illinois. New Jersey is typically credited for instituting modern common-law liability for commercial servers of alcohol. In the case *Rappaport v. Nichols,* the New Jersey Supreme Court extended liability to commercial servers to afford a fairer measure of justice to innocent third parties whose injuries are brought about by the unlawful and negligent sale of alcohol to minors and intoxicated persons. The New Jersey legislature, however, has since enacted a statute that provides the exclusive remedy for damages resulting from negligent service. *Rappaport* left room for servers to avoid responsibility by allowing the defense of due care on the part of the server. Most states have followed New Jersey and have since abandoned the traditional common-law rule, instead relying on evolving case law or dram shop statutes to determine liability.

Oklahoma, for example, enacted a dram shop statute in 1910 that imposed tort liability on servers of alcoholic beverages (Adkins 1995). This statute was designed to support the families of those who were frequently intoxicated and to discourage serving those who could not control their drinking. In 1959 Oklahoma passed its Alcohol Beverage Control Act, which did not provide for civil liability. The supreme court of the state then ruled that Oklahoma would follow the traditional common-law view with regard to dram shop liability and disallowed claims brought under the common law. In 1986, however, Oklahoma abandoned the traditional common-law stance and began to allow common-law claims.

Constitutionality of Dram Shop Statutes

The Twenty-first Amendment, which repealed Prohibition, shifted back to the states the power to regulate the alcohol industry, as part of their broad police power. The constitutionality of a dram shop statute hinges on whether the state legislature has enacted its police power reasonably under the powers granted to state governments. Thus the power to regulate the liquor industry lies with the state legislature, which may ultimately delegate this power to government agencies such as the state alcoholic beverage commission (ABC).

STATUS OF DRAM SHOP LIABILITY IN THE LATE 1990S
State Laws

In forty-three states in 1998, the injured party could also recover compensation by filing a negligence claim against the dram shop for serving alcohol to the drunk driver or by suing the server under the state dram shop statute, if available (see table 5.1). Thirty-six states had dram shop statutes that provided the basis for a dram shop claim. In eight states, dram shop liability was determined strictly through the common law, and in eighteen states an injured person could file a claim both under a dram shop statute and under common-law negligence.

Recent Trends

Beginning in the 1960s and continuing though the mid-1980s, there was a definite trend toward increasing tort liability for those who serve minors or obviously intoxicated adults. In the 1980s eleven states enacted dram shop statutes. As a result, bars in the middle to late 1980s began to face high insurance premiums and started to lobby legislatures to restrict their liability. In some states, such as California, Missouri, and South Dakota, the legislatures began to limit common-law liability by enacting statutes that now provide that drinking, rather than serving, alcoholic beverages is the proximate cause of injury by an intoxicated person. Courts in California and South Dakota, however, have found ways around these more restrictive legislative mandates (see *Cantwell v. Peppermill,* 25 Cal. App. 4th 1797 [1994] and *Baatz v. Arrow Bar,* 426 N.W. 2d 298 [1988]). Some states specified that the state dram shop statute is the exclusive remedy for an injured person. These states prevented an injured person from filing a common-law negligence claim against the dram shop.

Other states continued to broaden dram shop liability for those who serve minors or already intoxicated adults. In *Kelly v. Gwinnell,* 96 N.J. 538 (1984), New Jersey became the first state to impose liability on social hosts. In the 1990s, holding a social host liable for injuries caused by an intoxicated person who was served at a party or other social occasion has grown in popularity. For example, in 1995 New Hampshire recognized a common-law cause of action for social host liability, and in 1992 North Carolina recognized a cause of action for a social host who served a visibly intoxicated guest.

Parties Entitled to Sue

Under both dram shop statutes and common-law liability, there are potentially six types of injured parties who may bring a suit. These are innocent third parties, families of innocent third parties, complicitous (not innocent) third parties, the minor drinker, the adult drinker, and the family of the drinker (table 5.2).

Most dram shop statutes and common-law cases focus primarily on providing compensation for innocent third parties and their families. Language in most dram shop acts permits "any person" to sue, but "person" does not necessarily refer to every injured person. Historically, intoxicated persons have been precluded from suing bar owners for their own injuries. Some states go so far as to specifically state that the intoxicated person may not sue (see, e.g., Illinois Code Ann. 43 Section 135–6-21 and Oregon Rev. Statute Section 30.960.). However, most of the legal authority preventing parties from suing is found in the common law. The reasoning behind this disallowance is that, as a matter of public policy, drunk persons who harm themselves are responsible for their condition and should not prevail on either a common-law or a statutory basis.

Some states also deny recovery by plaintiffs who may have been drinking with the defendant under the rules of contributory negligence and the complicity doctrine. Complicitous (not innocent) third parties are prevented from suing in some states (see table 5.2) because they are viewed as actively contributing to the intoxication of the injurer. Thus complicitous third parties might include adults who purchase liquor for minors and drinking buddies who encourage consumption by buying drinks and accompanying the intoxicated person on barhopping adventures.

Potential Defendants

Modern dram shop common law establishes that a commercial vendor who sells alcohol for on-site consumption has a duty to exercise reasonable care not to serve a noticeably intoxicated person. A server who sells alcohol to someone who is already drunk should foresee the unreasonable risk of harm to others who may be injured by the person's impaired ability to, among other things, operate an automobile. This type of common law is designed to protect innocent third parties who may be injured as a result of service to an obviously intoxicated person.

Cases involving this principle are decided based on rules of negligence. These rules provide that it is negligent to permit a third person to use a thing, or engage in an activity, under the control of the actor if the actor knows or should know that the person intends or is likely to use the thing, or engage in the activity, in such a manner as to create an unreasonable risk of harm to others (American Law Institute, *Restatement (Second) of Torts* 1979, sec. 308). General negligence law also establishes that "one who sup-

Table 5.2 Who Has Standing to Sue the Dram Shop (1998)?

State	Minor Drinker	Adult Drinker	Innocent Third Party	Complicitous Third Party	Family of Drinker	Family of Innocent Third Party
Alabama			✓	✓	✓	✓
Alaska	✓	✓	✓	✓	✓	✓
Arizona	✓		✓			✓
Arkansas						
California	✓		✓	✓	✓	✓
Colorado			✓	✓		✓
Connecticut	✓	✓	✓	✓	✓	✓
Delaware						
District of Columbia	✓	✓	✓	✓	✓	✓
Florida	✓	✓	✓	✓	✓	✓
Georgia			✓	✓	✓	✓
Hawaii	✓		✓	✓		✓
Idaho			✓			✓
Illinois			✓			✓
Indiana	✓	✓	✓	✓	✓	✓
Iowa	✓	✓	✓		✓	✓
Kansas						
Kentucky	✓	✓	✓	✓	✓	✓
Louisiana	✓		✓			✓
Maine	✓		✓	✓		✓
Maryland						
Massachusetts	✓	✓	✓	✓	✓	✓
Michigan			✓			✓
Minnesota			✓		✓	✓
Mississippi	✓	✓	✓	✓	✓	✓

Missouri	✓	✓	✓	✓	✓	✓
Montana	✓	✓	✓	✓	✓	✓
Nebraska						
Nevada	✓		✓	✓		
New Hampshire	✓	✓	✓	✓	✓	✓
New Jersey	✓	✓	✓	✓	✓	✓
New Mexico	✓	✓	✓	✓		✓
New York	✓			✓		
North Carolina	✓		✓	✓		
North Dakota	✓	✓	✓	✓		✓
Ohio	✓	✓	✓	✓	✓	
Oklahoma	✓		✓	✓		
Oregon	✓		✓	✓		
Pennsylvania	✓	✓	✓	✓	✓	✓
Rhode Island	✓	✓	✓	✓	✓	✓
South Carolina	✓	✓	✓	✓		✓
South Dakota						
Tennessee	✓	✓	✓	✓	✓	✓
Texas	✓	✓	✓	✓	✓	✓
Utah	✓	✓	✓	✓		
Vermont	✓		✓	✓		
Virginia						
Washington	✓	✓	✓	✓	✓	✓
West Virginia	✓	✓	✓	✓	✓	✓
Wisconsin	✓		✓	✓		✓
Wyoming	✓		✓	✓		

Source: Our analysis of state statutes.

plies a chattel for the use of another whom the supplier knows or has rea-son to know to be likely because of his youth, inexperience or otherwise to use it in a manner involving unreasonable risk of physical harm to himself and others is subject to liability for physical harm resulting to them" (sec. 390). Based on the idea that vendors owe a duty to drinkers, dram shop statutes specifically outline categories of potential defendants. These po-tential defendants include commercial sellers of alcohol and may in some states extend to other categories such as employers and social hosts.

In states where it is a criminal violation to sell alcohol to a minor or an obviously intoxicated adult, courts may apply a negligence per se standard when determining the liability of the server or seller in both common-law and dram shop statute cases. To recover under negligence per se, the plain-tiff must prove that the injury was caused by the servers' violation of duty; that the injury was of a type intended to be prevented by the statute vio-lated; and that the injured party is one of the class intended to be protected by the statute. In most states commercial vendors owe no duty to an adult patron who voluntarily drinks alcohol and is subsequently injured. Minors, on the other hand, can recover under a negligence per se principle because minors, who lack experience and sound judgment, are in the class intended to be protected by the statute. In some expansive states, adult drinkers can recover under this type of negligence theory because intoxicated people, who have diminished reasoning capacities, can be considered members of the class of people dram shop laws were designed to protect.

Dram shop statutes and common-law principles apply not only to bars and other on-site establishments, such as restaurants, but also to liquor stores. A package store that sells to minors, for example, should be aware that they intend to drink the beer, and thus the resulting injuries are fore-seeable. According to this legal theory, where an injury is foreseeable as the result of a breach of duty, the breach constitutes proximate cause and the seller is liable. Other potential defendants include municipalities and police departments, particularly those that stop drunk drivers, fail to de-tain them, and allow them to drive on and injure innocent third parties. Colleges and universities and social hosts may also be liable for injuries caused by those who obtained alcohol at a party. Employers may also be held liable for the actions of intoxicated employees.

Imposing Liability on Bar Owners for Employees' Conduct

Bar owners and the bar as a corporate entity are typically liable if wait staff and bartenders serve minors and intoxicated adults. This type of liability, known as vicarious liability, is imposed on the bar owners and the bar itself for several reasons. First, bar owners are better informed about accident risks and legal regulations than their employees and are thus better able to avert bad behavior (Shavell 1987). Bar owners may be able to discipline their own employees for bad server behavior better than the court system. Additionally, bar owners and the bar may be more attractive as liability targets because law enforcement and plaintiffs may have more trouble identifying the server who actually committed the illegal act (Kornhauser 1982).

Special Statutory Provisions

Some state statutes contain strict requirements that a potential plaintiff provide notice of injury and intent to sue within a relatively short time after the accident. This time frame allows the defendant to gather evidence and assemble witnesses. Also, some states have shorter statutes of limitations for dram shop cases, which are distinct from those for common-law negligence. These provisions grant only one or two years from the time of injury for the plaintiff to file suit.

Since 1972, a provision requiring "name and retain" has been in effect in Michigan. Under this provision, an injured party may not bring an action against a retailer or wholesaler unless the injurer is also a named defendant and is retained as a defendant until the litigation is concluded by trial or settlement. This provision is designed to prevent the injurer, who may have enormous liability and limited assets and insurance, from settling with a plaintiff and then assisting the plaintiff with a suit against the dram shop. This scenario is most likely when the injurer and the plaintiff are friends.

Damages

Dram shop statutes allow plaintiffs to recover costs related to treatment of injuries and to loss of person, property, and means of support. Some permit recovery for emotional suffering. Plaintiffs in common-law cases are typically awarded damages for actual expenses, including injuries, loss of property, income, and services, and pain and suffering. In some states, including Alabama, Maine, Minnesota, New York, North Carolina, Utah, Virginia, and Wyoming as of 1998, punitive damages may have been awarded to plaintiffs who were injured by the reckless, willful, or wanton service of an intoxicated adult or a minor. For the plaintiff to be awarded punitive damages, the server's conduct must have demonstrated a reckless disregard for the safety of others.

Some states, as part of their dram shop statute, placed a dollar limit on recovery. Damage caps may have been a response to the insurance crisis for bar owners and an attempt to limit liability for noneconomic damages. The trend in tort seems to be to limit damages in all negligence cases, not just liquor liability incidents.

Potential Defenses

A breach of duty regarding the sale of alcohol to a minor may be excused if the vendor can establish that the purchaser appeared to be of age and that reasonable methods were used to verify that status (asking for valid identification as proof of age). This defense is a component of the broader responsible business practice defense. Most law-abiding servers or sellers will be protected from tort suits with this provision, but the burden of proof for excusability falls on the vendor. Through comparative negligence principles, the jury can choose to excuse the conduct of the vendor by allocating fault among the parties.

Contributory and Comparative Negligence

In some instances plaintiffs may be completely barred or limited in their recovery if they are partially responsible for their own injuries. Plaintiffs may be completely barred from recovery in the six states that, as of 1998, followed the traditional common-law doctrine of contributory negligence. Under this doctrine, plaintiffs are barred from recovery if their conduct falls below an objective standard of care necessary for their own protection and, along with the defendants' negligence, contributes to their harm. Plaintiffs whose negligence contributes to their own injury are barred from recovery unless the defendants had a last clear chance to avoid injuring them.

Most states in recent years, however, follow the more lenient modern rule of comparative negligence, which does permit recovery by a plaintiff who is partially at fault (Curran 1992). Under this determination of negligence, however, damages are reduced in proportion to the plaintiff's degree of fault. In modified comparative negligence jurisdictions, plaintiffs will be completely barred from recovery if their own negligence is shown to have contributed more than 50 percent to their own injuries.

In some states with dram shop statutes, courts have held that in a comparative negligence jurisdiction, a defendant may not introduce evidence of the plaintiff's negligence because the dram shop statute is governed by strict liability. Under this type of liability, when a server violates the dram shop act by serving an intoxicated adult or a minor, the dram shop is strictly liable for any injuries caused, no matter what the plaintiff's degree of negligence.

Responsible Server Practices

Dram shop liability in principle should provide incentives for implementing responsible server practices, with several areas of focus (see, e.g., Christy 1989; Mosher 1988). The implementation of any of these practices may be used by a commercial server to build a responsible business practice defense. The areas related to pricing and promotion include avoiding happy hours and, instead, subsidizing food as well as encouraging patrons to stay longer to eat more and drink alcohol at a regular price. Serving policies include never serving pitchers to single individuals and informing patrons about how to avoid impairment. Policies for service to minors include checking pockets for liquor (pat downs) during events likely to involve minors and detailed procedures for checking identification. Policies aimed at curbing service to obviously intoxicated persons include serving one alcoholic beverage at a time and refilling glasses only when empty, establishing procedures for cutting off excessive consumption, and having rules about employees' drinking on the job. Alternative transportation policies include designated driver programs, which may be combined with specific incentives for designated drivers, procedures requiring intoxicated patrons to give up their car keys, and procedures for ordering taxis. To carry out these policies, establishments may take precautions in hiring employees and terminating them when practices are violated, instituting server training, and maintaining internal surveillance systems, including decoys who check on employees' compliance with the establishment's rules and procedures.

Although it is possible to list responsible server practices as we have done, in reality it may be difficult to implement them effectively. Some commentators have expressed pessimism about their real potential to reduce harm from intoxicated patrons. For example, Jacobs (1989) stated:

> In a crowded bar, a bartender will have little opportunity to keep track of any particular patron's consumption. Indeed, he or she may have no way of knowing whether the patron had done any drinking before entering the bar, how long he intends to stay, or how much he has eaten. Monitoring consumption is further complicated by the common practice of purchasing rounds of drinks for several people, and of groups sharing communal pitchers of beer. Servers may have no way of identifying the drivers. Moreover, if customers are not cut off from drinking until they are identified as intoxicated it may be too late to prevent drunk driving.

No doubt bars could do more to refrain from serving the stereotypical drunkard. However, the vast majority of customers, including heavy drinkers, do not fall into this category. It will be awkward, to say the least, for bartenders to police their customers, interrogate "suspicious" patrons about their consumption, and require some sort of sobriety test before bringing the next drink.

Taverns, bars, and even many restaurants are in the business of selling alcoholic beverages. Profits depend upon creating an attractive atmosphere in which to drink. The goal is not to encourage long evenings of quiet conversations over two alcoholic drinks and several sodas. The best customers are the big drinkers; many run up huge bar tabs. It is highly unrealistic to expect most liquor establishments to police themselves. (140–41)

Fortunately, there is some empirical evidence on dram shop liability. It is to this evidence that we now turn.

REVIEW OF EMPIRICAL EVIDENCE ON DRAM SHOP LIABILITY
Evidence on Rationale for Server Intervention

One reason for focusing on the liability of alcohol servers is that, as we discussed earlier, many drunk drivers obtain their alcohol from establishments that sell it for drinking on the premises. In spite of the views to the contrary just noted, bartenders appear to be well positioned to control drinking and have been shown to understand drinking behavior and methods of deterring excessive consumption (Waring and Sperr 1982). However, bars are in the business of selling alcohol. As a result, not only is servers' intervention inconsistent with the owner's profit seeking, but it may also adversely affect the tips individual servers receive (Christy 1989; Berger and Snortum 1985). Especially among neighborhood bars, competition is based less on the quality of the product than on the feeling of intimacy or loyalty between patrons and bartenders. Bartenders develop loyalty by giving free drinks, such as offering "one for the road" or "one on the house" or offering a "last call" before the bar closes. To intervene may risk embarrassing regular patrons and reducing their use of alcohol, ultimately lowering the bar's profits (Gusfield, Rasmussen, and Kotarba 1984). Saltz (1987), however, reported that one server intervention program limited the drinking of the target population without reducing sales of the clubs studied, probably because the lighter drinkers consumed more.

Bartenders indeed may have trouble determining which patrons are intoxicated. Lagenbucher and Nathan (1983) tested the ability of bartenders, police officers, and social hosts to recognize levels of intoxication. The police officers demonstrated some degree of competence, but the bartenders and social hosts were unable to detect any differences. In this study, however, the drinkers were not allowed to exceed a BAC level of 0.10.

There is also uncertainty over whether servers should exercise reasonable care to avoiding serving an intoxicated patron or whether they must actively police and judge the sobriety of each patron (Heard 1986). Typical criteria include whether customers are so intoxicated as to be deprived of willpower or responsibility for their actions, are visibly intoxicated, are intoxicated to the point of being noticeable to a reasonable person, or are legally intoxicated according to their blood alcohol content.

Classification of Dram Shop Laws

In a comprehensive study of dram shop laws of all fifty states, Holder and his team identified the most relevant factors influencing server liability and its potential to reduce alcohol problems (Holder et al. 1993). The conceptual model for the study placed dram shop liability and alcohol-serving practices in a framework with regulatory systems, business climates, and individual behavior. Holder and his colleagues developed a method for quantifying liability exposure for each state by identifying twenty-six legal liability variables, which they grouped into five categories. The categories included server acts that give rise to liability; liability standards for judging the server's action; standing to sue (listing potential plaintiffs in a liquor liability suit); procedural or recovery restrictions (limitations on liability); and defenses that defendants can use to show that their actions were reasonable or that plaintiffs contributed to their own injuries. Each of the twenty-six factors included in these categories was given a weight by a panel of liquor liability experts. A positive score was assigned for increased liability exposure factors and a negative score for decreased exposure factors. Factors deemed most influential in increasing or decreasing liability included liability for serving minors, liability for serving a person who becomes intoxicated, strict liability, allowing an adult drinker to sue, allowing an innocent third party to sue, and limiting recovery to less than $100,000.

In the three states that had high exposure for liability—Indiana, Pennsylvania, and South Carolina—dram shop liability was based on common-law precedent. In states with the lowest exposure—Maryland, Virginia, Arkansas, Kansas, Nebraska, Nevada, and South Dakota—courts had consistently refused to allow liability for serving alcohol. States in the middle range tended to have liability by statute. Holder and his colleagues found that common-law states with no existing statutes concerning server liability fell into the extremes of very high or very low liability exposure.

Responsible Server Practices: Empirical Evidence

There is limited empirical evidence on the effect of specific server interventions that dram shop liability is designed to promote.

Pricing and Promotion

People drink more during happy hours (Babor et al. 1978, 1980), but evaluation of the ban on happy hours in Ontario found no statistically significant differences in alcohol use before and after the ban (Smart and Adlaf 1986). Studies of limitations on days and hours of sale of alcoholic beverages have not consistently demonstrated decreased alcohol use, alcohol-related mortality, or traffic accidents (Room 1984; Ashley and Rankin 1988). Mann and Anglin (1990) found evidence that alcohol consumption and alcohol-related collisions are influenced by alcohol availability, including day and hour limitations and per capita consumption.

Patron Education

Van Houton, Nau, and Jonah (1985) studied four drinking establishments in Nova Scotia, giving arriving patrons information on how to avoid impairment and informing departing patrons of their blood alcohol content levels. All the establishments catered to a working-class or mixed working- and middle-class clientele. This intervention did not reduce impaired driving. High percentages of impaired drivers left drinking establishments on Thursday through Saturday nights from 11:00 P.M. to 2:00 A.M. Over half of the patrons who left were legally impaired, suggesting that this group is an important target for measures against drinking and driving.

Employees' Drinking with Patrons

In an ethnographic study of fifty bars, Prus (1983) found a positive correlation between employees' and patrons' drinking. This finding provides a reason to ban employees' drinking on the job.

Hiring and Employment

The importance of management approval of server interventions is shown by servers' reluctance to interfere with customers' drinking. The servers believed that doing so was contrary to management goals, even if they are able to identify problem drinking and to intervene appropriately (Geller, Russ, and Delfphos 1987).

Server Training

Increasingly, states and localities are requiring that servers be trained in responsible alcohol service. More limited programs focus only on how to deal with intoxicated patrons. More comprehensive programs focus on servers, managers, and the bar's characteristics. Russ and Geller (1987) and Geller, Russ, and Delfphos (1987) evaluated the effectiveness of a six-hour program. The program, Training for Intervention Procedures by Servers (TIPS), teaches servers to identify intoxication from behavioral and psychological cues and suggests tactics for controlling alcohol flow. In the evaluation, research assistants visited and drank for two hours in two bars where about half the servers had received server training. Patrons served by trained personnel attained a much lower blood alcohol content level than did those served by untrained servers. Also, type and frequency of server interventions differed according to whether the server had been trained.

Howard-Pitney et al. (1991) conducted a larger study of the Responsible Beverage Service training program (RBS), which is more comprehensive than TIPS. RBS seemed to change servers' knowledge and beliefs but had little influence on their behavior. Establishments offering RBS followed more responsible alcohol-service practices, such as not serving drinks in pitchers and not serving doubles, but it is unclear that these policies were caused by RBS training.

McKnight (1991) assessed the effectiveness of server education administered to almost 1,100 servers and managers of one hundred establishments at eight locations in the United States. The author claimed that the program was similar enough to others to permit generalizing findings. Two types of effectiveness measures were employed. The first entailed observing server interventions. Observers ordered a beer while feigning intoxication, then noted the level of business, number of visibly intoxicated patrons, and whether such patrons were served. Observers were unaccompanied so as not to reveal that anyone was available to take them home or otherwise assist them. After being served or refused service, they left the establishment and recorded the information. The other measure was a written survey administered to servers and managers, which elicited information on knowledge, attitudes, and server practices. Overall, results were favorable to server intervention education programs. Knowledge, attitudes, and self-reported behavior of servers improved, and the number of observed server interventions increased.

Gliksman et al. (1993) reported results of a small-scale evaluation of a server training program that gauged program outcome in terms of improved server knowledge, server attitudes toward intervention, and changes in behavior. The results overall were favorable to server training.

One study's data suggest that server training can reduce alcohol-related traffic accidents. Holder and Wagenaar (1994) evaluated the effect of the first statewide mandated training program for alcohol servers in Oregon and found statistically significant reductions in single-vehicle nighttime crashes. With data from only one state, however, it is not possible to assess how stringency of dram shop liability influences the effectiveness of server training.

McKnight and Streff (1994) found that increased enforcement of laws covering service to intoxicated patrons can have a positive influence on server interventions and DUI arrests. In this study, plainclothes police officers monitored service of intoxicated patrons in Michigan bars over the course of one year. Before the official undercover observations, the police sent the establishments educational materials explaining the laws and describing signs of intoxication. The officers made 457 visits, half of them to the ten establishments that produced the largest number of intoxicated drivers. Over the year, the officers issued thirteen citations and eleven warnings for serving intoxicated persons. Service refusal rates for the observed bars were 34.2 percent before the educational materials were sent, 58.6 percent at three months after they were sent, 53.3 percent at six months, and 53.0 percent at one year. In the comparison area, refusal rates were 23.3 percent before, 34.5 percent at three months, 32.7 percent at six months, and 25.7 percent at one year. Notably, the officers observed that refusing service was related to business volume, with refusals more likely when the establishment was one-fourth to one-half full. Server intervention rates were not related to establishment or clientele characteristics. DUI arrests were fifteen times more likely to come from blue-collar and college hangouts than from restaurants or cocktail lounges.

Bar Server Perceptions and Attitudes

Turissi, Nicholson, and Jaccard (1999) used a social-psychological framework to assess the effects of server intervention policies. According to this framework, individuals' behavior primarily depends on their attitude toward performing the behavior. Attitude depends on the subjective probability that the behavior will lead to a particular outcome. Such perceptions are in turn influenced by personal experiences, observational learning, and information from other sources.

The authors surveyed 185 owners and 185 servers of college bars (Turissi, Nicholson, and Jaccard 1999). They first examined which server intervention policies were viewed favorably or unfavorably by owners and servers. Policies that were rated favorably included offering to call a taxi for intoxicated patrons and training employees in alcohol awareness. These policies were oriented toward preventing patrons from leaving the establishment too drunk to drive. By contrast, policies that respondents rated unfavorably included limiting the number of persons in the bar, posting drink limits, and discontinuing alcohol sales one hour before closing. The latter policies were oriented toward reducing sales of alcohol. Policies that were rated neutrally were serving beer by the glass and not by the pitcher, having security personnel circulate within the bar, serving free nonalcoholic drinks to designated drivers, sponsoring nonalcoholic promotions, and posting information on the consequences of DUIs and alcohol-related accidents. These policies are more difficult to characterize as a group than the others.

The authors conducted path analysis to assess determinants of attitudes about server intervention policies (Turissi, Nicholson, and Jaccard 1999). This analysis revealed that as the perception that a policy was a hassle increased, respondents' attitudes about it became more negative. By contrast, as the perception increased that a policy reduced DUI or that it would attract more customers, attitudes toward it improved. The authors stressed that the view that owners dislike all server intervention policies did not receive empirical support. Rather, support depends on the costs versus the benefits of the policy. Not all of the benefit, however, was likely to be realized in terms of the owner's or server's immediate financial interest.

Preventing Alcohol Trauma: A Community Trial

The largest intervention project designed to reduce alcohol-related injuries in the United States was conducted over a five-year period in three communities (Holder, Saltz, Grube, Voas, et al. 1997; Holder and Reynolds 1997; Holder, Saltz, Grube, Treno, et al. 1997). Several of the study's components involved administrative and criminal law, as discussed in previous chapters. In this section we focus on the responsible beverage service component, which established standards for servers and owners or managers of on-site alcohol outlets to reduce the risk of having intoxicated or underage patrons in bars and restaurants.

The intervention consisted of obtaining local industry association support for Responsible Beverage Service (RBS) training and gaining endorsement of RBS from local civic groups; teaching server training to managers and employees using a standard curriculum; developing a process to increase enforcement of existing laws regarding service to obviously intoxicated patrons; and actively exploring the use of local licensing or zoning authority to require RBS. Details of implementation have been described by Saltz and Stanghetta (1997).

Since RBS was only one of the interventions it was not possible to isolate its individual role, but some of the data collected do suggest its effects. The researchers conducted short interviews with managers at the baseline and again in the early stages of the program. The managers seemed supportive of server training, even before the intervention was implemented, and were more likely than the general public to support the view that servers should prevent patrons from becoming intoxicated.

In addition, using "pseudopatrons," the study attempted to see whether servers would refuse to serve obviously intoxicated persons. This approach was limited because of concerns for the patrons' safety, but there was little support for the notion that the servers, presumably trained, impeded heavy drinking. Analysis of how server training affected service to minors in off-site establishments revealed no effect of server training per se, although overall the intervention (and presumably other aspects) decreased sales to customers who were obviously minors in two of the three experimental communities (Grube 1997).

Empirical Evidence on Effects of Dram Shop Laws on Roadway Safety and Driving under the Influence of Alcohol

In several studies of motor vehicle fatalities, dram shop liability had a negative and statistically significant effect on the dependent variables. For example, in an empirical analysis by Chaloukpa, Saffer, and Grossman (1993), total motor vehicle fatality rates, fatalities occurring at night (which are more likely to involve alcohol), and those involving intoxicated drivers were lower in states that recognized dram shop liability. When the sample was limited to eighteen- to twenty-year-olds, the parameter estimates remained statistically significant at the 10 percent level, rather than at the 1 percent level as when drivers of all ages were included. The authors explained these results by noting that during the observational period the minimum drinking age would have made it difficult for such persons to obtain service in on-site drinking establishments where dram shop laws are expected to have an impact.

The results were confirmed by Sloan, Reilly, and Schenzler (1994b) and by Ruhm (1996). Ruhm's specification of the mortality equation was the most complete of any of the studies of dram shop liability. He varied the specification to gauge the sensitivity of results to changes in equation specification. Except for his result on alcohol taxes, the most robust finding was for the effectiveness of dram shop liability laws. Sloan, Reilly, and Schenzler (1994a) found that implementing dram shop liability lowered death rates not only from traffic accidents but also from primary alcohol causes and homicides. Primary alcohol-caused deaths included chronic liver disease and cirrhosis, alcoholic cirrhosis of the liver, alcoholic liver damage, unspecified, and other mortality with alcohol as primary cause.

In contrast to these findings, one study did not find that dram shop laws were effective. In a study of self-reported binge drinking and drinking and driving, based on data from Behavioral Risk Factor Surveys, Sloan, Reilly, and Schenzler (1995) found no statistically significant effects for dram shop liability. With negative findings from only one study, it is probably safe to assume that dram shop laws are effective. It is difficult to speculate about the contradictory results found in a single study.

New Empirical Evidence on Dram Shop Liability
Views of Bar Owners from Our Focus Groups

Before the Survey of Commercial Servers, we conducted focus groups with eleven owners and managers of large drinking establishments (more than ten employees) and nine owners and managers of smaller establishments in order to develop our survey and learn more about their perspectives on alcohol regulation. The participants, all from the area of Princeton-Trenton, New Jersey, volunteered to participate after receiving a mailed invitation. Four interviewers led the focus groups. The bar owners in our groups criticized the tort system because it makes them responsible for other people's actions. The views of one bar owner are illustrative:

> The way the system works doesn't seem fair in order to defend yourself. It's like somebody goes out and gets into an accident, nine months later you get the papers that you're being sued over an incident that you never even knew happened. You've got to try to find witnesses that say the guy wasn't intoxicated when he left. I had a nightmare scenario happen to me. Had this old guy, World War II veteran, who was part of a group of guys who was in every night. They'd watch the news, they'd watch *Jeopardy,* he'd leave at 7:30. So one night he's coming out of the street from where his Veterans of Foreign Wars chapter is, 9:30 at night. He goes through a green light, a motorcycle running a red light hits him in the rear end, and I get sued over that. And they held me liable, 40 percent liable. They couldn't even prove that he was in my bar. They held me, my insurance company, 40 percent liable.

Another asked, "Why are we held responsible for other people's actions? What ever happened to being responsible for your actions? If you're twenty-one, you're old enough to drink, you should be old enough to be responsible."

Results from Our Survey of Commercial Servers

About one-fifth of establishments that responded to our Survey of Commercial Servers reported that a tort claim, including all types of civil liability, had been filed against them during 1990–96 (table 5.3). However, almost 80 percent had never had a tort claim brought against them. About one-tenth of respondents had had one claim, fewer than 5 percent had had more than one, and about an equal number did not know their establishment's claims history.

The survey asked how the threat of being sued had affected business practices. From these responses, it is evident that owners are very much aware of the potential for liability and act in response to this threat. We classified the responses into three categories: increased precaution level, reduced profitability, and other (box 5.1).

Under increased precaution, thirty respondents said they were more careful about serving people. Others said they "are more aware of the threat of suit" (8), "closely monitor customers" (7), and "have increased awareness of the laws" (5). Very few mentioned that suits lowered their profits. Six stated that they were "scared of suits by our own customers." Three were concerned that "insurance goes up." Under "other," respondents reported that the threat of a lawsuit affected their business practices "not very much" (12), yet one respondent said he would "rather be safe than sell another beer" (1). Overall, there was a wide range of responses from the commercial servers, from an increased general awareness of the threat to instituting policies and greater education for both employees and patrons about alcohol issues.

Our Survey of Commercial Servers also obtained owners' or managers'

Table 5.3 Frequency of Tort Claims
Brought against Establishments,
1990–1996

Number	Percentage
None	79.8
One	10.3
Two	3.1
Three or more	1.4
Don't know	5.4

Source: 1996 Survey of Commercial Servers.

Box 5.1 How threat of lawsuit has affected business practices.

Increased Precaution Level

More careful about serving people	30	Paranoia among employees	1
More aware of threat of suit	8	We are living in a victim society	1
Closely monitor customers	7	Make sure there is no drunk driving	1
Increased awareness of the laws	5	Developed liability avoidance strategies	1
Increased server training	5	Emphasizing threat to bartenders	1
Cut people off sooner	5	More aware of police stings	1
Follow policies/don't take chances	4	Keep incident reports	1
More careful because want to keep the business	3	Do not serve anyone who has threatened to sue	1
Have been threatened with suit	2	Fear of being closed down	1
Educate patrons about consumption	1	Increased security	1
Educate employees about laws	1	Employees instructed not to serve minors	1
Employee intervention	1		

Affected profitability

Scared by suits by our own customers, they are the enemy	6	We pay for cabs for those who shouldn't drive	2
We were sued	5	Don't serve as much—afraid of drunk driving	1
Insurance goes up	3		
Purchased insurance	2	Increased costs of operation	1

Other

Not very much	12	Rather be safe than sell another beer	1
Don't know	1		

Source: 1996 Survey of Commercial Servers. Numbers are number of responses.

perceptions of the probability of being sued for serving an obviously intoxicated adult or a minor. Possible responses were given on a five-point scale ranging from "not at all likely" to "very likely." It must be clarified, however, that such terms as "very likely" cannot be taken literally because the true probability that any instance of serving an obviously intoxicated adult or a minor would result in a claim is very small. However, this type of ranking may in fact indicate the *relative* perceived probability of being sued.

Overall, 33.0 percent said they thought a suit would be "very likely" if they served a minor (fig. 5.1). 22.9 percent thought a suit would be "not at all likely." The remaining responses—almost half—fell between the two extremes. The perceived threat from serving an obviously intoxicated adult was somewhat lower: Only 21.9 thought a suit would be "very likely," and 25.4 percent thought it would be "not at all likely."

Responses to the risk perception questions pertaining to citations from

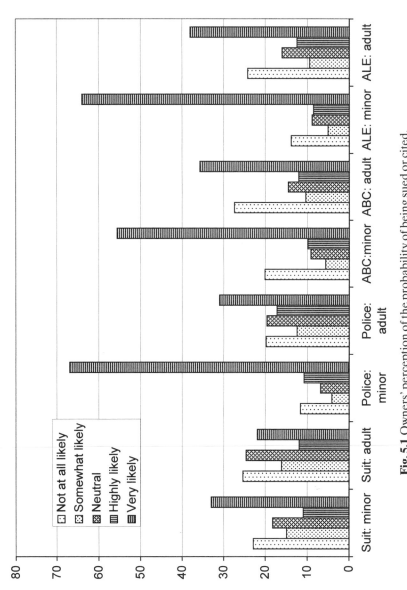

Fig. 5.1 Owners' perception of the probability of being sued or cited.

police, ABC, and ALE for serving minors and obviously intoxicated adults provide an interesting comparison with those for suits. Uniformly, the threat of consequences from these public agencies was higher for serving minors than for serving obviously intoxicated adults. For the perceived threat of citation by the police, ABC, and ALE, the proportion of respondents stating that a citation was "very likely" was higher than the same level of probability ("very likely") for a suit. This result suggests, as seems plausible, that this population may regard a citation as a more certain event than a suit. At the other end of the spectrum, however—the "not at all likely" category—responses for some types of citations were about the same as for suits or even more frequent.

Comparisons of risk perceptions do not by themselves imply the relative effectiveness of policies as deterrents. To link perceptions to deterrent effects, one should first validate the risk perception measures—that is, show that they bear some relation to objective measures of risk. And second, one should show that variations in risk perceptions actually affect behavior. In our Survey of Commercial Servers, we found that 15.6 percent of establishments had had a tort claim brought against them in the six years before the survey (1990–96), and 6.0 percent had been disciplined by a state or local liquor authority in the past year. We found that 88.6 percent also reported that the police were on patrol outside, while 27.4 percent said alcohol law enforcement personnel never entered their establishment.

To ascertain whether differences in tort law by state could explain variation in the perceived probability of being sued, we regressed responses to the risk perception questions on tort law variables and on variables representing other potential influences. We defined separate variables for tort laws that applied to adults and to minors. For each, we first determined whether the state had dram shop liability for adults or minors. We then split the states that did into those with "strict" laws and others. "Strict," was interpreted to mean strict from the perspective of the defendant. Consequently, a "strict" law would be considered pro-plaintiff.

Within this framework, we used five aspects of the law to determine strictness. Subsequently, a particular dram shop law was considered strict if it had more than two of these pro-plaintiff provisions. Otherwise such laws were considered "not strict." The omitted reference group was no dram shop law. The adult and minor versions were the same on the criteria for strictness, differing only on the adult versus minor distinction. The equations were estimated with ordered logit analysis.

The questions used to determine strictness of the laws sought to determine whether the laws of an individual state contained each of five provisions. First, did the state have a responsible business practices defense? A responsible business defense would give the bar a defense if it could prove it had adhered to the responsible server practices described above. Second, did the state uphold the doctrine of comparative negligence, generally thought to be more favorable to plaintiffs than contributory negligence? Under contributory negligence rather than comparative negligence, a bar could escape liability if it could prove that patrons contributed to their own intoxication. Such proof should not be difficult in many cases. Third, did the state implement a damage cap on liability awards? A limit on damages would make bringing suit less attractive to potential claimants and their attorneys. Fourth, did the state uphold restrictions on notice? Fifth, did the state have a statute of limitations? In defining strictness, we considered only special damage caps, restrictions on notice, and statutes of limitations—that is, dram shop–specific limitations. Without restrictions on notice or statutes of limitations, injury victims are free to file claims many years after an injury occurs.

Overall, we found correspondence between the probability of being sued as perceived by the bar owners or managers and the actual status of dram shop laws in the states. That is, in states with strict dram shop laws, respondents perceived a higher probability of being sued for serving an intoxicated adult (table 5.4). The parameter estimate on this variable was positive and statistically significant at better than the 1 percent level. In the regression for perceived threat of tort for serving minors, the parameter estimate for not strict dram shop laws was also positive and almost as large as its counterpart for strict laws, but the parameter estimate for not strict laws was statistically significant at only the 0.13 level.

Other variables had statistically significant effects on the perceived probability of being sued for serving an obviously intoxicated adult: being incorporated (+) and the fraction of patrons who come alone (+). The net worth of the alcohol establishment did not affect the perceived probability, but the binary variable identifying those establishments that did not report net worth was positive and almost statistically significant ($p = 0.057$).

For the perceived probability of being sued for serving minors, having a strict dram shop law again had a positive effect. Here, however, the parameter estimate was statistically significant at only the 0.12 level. Having dram shop laws that were not strict also had a positive effect on the perceived probability of being sued for serving a minor. Other determinants related to the establishment were being incorporated (+) and years in business (−). The variable for net worth missing also had a statistically significant effect (+).

Table 5.4 Owners' Perception of Likelihood of Being Sued for Serving an Intoxicated Adult or a Minor

Explanatory Variables	Intoxicated Adult			Minor		
	Coeff.	Std. Err.	M.E.	Coeff.	Std. Err.	M.E.
Tort law						
Strict	0.43[a]	0.16	0.073	0.32	0.20	0.069
Not strict	0.41	0.27	0.069	0.16	0.22	0.035
Establishment Characteristics						
Net worth $150,000–$500,000	0.16	0.17	0.027	0.18	0.17	0.040
Net worth $500,000+	0.081	0.28	0.014	0.44	0.29	0.096
Net worth missing	0.52	0.27	0.088	0.72[a]	0.26	0.16
Incorporated	0.58[a]	0.15	0.099	0.50[a]	0.16	0.11
Part of chain	0.0076	0.36	0.001	0.25	0.38	0.54
Age of establishment	-0.0049	0.0040	-0.0008	-0.010[a]	0.0040	-0.0023
Fraction of sales from food	0.47	0.38	0.08	0.41	0.41	0.090
Clientele characteristics						
Fraction of						
Customers aged 25–40	-0.20	0.61	-0.034	-0.58	0.61	-0.126
Customers aged 40+	-0.57	0.60	-0.096	0.17	0.62	0.037
Students	0.030	0.78	0.0050	-0.53	0.76	-0.12
Blue-collar workers	-0.32	0.28	-0.054	-0.080	0.28	-0.018
Regular customers	0.20	0.33	-0.033	-0.18	0.34	-0.040
Men	-0.26	0.53	-0.044	0.43	0.53	0.093
Customers who come alone	1.08[b]	0.50	0.18	0.49	0.50	0.11
Customers who come in groups	-0.61	0.53	-0.10	-0.36	0.54	-0.078
Customers who come by car	0.069	0.25	0.012	-0.18	0.26	-0.039
Population density	-0.0009	0.0014	-0.0002	-0.0006	0.0017	-0.0001
Constant	1.00	0.75	0.17	0.99	0.79	0.21
	N = 629			N = 626		

[a]Statistically significant at 1 percent level.
[b]Statistically significant at 5 percent level.
Coeff. = coefficient; Std. Err. = standard error; M.E. = marginal effect.
Table reports nonstandardized regression coefficients.

We also assessed the probability that the establishment had had one or more claims during 1990–96 using logit analysis (table 5.5). The question in the survey did not distinguish between having a claim for serving an obviously intoxicated adult, for serving a minor, or for some other type of dram shop claim—with the benefit of hindsight, a regrettable omission. We assumed that the adult dram shop laws would be most pertinent and therefore included explanatory variables only for such laws.

Both strict and not strict laws had positive effects on the probability of having been sued. Both parameter estimates were statistically significant at better than the 1 percent level. For reasons we cannot explain, the not strict laws had a greater marginal effect than the strict ones.

Other factors explaining the actual probability of having been sued

Table 5.5 Probability of Having Had a Dram Shop Suit between 1990 and 1996

Explanatory Variables	Coeff.	Std. Err.	M.E.
Tort law			
Adult law: strict	0.73[a]	0.28	0.079
Adult law: not strict	1.19[a]	0.40	0.13
Establishment Characteristics			
Net worth $150,000–$500,000	0.28	0.28	0.030
Net worth $500,000+	0.50	0.42	0.054
Net worth missing	−0.72	0.47	0.078
Incorporated	0.98[a]	0.26	0.11
Part of chain	−0.14	0.55	−0.015
Age of establishment	0.018[a]	0.0057	0.0019
Fraction of sales from food	−0.91[a]	0.62	−0.098
Clientele characteristics			
Fraction of			
Customers aged 25–40	−1.58	0.91	−0.17
Customers aged 40+	−2.61[a]	0.96	−0.28
Students	1.87	1.09	0.20
Blue-collar workers	1.30[b]	0.51	0.14
Regular customers	−0.34	0.54	−0.037
Men	−0.55	0.91	−0.059
Customers who come alone	0.35	0.83	0.038
Customers who come in groups	−0.11	0.92	−0.011
Customers who come by car	−0.31	0.40	−0.034
Population density	−0.0011	−0.0022	−0.0001
Constant	−1.81	1.23	−0.19
	N = 650		

[a]Statistically significant at 1 percent level.
[b]Statistically significant at 5 percent level.
Coeff. = coefficient; Std. Err. = standard error; M.E. = marginal effect.
Table reports nonstandardized regression coefficients.

were being incorporated (+), years in business (+), clientele aged twenty-five to forty (−) ($p = 0.084$), clientele over age forty (−), student clientele (+) ($p = 0.087$), and blue-collar clientele (+). Net worth did not affect the probability of having been sued. Overall, the results are highly plausible.

In one regression, we included the number of dram shop suits the establishment had had between 1990 and 1996 as an explanatory variable in the tort risk perception analysis. The coefficient on actual suits was not statistically significant at conventional levels.

CONCLUSION

Dram shop liability represents an expansion of tort law to include parties who may be in a position to influence the wrongdoer's behavior. The motives for adopting dram shop liability may have been a combination of deep pockets and a perception that drunk drivers lack the capacity to act responsibly. Indeed, many drunk drivers obtained their alcohol from bars.

There is limited empirical evidence on the impact of specific kinds of "responsible server practices" that dram shop laws are designed to promote. With the notable exception of a large community trial, most studies of effects of specific server interventions have been small scale and localized. With this caveat duly noted, the literature indicates what servers and their establishments should not do and what they should do. In the former category, employees' drinking on the job promotes patrons' drinking, as do "happy hours." This is not surprising, since making a profit is logically a goal of bars. With one notable exception, the empirical evidence from several studies found evidence that server training is effective.

Interestingly, several previous empirical studies have found that implementing dram shop liability lowers motor vehicle fatalities as well as fatality rates for other alcohol-related causes such as liver cirrhosis and homicides. In these studies a link has been made between implementing statutes or case law and reducing harm.

There is a substantial amount of writing on how dram shop liability should be carried out, including model laws, but to date no one has presented direct evidence on how imposing such liability influences the commercial server of alcoholic beverages. In this chapter we presented new evidence on how dram shop laws influence servers' perceptions of being sued if they engage in bad server practices. We found that in states with dram shop liability, servers do indeed perceive a greater threat of suit, implying that at least part of the signal is getting through to the relevant decision makers. Because of the infrequency of server citations by the police and of citations and alcohol license revocations by the ABC, as discussed in chapters 2 and 3, there is a role for the threat of suit as a deterrent from serving minors and obviously intoxicated adults. Of course suits against bars are also rare, in fact less common than citations by public agencies. But the financial consequences of lawsuits are potentially greater, especially for establishments without liability insurance covering dram shop claims. In addition, bar owners or managers likely have less experience in dealing with defense attorneys and protracted litigation than with regulatory agents.

We also found correspondence between the laws and the server-reported suit histories. It will be the task of the later chapters to probe more deeply into the relation between dram shop laws and other forms of regulation and of server and employee behavior.

6

Liability Insurance for Commercial Servers

Any business involves risk. Firms cope with such risk in part by purchasing insurance policies to cover various liability losses or, alternatively, by self-insuring. Liability insurance covers only damages deemed the legal responsibility of the insured policyholder. The amount of damages is also determined by legal rules. Civil liability, which includes dram shop liability, differs from administrative and criminal liability in that financial risks can be mitigated by purchasing insurance. By contrast, there are no insurance contracts that protect a bar from a fine (criminal liability) or license revocation (administrative liability). Liability insurance is also called third-party insurance in that the insurance is to cover the loss incurred by someone else.

When any type of liability is imposed, the cost of doing business rises. Consequently some bars that are found liable in a tort action go out of business, leaving the remaining establishments with greater market power. These bars will in turn raise prices and take other steps that reduce their expected cost. In particular, they may engage in risk prevention (increased monitoring to reduce injury rates or to prevent tort claims from being filed, given that injury has occurred), obtain insurance, or both. The changes surviving firms adopt will depend on their market niche, assets, and other characteristics. Imposing liability may reduce heavy drinking at bars both directly (by reducing the number of bars and causing an increase in beverage prices, thus lowering alcohol consumption in general and heavy drinking and driving under the influence of alcohol in particular) and indirectly (by providing an incentive to discourage heavy drinking among patrons and mitigating its external effects if it occurs). Large enterprises are more likely to self-insure because they can pool risks internally (see, e.g., Schwartz 1998).

This chapter has five goals: to describe the general functions of liability insurance and the decision to purchase such insurance; to describe practices of dram shop insurers based on responses to our Survey of Dram Shop Insurers; to examine the industry structure as it applies to this small line of property casualty insurance; to discuss the role of state insurance departments based on evidence from our Survey of State Departments of Insurance; and to analyze demand for dram shop insurance with data from our Survey of Commercial Servers.

Functions of Liability Insurance and the Decision to Purchase It

Liability insurance finances payments to injured parties on behalf of policyholders determined to be responsible for those injuries. In addition to bearing risk, liability insurers perform two other roles. The first is loss prevention. The insurer may oversee actions of the potential defendant in order to prevent injury. Insurers may gain experience that can be fruitfully applied to preventing claims. Methods adopted may be safety strategies for preventing injuries or strategies for preventing claims once the injury has occurred. Sometimes the insurer may explicitly link premiums to certain preventive actions by the insured, or it may refuse to underwrite coverage at all. "Loss prevention" may be highly feasible for commercial servers. Whether insurers contribute to loss prevention is an empirical question.

Second, liability insurers typically take an active role in cases against insured defendants. The legal defense of the insured, including the competency of the lawyers and the litigation strategy, can greatly affect the cost of paying claims. For this reason liability policies commonly provide that the insurer will select the attorney and control the litigation, including settlement negotiations and awards.

In the traditional theory of demand for insurance, risk-averse individuals demand insurance coverage, depending on its price. In the context of liability insurance, risk aversion is not a necessary condition for purchasing coverage. Because loss prevention and litigation management are "bundled in," insurers, especially in specialized lines such as dram shop insurance, may have a comparative advantage. Even risk-neutral firms may demand such coverage.

As with insurance for individual drivers, lack of experience rating blunts the full deterrent effects of tort liability (Shavell 1987, chaps. 7–9). With a very small line of insurance such as dram shop liability, there is a question whether risk pooling by insurers is achievable. Tort claims per insured may not be frequent enough to allow experience rating at the level of the individual insured. Also, risk may not be fully diversifiable because, unlike a well-established line such as automobile liability insurance, a single court decision in a state may dramatically alter future insurer liability.

The availability of liability insurance to a commercial server depends in part on state regulations governing insurance and on how often lawsuits against bar owners are filed and result in compensation. The owners' decision to insure against this form of liability should be influenced by the premium structure, the assets at risk, and whether the bar is owned by an enterprise that is large enough to self-insure.

BACKGROUND ON DRAM SHOP LIABILITY INSURANCE

A common form of insurance for on-site commercial alcohol establishments is dram shop liability insurance. Policies cover most dram shop violations, including service to minors and to obviously intoxicated adults. Some businesses may have general liability insurance policies and premises liability policies that they believe cover some liquor liability claims, but these are often poor substitutes for a specific dram shop liability policy, given exclusions from coverage (Mosher 1988 and 1997 supplement). Dram shop insurance, however, typically excludes coverage for assault and battery or for intentional acts of the insured.

There are alternatives to purchasing dram shop insurance directly from a commercial insurer. Several major trade associations formed a consortium to manage their own insurance retention group, called Beverage Retailers Insurance Company (BRICO) (Christy 1989). In some states there are state-operated insurance pools that make liability insurance available to all commercial servers by dividing the risk among servers (Goldberg 1987). Pools are necessary when insurance is compulsory. In addition to state risk pools, there are examples of liquor manufacturers' organizing an insurance group (e.g., a group organized by Joseph E. Seagram and Sons) to provide alcohol liability insurance to establishments that have difficulty obtaining it (Holder et al. 1990).

Given that dram shop liability insurance and alternative sources of coverage are such small lines of insurance, data on industry underwriting practices and premiums are rare. The problem is compounded because "surplus line" or "excess line" insurers often provide coverage, and such insurers do not have to be licensed by states. Also, they tend not to belong to insurance associations.

Dram shop insurance premiums sometimes bear little relation to measures of liability risk (Saltz 1993). For example, in Maryland premiums actually rose for one year directly after the state passed severe restrictions on liquor liability. Although some insurance companies provide discounts for bars that provide server training, the base rates for these companies are usually a great deal higher than those of insurance carriers that do not offer discounts. The arbitrariness of premium rate structures, the high cost of coverage, and the absence of any real means of controlling these costs make bar owners dissatisfied with dram shop insurance.

POLICIES AND PRACTICES OF DRAM SHOP INSURERS
Survey of Dram Shop Insurers

The Survey of Dram Shop Insurers gathered information on underwriting practices, premiums, and loss prevention practices. We surveyed insurers identified from secondary data sources as among those that provided dram shop insurance to drinking establishments. In the spring and summer of 1996 we received survey responses by mail from fourteen dram shop insurance providers that supplied state-specific information on dram shop insurance.

Premium Income and Premiums

On average, the fourteen insurers that responded to our Survey of Dram Shop Insurers derived little premium income from sales of dram shop insurance. In 1995 the median respondent obtained $2 million from this line of coverage (table 6.1). Premium income ranged from as little as $50,000 to $8 million. Premiums for such insurance were based in part on the establishment's annual sales of liquor. Many of the insurers sold policies in only a single state or a few states, and only a few could be considered national companies. For one national insurer that quoted premiums by state for most states, the median premium for coverage with a $500,000 liability limit was between $4 and $5 per $1,000 of liquor sales in 1995. In only a very few states were premiums for such coverage over $6. All the multistate companies reported that underwriting practices differed among the states where they sold coverage. Such insurance was mostly sold through brokers rather than directly by insurance company agents.

Underwriting Practices

We asked the companies whether they sold coverage in each of fifteen situations (table 6.2). The responses were on a five-point scale: never, rarely, sometimes, often, and always.

Insurers were generally not willing to sell coverage in the following circumstances: servers with a criminal record; establishments with police

Table 6.1 General Policies and Business Practices
of Dram Shop Liability Insurers

Premium income, FY 95	
Median	$2 million
Range	$50,000 to $8 million
How liability insurance is sold (%)	
Company agents	35.7
Brokers	57.1
Percentage of insurers selling coverage in	
1 state	58.3
2–35 states	25.0
35+ states	16.7
Underwriting practices differ by state when company	
sells liability insurance in more than one state (%)	100.0
Basic premiums for liquor liability insurance based on	
a national insurer's average policy with $500,000 limit and	
$1,000 deductible	
Rates per $1,000 of liquor sales (%)	
<$4.00	21.1
4.00–4.99	36.8
5.00–5.99	39.5
6.00+	2.6

Source: 1996 Survey of Dram Shop Insurers.

problems or known to have firearms on the premises; biker bars; establishments without a bartender; and those with previous dram shop suits involving minors. By contrast, insurers were much more willing to cover establishments with previous tort claims involving intoxicated adults and administrative violations.

Premium Surcharges and Discounts

Some insurers covered establishments with practices they considered undesirable by adding a premium surcharge (table 6.3). Other insurers were unwilling to write coverage in such circumstances at any price. For example, most of the respondents did not cover bars with bouncers or security guards, exotic or nude dancers, athletic contests or events, or mechanical rides. Some insurers that did cover such establishments imposed premium surcharges of up to 25 percent, but other insurers were willing to sell them coverage without a surcharge. Conversely, some insurers granted premium discounts for safe drinking practices such as server training, providing free rides to intoxicated patrons, deriving less than 30 percent of revenue from alcoholic beverages, and having no tort claims in the recent past (table 6.4).

Table 6.2 Underwriting Practices (% Responding)

Practice	Never	Rarely	Sometimes	Often	Always	Total
Sell coverage to commercial servers with liquor license violations	28.6	28.6	21.4	14.3	7.1	100.0
Sell coverage to commercial servers with past criminal sanctions for selling alcohol to obviously intoxicated persons	64.3	7.1	14.3	14.3	0.0	100.0
Sell coverage to establishments with liquor license suspensions in past three years	45.4	9.1	36.4	9.1	0.0	100.0
Sell coverage to establishments with any liquor liability claims in past three years	18.2	36.3	18.2	18.2	9.1	100.0
Sell coverage to establishments with known police problems	58.3	33.3	0.0	8.4	0.0	100.0
Sell coverage to establishments with firearms on premises	66.7	25.0	8.3	0.0	0.0	100.0
Sell coverage to biker bars (motor-cycle)	50.0	16.7	25.0	0.0	8.3	100.0
Sell liquor liability coverage to establishments without an employed bartender	61.5	0.0	7.7	0.0	30.8	100.0
Sell liability coverage to commercial servers with past criminal sanctions for selling alcohol to minors	69.2	15.4	7.7	0.0	7.7	100.0
Sell liability coverage to commercial servers with dram shop claims involving intoxicated adults	27.3	27.3	27.3	0.0	18.1	100.0
Sell liability coverage to commercial servers with past dram shop claims involving intoxicated minors	53.8	15.4	30.8	0.0	0.0	100.0
Willingness to sell liability coverage depends on location (near university, bad neighborhood, etc.)	42.9	14.3	7.1	7.1	28.6	100.0
Willingness to cover an establishment depends on clientele mix (of establishment)	42.9	7.1	7.1	7.1	35.8	100.0
Differentiate willingness to cover an establishment based on ratio of sales of alcohol to sales of non-alcoholic beverages and food	21.6	0.0	7.1	14.2	57.1	100.0
Differentiate willingness to cover based on whether establishment has server training program	23.1	0.0	15.4	8.0	53.8	100.0

Table 6.3 Surcharges on Premiums

Establishment Characteristics	Percentage Debit			Don't Cover (%)
	Low	Median	High	
Customers predominantly aged 26–35	0	0	40	14.3
Customers predominantly aged 21–25	0	0	25	0.0
Dance floor	0	0	25	28.6
Live music	0	0	25	14.3
Bouncers or security guards	0	0	0	57.1
Exotic or nude dancers	0	0	25	57.1
Athletic concerts or events	0	0	0	57.1
Mechanical rides	0	0	25	57.1
Sports bars	0	0	25	42.9
Alcohol sales for more than fourteen hours per day	0	0	25	33.3
Located in resort area	0	0	25	28.7
Banquet facilities	0	0	0	42.9
Security guards (insured by independent contractors)	0	0	0	57.1
Establishment sponsors or provides "ladies' night"	0	0	25	28.6
Establishment sponsors or provides doubles for single prices	0	0	25	28.6
Establishment sponsors or provides two for one drinks	0	0	25	28.6
Establishment sponsors or provides free alcoholic drinks	0	0	25	28.6
Establishment sponsors or provides singles night	0	0	25	28.6

Source: 1996 Survey of Dram Shop Insurers.

INDUSTRY STRUCTURE

Since 1991, Michigan's Commissioner of Insurance has issued an annual report on the availability and pricing of liquor liability insurance in that state (Michigan Commissioner of Insurance 1996). Michigan is one of the few states requiring that commercial sellers show proof of financial responsibility, such as dram shop insurance or having sufficient net worth to self-insure, in order to obtain a license. Michigan has many commercial servers in relation to its population, and tort claims tend to be relatively frequent there (Posner 1997). Nevertheless, the Michigan reports provide a valuable source of information on dram shop insurance, particularly given the paucity of literature on this type of insurance.

The latest underwriting crisis to affect the liquor liability insurance market was in 1985–86, in part reflecting more frequent dram shop claims and the adverse impact of the underwriting cycle more generally. Although

Table 6.4 Discounts on Premiums

Description	Percentage Credit		
	Low	Median	High
Server training	0	10	25
Provides free rides to intoxicated patrons	0	0	25
Sells beer and/or wine only	0	0	5
Less than 30 percent alcohol sales	0	0	30
30 percent to 49 percent alcohol sales	0	0	0
Loss-free past two years	0	0	10
Loss-free past three years	0	0	15

Source: 1996 Survey of Dram Shop Insurers.

other types of liability insurance were also affected (Bovbjerg 1995), this line was hit particularly hard given its tendency toward greater volatility owing to the relatively small number of insureds. Before a liquor liability pool was instituted in Michigan, during the contracting phase of the underwriting cycle, retail establishments in this sector had to either do without coverage or obtain liability insurance through surplus line insurers. These insurers are not subject to regulatory oversight by states, may limit the amounts of coverage offered, may charge higher premiums, and might be subject to greater insolvency risk. In 1986 surplus line carriers sold virtually all dram shop insurance offered in Michigan. Few licensed insurers offered such coverage and, if so, only in conjunction with a general liability policy. The crisis in Michigan was alleviated at least in part in 1986 by passage of legislation requiring dram shop insurance.

By 1996 there were 141 insurers providing some liability coverage to over 17,000 off-site and on-site alcohol establishments in the state, either as a liquor liability policy or as an endorsement onto a commercial general liability policy. This rise in the number of insurers led to a cut in premiums by over 70 percent between 1987 and 1996.

At least in Michigan, entry into this line of insurance by traditional insurance firms appears to have been relatively easy. Yet analysis of insurers' market shares reveals considerable change over time in the dominant insurers. Although ease of market entry is typical of property liability insurance in general, entry of companies with low financial ratings, such as those offering liquor liability coverage, is not as easy. Michigan in 1996 was thus atypical, since many of the dominant insurers in this line had low financial ratings. During this time, 28 percent of liquor liability insurance premiums in Michigan were written by A-rated carriers, in contrast to 90 percent of premiums for property liability.

In spite of the low ratings of liquor liability insurers, insurer insolvency was not yet widespread. The high turnover of insurers offering dram shop liability insurance in this market may account for their failure to take loss prevention measures, evident from our Survey of Commercial Servers. Since the gain from loss prevention occurs in the future, it stands to reason that an insurer that does not plan to remain in the line would see little to be gained from such an investment.

STATE REGULATION OF LIQUOR LIABILITY INSURANCE
Survey of State Departments of Insurance

In 1996 we surveyed state departments of insurance to obtain names of dram shop insurers, information on premium volume and premiums for particular liability limits, state guidelines for reporting incidents covered by dram shop insurance, and state requirements for minimum liability coverage. Mail surveys were completed and returned by forty-eight states and the District of Columbia (see the appendix).

Survey Findings

Dram shop coverage is subject to the same overall rules governing insurance policies in general. According to responses to the Survey of State Departments of Insurance, only four states had dram shop–specific regulations (table 6.5). In these circumstances we obtained information specific to dram shop insurance. Otherwise the responses applied to other lines of insurance as well.

Overall, based on the responses of the state insurance departments, neither premium regulation nor regulation of underwriting practices appeared to be restrictive. Perhaps insurers, if queried about regulation, would have been less sanguine about the regulatory practices of the states.

In general, rate filings were approved quickly. Some states limited the number of times a year an insurer could file for a premium increase or the maximum percentage increase allowed per filing with the state department of insurance. Some states limited insurers' ability to classify risks. Subsequent limits on risk classification focused on banning the policy of "redlining"—charging more for insurance in particular neighborhoods (e.g., low income, high crime). In addition, limits were imposed on how far experience rating could be used, as well as on other discriminatory practices such as basing premiums on the racial composition of a bar's clientele. Only one state required that insurers take all customers who apply for coverage. Very few states had statutory requirements for periodic reporting on dram shop liability and coverage for such loss or for system-

Table 6.5 Summary of Results from Survey of Insurance Departments

	minimum	median	maximum
State has dram shop insurance–specific regulations			4
Premium regulations			
Limit on percentage increase in premiums insurer can obtain from single filing			4
Limit on number of times a year insurer can apply for premium increase			5
Limit on number of times insurer can apply for premium increase			7
Number of states in which department of insurance denied a premium increase for dram shop insurance during 1995			5
Number of states in which department of insurance denied a premium increase for dram shop insurance during 1990–94			7
Insurers must accept all establishments that want coverage ("take all comers")			1
Length of time it takes rate filings to be approved (months)	0	1.5	11
Maximum percentage increase allowed	15	25	25
Number of times insurer can apply for premium increase	1	1	1
Reporting requirements			
State required by statute to submit periodic reports on dram shop liability			4
Department of insurance collects data on dram shop cases			4
State makes data on dram shop cases publicly available			1
			(Iowa)

Source: 1996 Survey of State Departments of Insurance.

atic data collection. Only Iowa made data on dram shop cases publicly available.

We reviewed state financial responsibility laws and dram shop liability laws for statutory minimum liability limits in mid-1998. Five states had laws specifying a minimum dollar amount that commercial establishments had to have to cover dram shop liability claims before they could be licensed to serve alcoholic beverages (table 6.6). Of these states, only Maryland's financial responsibility requirement was determined at the county level. Although financial responsibility could be demonstrated by showing that the minimum required assets were held in reserve, most establishments satisfied the requirement by obtaining minimum liability coverage (see discussion below). In addition, three states required proof of financial responsibility from commercial establishments before granting a liquor license, but no specific dollar minimum was included in the statute.

Nine states imposed minimum liability limits on dram shop insurance policies. This means that all policies sold must offer the specified minimum coverage. This is in contrast to a statutory requirement that insurance be purchased. Such laws apply to motor vehicle liability coverage, but not to firms. Financial responsibility laws are more permissive in allowing for self-insurance. The rationale for imposing such limits is to ensure that the insured has adequate liability insurance to cover most claims. An unintended side effect of imposing such minimums is that some establishments may decide not to insure because the required minimum coverage is so high that the insurance is too expensive.

DEMAND FOR DRAM SHOP INSURANCE
Description

The Survey of Commercial Servers, a national survey of 778 bars, included some questions on dram shop liability coverage. The vast majority of establishments we surveyed (93 percent) had some form of liability insurance (table 6.7). Unfortunately, the survey question referred to liability insurance rather than specifically to dram shop coverage, and so the responses may include insurance obtained through a general liability policy and not necessarily specific "dram shop" insurance. For this reason we cannot exclude the possibility that some liability policies covered accidents on the premises and other torts but not specifically dram shop suits. Of those with coverage, about one-fifth knew their insurers offered a premium discount if the establishment provided server training. Of course, if they had general liability rather than dram shop coverage, it is very unlikely that they would have been offered a premium discount for server training. Relatively few insurers seem to engage

Table 6.6 Minimum Financial Responsibility and Liability Limit Laws, 1998

Financial responsibility
Minimum dollar amount specified
  Iowa
  Maryland (partial)
  Michigan
  Minnesota
  Vermont
No minimum dollar amount specified
  New Mexico
  New York
  Oregon
Statute specifies liability limits
  Colorado
  Connecticut
  Illinois
  Indiana
  Kentucky
  Pennsylvania
  Tennessee
  Texas
  Utah

Source: Our analysis of state statutes.

Table 6.7 Characteristics of Liability Insurance Policies: Establishments

Item	% Yes	% Missing
Had a liability insurance policy	93.3	0.6
Insurer offered discount for server training	20.2	22.0
Insurer provided advice on dealing with intoxicated persons	14.1	11.5

Source: 1996 Survey of Commercial Servers.

Table 6.8 Net Worth of Firm (%)

Net Worth	All	With Dram Shop Insurance	Without Dram Shop Insurance	Refused to Answer
Less than $150,000	40.7	37.9	81.1	33.3
$150,000–$500,000	36.2	38.5	11.3	22.2
$500,000+	10.3	10.9	3.8	5.6
Don't know	12.8	12.7	3.8	38.9

Source: 1996 Survey of Commercial Servers.

in loss prevention. Only 14 percent of respondents said their insurers gave them advice on how to deal with intoxicated patrons. Sizable numbers did not know whether their insurers took these loss prevention measures.

A large tort claim would bankrupt many bars if they did not have liability coverage. About three-quarters of the establishments reported they had a net worth of less than $500,000 (table 6.8). When asked in a separate question whether the company had sufficient reserves to cover a half-million dollar tort claim against it, 79 percent said no.

Among survey respondents, there was an appreciable difference in the propensity to have coverage depending on the net worth of the firm. Of those firms without liability insurance, 81.1 percent had a net worth under $150,000. By contrast, of those with coverage, only 38 percent had a net worth less than this amount.

We asked commercial establishments that did not have liability insurance why they did not carry it. The most frequent response by far was "too expensive/cannot afford" (box 6.1). Other responses included "business is too small to bother," "in between companies," "monitor ourselves," and "bar is in the middle of nowhere," suggesting little liability risk. Of those with insurance, a few commercial establishments had positive things to say about loss prevention requirements of their insurers (box 6.2). Although the bars perhaps did not like what the insurers mandated, they at least indicated that insurers' efforts might have increased servers' precaution levels. The most frequent responses regarding loss prevention measures by insurers were "[we] have to play by their rules," "[they] made us aware of a

Box 6.1 Reasons establishments did not have liability insurance.

Too expensive/cannot afford	34	Insurance companies are thieves	1
Business is too small to bother	2	Waste of money	1
In between companies	2	Own property and am self-insured	1
Monitor ourselves	1	Comparing rates now	1
Bar is in the middle of nowhere/no need	1	Just don't have it	1
Business is incorporated	1	I don't know	1
Customers are socialized not to get drunk		Liability insurance is too expensive,	
and drive, rely on law enforcement	1	would just declare bankruptcy	
		if sued	1
and drive, rely on law enforcement	1	Do not have a problem	1
Not enough business	1		
Never felt we needed it	1		

Source: 1996 Survey of Commercial Servers. Numbers are number of responses.

possibility of a lawsuit," "[we] had to improve bar safety," and "[we] have to take required server courses."

Despite recognizing the positives of loss prevention, many commercial establishments made unfavorable remarks about insurers. On balance, unfavorable remarks were more frequent than favorable ones. Many bars complained that such insurance "[is] expensive/costs a lot/[had] high premiums/[has] rates [that] always increase"; that it "increases exposure to liability if customers know establishment has such coverage"; "[we] had to raise our prices to cover premiums," and that "[we experience] higher insurance rates when there is trouble." Some commercial servers said that insurance companies had "no effect" on their practices.

Focus Group Reactions to Liability Insurance

As we mentioned previously, to develop questions for our Survey of Commercial Servers we conducted one-day focus groups composed of owners of large and small establishments. Each group contained ten owners of bars in New Jersey, who were asked questions about their businesses. One group included large establishments, defined as having ten or more employees; the other consisted of owners and managers from small establishments. Comments from these groups showed that owners had strong opinions about liability insurance.

Liability Insurance

Discussion in focus groups revealed that all owners of small establishments carried general liability and fire insurance. These owners all recognized

Box 6.2 Ways insurance companies have affected commercial servers' behavior.

Loss Prevention

Have to play by their rules   12

Made us aware of a possibility of a
   lawsuit   11

Made us more cautious   6

Had to improve bar safety   5

Have to take required server
   courses   3

Careful not to have infractions   3

More careful in dealing with intoxicated
   patrons   2

More attention to server training   2

Do whatever company says to keep
   insurance   1

The insurance company is always
   around   1

Not to serve minors   1

Increased awareness of drunk driving   1

Cut out employee drinking   1

No employee meals allowed   1

No happy hours   1

More aware of serving and watching
   people as they leave   1

Forced to monitor more closely   1

Reduced Profitability

Expensive/costs a lot/high premiums   49

Rates always increase   33

Increases exposure to liability if customers
   know you have insurance   6

Had to raise our prices to cover
   premiums   5

Higher insurance rates when there is
   trouble   3

No more live entertainment   1

Made us restructure the building   1

Had to move business out of nightclub
   setting   1

Must sell more to afford premiums   1

Reduces business   1

Have cut back on number of employees   1

More expensive to do business   1

There are improvements I would like to
   make but insurance is too expensive   1

Have added food serving   1

Have cut business down because of risk
   the of DUI   1

Other

No effect   5

Takes care of liability   5

A little bit   2

None—only required to have fire
   insurance   1

Don't know   1

Our insurance does not cover a lot that
   should be covered   1

Afraid to insure business—too
   expensive   1

Required by state   1

Source: 1996 Survey of Commercial Servers. Numbers are number of responses.

the risk of being sued in a dram shop action. For varied reasons, some chose to purchase dram shop liability insurance in addition to general liability and fire insurance. Others, however, decided to chance being sued.

   The experiences of small establishment owners with dram shop liability insurance varied. Many claimed they could not afford it. One claimed that he "did away with insurance about five years ago when we couldn't afford it." Others thought they might be shielded from liability if the bar was incorporated. One owner thought he would be safe because he held the real property under a realty company and the tavern was organized as a corporation. After consulting his lawyer, however, this man decided he was running a 0.5 percent chance of being sued and took out dram shop insurance. One owner reported he did not want to risk being sued without insurance: "It's like I don't want to operate and have that gun at my head." After being sued in the early 1980s, another owner without insurance took out a liquor liability policy. Although he was found not liable in the suit, he still spent $7,000 in attorney's fees for his defense. Another reported trouble finding a company to insure his establishment and claimed, "I could never receive a quote, and I asked at least three people."

Larger establishment owners who participated in our other focus group were more likely to have dram shop insurance. Some said they bought the insurance to defend against lawsuits. Additionally, some servers in large establishments carried their own individual insurance. Some large establishments, however, did not have dram shop liability insurance. One owner formed a shadow company in another state to hide his assets in case of a suit. He said that if he was sued he would just close the bar and open another one with the assets from the shadow company. The insurance companies imposed business practices on the large establishments, whose owners reported that some insurers regularly visited them to check the ratio of food to alcohol sales.

Owners and managers of large establishments reported a shift in their business from serving mostly liquor to placing more emphasis on food, a change they primarily attributed to the focus on liability and drunk driving. The owners noted a decrease over the past twenty years in those coming to the bar solely to drink. Although the large establishment owners claimed most of their revenue was from liquor, they reported that this new focus on dram shop liability placed them in a difficult position. According to one, "You want to sell the liquor to make money, but yet you're not going to put somebody out on the street that's going to go out and get in an accident and come back and wipe out your entire business that you worked so hard for." Another said, "It's almost against your grain to be sitting there trying to sell drinks and then sit there and tell people not to drink."

Server Training

None of the owners with dram shop insurance reported that their insurers required specific server training. However, all establishments reported having some sort of training. Several small owners reported using a video-tape issued by a previous insurer to educate new employees. Another re-ported taking employees to a three-hour alcohol-training seminar for server certification. The owners claimed that having certified employees aids their defense if anything happens in the bar. The course recommended documenting all incidents in case a suit arises, but bar owners found this burdensome and typically did not follow this advice.

Server training included teaching bartenders to be attentive to whether customers show signs that they have already been drinking, and bartenders changing shifts were taught to point out to the next shift of bartenders those customers who have been drinking for a while. Other bars offered classes in server training that taught about consumption rates and absorp-tion rates. Both large and small establishments adopted server training when they began to recognize the potential for liability and litigation.

Demand for Liability Insurance

To further assess the demand for liability insurance, we specified and esti-mated an equation using logit analysis for whether the commercial server had coverage, using several explanatory variables: premiums, whether the state had dram shop liability for obviously intoxicated adults and for mi-nors, net worth of the establishment, and the presence of regulatory poli-cies on coverage (i.e., minimum financial responsibility and minimum liability limits), as well as other factors potentially affecting demand for li-ability insurance (table 6.9). We estimated two specifications, one includ-ing the type of entertainment provided by bars and one without the entertainment variables. The premium data came from one of the fourteen insurers that responded to our 1996 Survey of Dram Shop Insurers and sold dram shop liability insurance in most states.

Overall, with two important exceptions, the results were very plausible and consistent with evidence we have already presented. The two excep-tions were the binary variables for dram shop liability. Both parameters were positive, implying higher demand for insurance in states with dram shop liability, but neither parameter estimate was even close to statistical significance at conventional levels. This result suggests that some respon-dents who had liability coverage for suits other than dram shop liability, such as premises liability, responded positively to our question. Statisti-cally significant determinants of having coverage were premiums ($-$); hav-ing a statutory minimum financial responsibility requirement ($+$); having net worth of \$150,000 to \$500,000 ($+$) relative to the omitted reference group, which was net worth under \$150,000; fraction of customers aged

Table 6.9 Probability of Having Dram Shop Liability Insurance

Explanatory Variables	Coeff.	Std. Err.	M. E.	Coeff.	Std. Err.	M. E.
Insurance variables						
Premium	−0.78[a]	0.29	−0.035	−0.86[a]	0.30	−0.023
Premium missing	−4.64[a]	1.51	−0.21	−4.89[a]	1.54	−0.13
Minimum liability limit	−0.16	0.39	−0.0070	−0.065	0.40	−0.0017
Financial responsibility	2.64[a]	1.01	0.12	2.82[a]	1.03	0.076
Adult	0.081	0.53	0.0036	0.083	0.54	0.0022
Minor	0.35	0.52	0.016	0.31	0.53	0.0084
Establishment characteristics						
Net worth $150,000–$500,000	1.42[a]	0.41	0.063	1.50[a]	0.42	0.041
Net worth $500,000+	0.82	0.69	0.037	0.78	0.71	0.021
Net worth missing	0.35	0.45	0.016	0.40	0.46	0.011
Incorporated	0.58	0.32	0.026	0.52	0.33	0.014
Part of chain	0.33	1.08	0.05	0.24	1.12	0.0066
Age of establishment	−0.0002	0.0078	−0.0000	0.0011	0.0080	0.0000
Fraction of sales from food	1.84	0.99	0.082	1.81	1.03	0.049
Clientele characteristics						
Fraction of						
Customers aged 25–40	2.12	1.16	0.094	2.38[b]	1.19	0.064
Customers aged 40+	1.02	1.07	0.045	1.41	1.13	0.038
Students	0.53	1.50	0.023	0.029	1.57	0.0008
Blue-collar workers	0.23	0.56	0.010	0.13	0.57	0.0036
Regular customers	−0.62	0.73	−0.028	−0.61	0.74	−0.017
Men	−0.53	1.02	−0.024	−0.57	1.05	−0.015
Customers who come alone	1.43	0.96	0.064	1.44	0.98	0.039
Customers who come	2.51[b]	1.21	0.11	2.46[b]	1.25	0.066
in groups						
Customers who come	−0.13	0.50	−0.0057	−0.14	0.51	−0.0038
by car						
Population density	−0.0053	0.0031	−0.0002	−0.0054	0.0032	−0.0001
Entertainment						
Pool table				0.26	0.41	0.0071
Video games				−0.30	0.38	−0.0082
Television				−11.01	209.35	−0.30
Jukebox				−0.41	0.54	−0.011
Live entertainment				0.69	0.39	0.019
Dancing				−0.39	0.38	−0.011
Internet access				10.73	192.11	0.29
Constant	2.86	2.00	0.13	14.28	209.36	0.39
	N = 650			N = 650		

[a]Statistically significant at 1 percent level.
[b]Statistically significant at 5 percent level.
Coeff. = coefficient; Std. Err. = standard error; M.E. = marginal effect.
Table reports nonstandardized regression coefficients.

twenty-five to forty ($+$) relative to the omitted reference group, which was fraction under age twenty-five; and fraction of customers who come in groups ($+$). Fraction of sales from food was nearly significant in both estimations ($p = 0.061$ and $p = 0.080$). The price elasticity of demand for insurance, evaluated at the observational means, was -1.40 (without entertainment variables) and -0.94 (with entertainment variables). These elasticities indicate substantial demand for liability insurance in response to changes in premiums.

Establishments in one of the twelve states for which we had no premium data from the insurer were less likely to have coverage; in several of these states there was no dram shop statute or case law supporting the existence of dram shop liability. As we noted in chapter 5, not having dram shop liability in a particular state does not totally eliminate the chance of a suit, since cases may be brought under other legal principles such as wrongful death.

Establishments in the middle net worth category were more likely to have such insurance than either the less wealthy or the more wealthy, holding other factors constant. This is plausible in that the low-wealth firms can just declare bankruptcy if forced to pay a large tort claim. The wealthier firms can self-insure against such risk.

The positive coefficient on the percentage of sales from food seems implausible at first glance, but insurers grant discounts based on this fraction. The premium variable in our analysis did not take account of various debits and credits.

CONCLUSION

Liability insurance serves the dual purpose of risk spreading and loss prevention. According to the information collected in our focus groups, however, dram shop liability insurers took few measures to prevent loss. Rather, their visits to the large establishments seem to have been more to determine premiums than to encourage loss prevention. Dual explanations for their lack of loss prevention initiatives are the small volume of such business underwritten by most insurers and the high rate of insurer turnover in this line.

Some establishments operated without dram shop liability insurance. A few stated that if they had to pay a claim, they would just declare bankruptcy. Others were large enough to self-insure. There was a clear link between purchasing insurance and premium changes, with higher premiums reducing the likelihood of having such coverage.

The possibility that the defendant will not have sufficient funds to cover the victim's loss is one deficiency of tort liability. Mandatory coverage, commonplace in automobile liability, is the exception rather than the rule for businesses. Given the small size of this line of insurance, it goes virtually unnoticed by state insurance departments. Many bars obtain their insurance from surplus line carriers who are not subject to state insurance regulation, and others self-insure.

If there is to be insurance reform, it likely to be "generic," that is, applicable to all lines of liability insurance or focused on a few lines, such as professional liability and products liability, that command much greater attention from the public and focused political constituencies. For now, as far as dram shop liability insurance is concerned, the best policy seems to be watchful waiting.

7

Effects of Administrative, Criminal, and Tort Liability on Server Behavior

INTRODUCTION

In previous chapters we investigated various approaches designed to curb hazardous behavior associated with excessive alcohol consumption. In this chapter we present empirical evidence on the effects of these approaches on alcohol servers (owners or managers), based on data from our national Survey of Commercial Servers. These server behaviors are likely to affect drinking and driving by customers. We first present descriptive evidence from our survey of owners' or managers' self-reports about their behaviors, then we test specific hypotheses about the effects of various public policies on server behavior. Finally, we evaluate our findings and discuss the public policy implications as well as the limitations of our analysis.

Bar owners and managers make a number of decisions that either promote or discourage heavy drinking by patrons. These choices may be categorized in terms of "location and ambiance," "pricing," and "monitoring." The bar's location, decor, food service, entertainment, and other features influence the drinking proclivities of its patrons and the amount they actually drink. Thus, for example, a bar oriented to college students and the "party scene" should attract a more rowdy, hard-drinking clientele than one oriented to middle-aged couples. Other things being equal, higher prices tend to reduce heavy drinking (Cook and Tauchen 1982; Kenkel 1993; Leung and Phelps 1993; Mullahy and Sindelar 1994; Sloan, Reilly, and Schenzler 1994a; Cook and Moore, n.d.), both by lowering the number of heavy drinkers who patronize the bar and by curtailing patrons' drinking. Whether an establishment can set prices depends on competition in its market area. If the bar has some market power, it sets price. If the market is competitive, price is exogenous to the firm. Additionally, "monitoring" in a drinking establishment may take the form of spacing service, serving one drink at a time, watering drinks, or refusing service. Other policies, such as calling a taxicab for inebriated patrons, are also forms of monitoring and may be included with those above in a training program that instructs servers how to serve drinks in a safe manner.

As we explain below, even without various forms of public intervention, bars would probably engage in some monitoring, given the profit motive. In addition, they may cater to clientele less prone to heavy drinking. However, public intervention may encourage such firms to do more to deter patrons' unsafe behaviors.

Three Hypotheses

In this chapter we test three hypotheses:

> H1. *Imposing administrative, criminal, and dram shop liability on commercial servers raises the price they charge for alcoholic beverages, increases monitoring of patrons, and changes product mix in ways that are likely to improve public safety.*

Because of offsetting indirect effects, imposing liability on an establishment may not have the intended effect on all measures. For example, when a bar sells more food there may be fewer drinkers to monitor, thus lowering the return from monitoring heavy drinkers. Thus it is possible that the level of monitoring bars undertake could decrease in response to more stringent dram shop liability. Yet most measures should be in the intended direction. Further, there are important potential interactions between some policies and servers' incentives. For example, server training is likely to be more effective if the establishment has an incentive to monitor patrons' behavior.

In previous chapters we reported on empirical analyses relating objective measures of the threat of liability to the threat as perceived by the servers. One advantage of our perception measures is that we asked about the threat in response to a hypothetical deviation of servers' behavior from the legal standard. An alternative measure would have been to ask about the threats conditional on actual behavior of the bar. By posing the questions as we did, we mitigated a potential problem of endogeneity of threat. As discussed below, however, some endogeneity problems remain.

> H2. *The availability of liability insurance reduces the effectiveness of dram shop liability, especially when premiums are not tied to*

the server's past claims experience and current loss prevention practices.

Because the dram shop insurance will most likely cover a bar's expenses in full or in part if it is sued, the effectiveness of dram shop liability is limited for these establishments. Contrary to the intent of dram shop laws, we expect to find that when commercial establishments have liability insurance, they are less careful about serving minors and intoxicated adults.

> H3. *Increased competition among commercial servers reduces the price they charge for alcoholic beverages. However, holding ambiance constant, the effect of increased competition on monitoring excessive drinking is ambiguous and must be determined empirically.*

Knowing the effect of competition among sellers of alcohol is important for public policy purposes. Insofar as competition causes a "race to the bottom," with bars competing for customers by offering an environment that encourages heavy drinking, additional regulation may be warranted, including restrictions on entry.

Accident Prevention and the Profit Motive

Bars are in business to make a profit. Since our study's focus is on monitoring, we start with this decision variable. We assume initial homogeneity among consumers. Order can be produced by monitoring. The server knows that many people do not want to visit a very unruly establishment. However, they do want to have fun. The hourly wage of monitors is fixed. Thus, starting at a very negative value—total bedlam—increasing order by monitoring is initially profitable; that is, the added revenue exceeds the added cost. As order is increased, however, a point of zero marginal profit is eventually reached. Thereafter, further increases are unprofitable.

Now assume heterogeneity among consumers. There are two groups: graduate students (students past the minimum drinking age) and yuppies. The students live near a university, and the yuppies live in the suburbs. Neither the students nor the yuppies like total bedlam, but the students are more tolerant of a little disruption. Reflecting this, the relation between order, monitoring, and profit differs for the two groups. Students will prefer less order, and the profit-maximizing amount will be lower. Because it may take more monitors to produce a given level of order in the student-oriented bar, order will be lower there. Ambiance may differ as well. The students may like loud music, whereas the yuppies may prefer watching sports on television.

A potential entrant into the on-site commercial server market faced with the choice of bar location will plausibly pick the more profitable one, given the profit-maximizing level of order for that type of establishment. If there is positive (economic) profit and free entry, entry will occur until profit becomes zero. For a given population served, the level of order and monitoring by competing bars will be the same.

Imposition of Liability, Monitoring, and Effects of Competition

Imposing liability may lead sellers to set order (monitoring) at the socially optimal level—higher than would prevail in the absence of liability. Since the higher level of care is not the one consumers prefer, then if that level is required by law or regulation but the rules are not enforced, firms will be tempted to offer a lower level and hence attract patrons from competitors. Lack of enforcement may take a number of forms, including little patrolling by police, low conviction rates, low criminal penalties, and few tort claims.

COMMERCIAL SERVERS' SELF-REPORTS OF ACTIONS LIKELY TO INCREASE OR REDUCE THE EFFECTS OF HEAVY DRINKING
Ambiance

In our focus group discussions with commercial servers (see the appendix and chapter 5 for descriptions), we learned that their clientele has changed over the years. Some decades ago it was common for workers to walk to a neighborhood bar after the workday and then walk home. With the decline in the manufacturing sector, fewer bars are near a plant. Today, although some neighborhood taverns still exist, many patrons drive to bars. Although this neighborhood quality is no longer so prevalent, the owners of smaller establishments in our focus group reported that the owner or server recognized most customers. Overall, 65.7 percent of the patrons in our national sample were regulars.

Virtually all bars in the focus groups reported offering some form of entertainment (table 7.1). Television was a universal fixture in these establishments, whereas only 3 percent offered patrons Internet access. About half of responding establishments had some form of live entertainment or dancing. According to focus group respondents, the purpose of offering live entertainment was to lure customers, even if a very secondary purpose was to occupy patrons so they did not drink excessively (Christy 1989). Some small establishment owners were annoyed by people who came to listen to entertainment but did not buy anything. "They pay their five dollar cover charge, they come in, and they want to sip on water. So then we got

Table 7.1 Types of Entertainment Offered
by Commercial Establishments

Type	% Offering
Pool tables	70.8
Video games	70.8
Television	97.3
Jukebox	81.4
Live entertainment	47.6
Dancing	44.3
Internet access	3.0

Source: 1996 Survey of Commercial Servers.

smart, and we put in bottled water. Now we charge them a dollar fifty for a bottle of water that costs us twenty-nine cents."

The availability of food in a drinking establishment may also influence how much alcohol patrons consume. Participants in the focus group for larger establishments (those with ten or more employees) reported a shift in their business over the past decade from serving mostly liquor to selling more food. Also, the owners noted a decrease over the past two decades or so in patrons who come to the bar solely to drink.

A recent newspaper story about Chicago titled "Socializing amid the Suds: Corner Bars Are Also Community Centers" (Novak 1998b) further illustrates this point. According to the story, "For much of Chicago's history, the neighborhood bar was a fixture, a place where a man could stop for a drink after breaking his back at a mill, a factory or the stockyards. In many neighborhoods, it seemed every corner had a bar. . . .An awful lot takes place in a bar other than drinking. Calling them a poor man's social club isn't too far off" (4A). Recognizing that more customers are driving to bars outside their neighborhoods, the article continued, "The neighborhood bar as a hangout has been on its way out for a long time. The steel industries are gone, the farm equipment is gone, the stockyards . . . we are no longer that kind of town" (4A–5A).

Fights

Fighting among adults in public is exceedingly rare. However, 44 percent of the commercial servers who responded to our survey said there had been a disturbance or fight during the past year in which patrons were removed from the bar (table 7.2). In nearly a quarter of these cases someone was injured, and police were called almost three-fourths of the time.

Our focus group participants said that bar owners expect rowdy patrons and fights, since such conduct often is at least partially due to drinking alcohol. According to them, this is the nature of the business. Owners reported that the biggest problem is that one never knows how much customers have had to drink before coming to the bar, what medications or other drugs they are taking, and how these will affect their tolerance for alcohol and their subsequent behavior.

Pricing

Reducing the money price for alcohol and increasing the convenience of consumption are ways to encourage drinking. Over half of the respondents to our Survey of Commercial Servers said they offered two mixed drinks for the price of one (table 7.3). Almost half reported sponsoring "happy hours," and nearly a third ran up bar tabs. Fewer (6.1 percent) put more than one shot in standard mixed drinks.

Monitoring

Many aspects of monitoring (and lack of monitoring) by a bar have the potential to influence patrons' drinking patterns. Perhaps most surprising is the lack of strict internal policies disallowing alcohol consumption by employees. Consequently, nearly one-fifth of commercial establishments reported that their employees were allowed to drink on the job. We asked in what circumstances servers were allowed to drink with patrons (box 7.1). The most

Table 7.2 Public Disturbances or Fights in Past Year

Item	% Yes
Had disturbances or fight that resulted in having to remove patrons involved	44.3
Someone injured in bar reporting disturbance or fight	24.1
Police called in bar reporting disturbance or fight	73.6

Source: 1996 Survey of Commercial Servers.

Table 7.3 Five Practices That May Increase Patrons' Drinking

Practice	% Yes
Offers doubles on mixed drinks	52.0
Has "happy hour"	49.0
Runs up bar tabs	29.2
Employees are allowed to drink on job	18.5
More than one shot put in standard mixed drinks	6.1

Source: 1996 Survey of Commercial Servers.

Box 7.1 Circumstances under which servers are allowed to drink on the job: most frequent responses.

Toward end of shift   24
Special occasion (birthday party, New Year's Eve, etc.)   21
When the server wants to   19
When the server gets thirsty   19
If someone buys them a drink   16

Source: 1996 Survey of Commercial Servers. Numbers are number of responses.

frequent response was "toward the end of shift," followed by "special occasions" such as birthday parties. There were also some frequent inappropriate responses: "when the server wants to," "when the server gets thirsty," and "if someone buys them a drink." That such behavior exists reinforces the conflict commercial servers face: selling drinks and making a profit versus monitoring excessive drinking and potentially lowering profits.

Virtually all commercial servers in the focus groups reported that to some degree they monitor drinking by minors (table 7.4). In addition, almost all establishments checked identification, instructing employees in how to do so. About two-fifths of establishments stationed an employee at the front door specifically for this purpose. In addition to checking identification, about three-fifths reported assigning specific employees to monitor drinking by minors. Only 9 percent used "pat downs" to check for minors bringing alcohol into the bar.

All focus group participants were concerned about serving minors, and almost one-quarter said they did not allow minors in the bar at all. Respondents reported that trying to monitor the presence of minors and related serving practices was frustrating. Of those allowing minors to enter, if they came in with parents or spouses of legal drinking age virtually all served alcohol to the adult patrons. In other situations involving minors, adults were served but somewhat less frequently. One owner stated: "I serve a table if they're [minors] accompanied by a parent or guardian. If there's a doubt, card them. If they present you with a false ID, what do you do? Who's liable? I met the criteria. I carded this person. This is the identification they gave me. Now, they falsified the identification. So now they're buying it under false pretenses. Now, whose fault is it? It's their fault, not my fault. Everybody's trying to beat the system."

In addition to monitoring alcohol use by minors, alcohol-serving establishments also monitor adults' consumption and try to prevent excessive drinking. Such monitoring can take many forms, including various types of patron education. Nearly two-thirds of bars posted signs warning about the dangers of excessive drinking (table 7.5). Almost as many listed nonalcoholic drinks on the menu. A minority (15.6 percent) of establishments had employees wear buttons with cautionary messages or used menus for this purpose (23.4 percent). Half of the bars also provided pamphlets and other reminders about naming a designated driver. In addition to patron education, participants from the focus group of small establishments described other policies for controlling consumption. For example, one establishment had a two-shot maximum for those sitting at the bar.

Monitoring by bars and other alcohol-serving establishments also includes keeping patron drunkenness down to an acceptable level. Owners trained their servers to control rowdiness. To handle a really loud person, the manager or owner usually went over to the table rather than sending a bartender with less authority. Most small establishments did not have bouncers or security guards because "it wouldn't pay to bring in anybody." We asked respondents what they instructed their servers to do if an intoxicated patron appeared to be dangerous (box 7.2). Most said they told them

Table 7.4 Procedures for Detecting Minors

Procedure	% Yes
Person at door checks IDs	39.2
Server checks IDs	94.6
Provides instructions to employees checking IDs	92.3
Designates specific employees to monitor drinking by minors	60.4
When group ordering drinks has minors, alcohol is served to anyone in party	35.6[a]
If group includes parents or spouses of minors, alcohol is served to adults	97.5[a]
If group includes adults and underage persons, alcohol is served to adults	80.5[a]
Uses "pat downs"	8.6

Source: 1996 Survey of Commercial Servers.
[a] 23.1 percent reported they have no minor patrons.

Table 7.5 Patron Education

Practice	% Yes
Employees wear buttons	15.6
Uses menu messages	23.4
Nonalcoholic drinks on menu	61.3
Displays information about importance of designated driver	50.5
Posts signs warning about dangers of excessive drinking	64.8

Source: 1996 Survey of Commercial Servers.

to "call police" (81 respondents), "refuse service" (55), or "call manager" (50). All responses to this question were appropriate.

In their open-ended responses bar owners and managers listed several other techniques for dealing with obviously intoxicated adults (box 7.3). The most frequent were serving coffee (which is of doubtful effectiveness); allowing patrons to sleep it off in the bar or in their cars; letting them sit in the bar and rest; and serving them food. Focus group participants gave vivid examples of trying to serve as their own security guards. Colorful anecdotes are retold in box 7.4.

In the focus group meeting with large bar owners, participants reported that by the time many patrons leave bars and restaurants, they are probably close to the legal limit of alcohol. These bar owners thought the situation was much worse in nightclubs than in restaurants that serve alcohol.

Box 7.2 Actions taken by server to handle the obviously intoxicated patron who appears dangerous.

Call police	81	Monitor the situation	4
Refuse service	55	Throw them out	2
Call manager	50	Use best judgment	2
Serve coffee/soda/food	7	Call a cab	2
Call security	5		

Source: 1996 Survey of Commercial Servers. Numbers are number of responses.

Box 7.3 Other actions servers have taken to deal with obviously intoxicated persons.

Serve coffee	45	Send them to a friend's house	10
Give them a ride home	40	Take their keys	9
Allow to sleep at bar	29	Call a cab	9
Allow to sit in bar and rest it off	25	Make them walk home	8
Allow them to sleep in cars	21	Do not let them get intoxicated	7
Serve food	17	Take them for a walk	7
Stay at employee's home	16	Go home with other patrons	6
Call their relatives	16	Sober them up	6
Call police	15	Detain until they find a ride	4
Make them leave the bar	14	Call friends to pick them up	1
Whatever it takes to make sure they are safe	13	Bar has car service to take them home	1
Make sure their friends take them home	13	Slow down service	1
Cut off service	13	Make sleeping arrangements for them	1
Serve soda	10		

Source: 1996 Survey of Commercial Servers. Numbers are number of responses.

Box 7.4 Owners trying to protect their establishment.

"I've been stabbed, I was shot. One time, I was being held up, I got stabbed during the process. I beat the guy silly with a six-pack. I got arrested for excessive force." Another reported, "$3,400 worth of teeth he knocked out of my mouth. He came into the bar all drunk. I said, 'Norman, you're stone drunk, get out.' 'I just want a six-pack.' 'I'm not serving you anything, leave.' He put a gun to my head. He said, 'I'm taking a six-pack.' Stupid me, I jumped the guy. He slugged me in the mouth with the butt of the gun, he walked out with the six-pack. I ran after him, wrestled him down on the sidewalk, broke the six-pack. I lost the six-pack, lost half of my teeth. When the police came, ten cars pulled up. One cop tripped over his flashlight getting out of the patrol car. He said it was my fault that he got injured, If I hadn't caused the ruckus, I caused the ruckus; he wanted me to pay for the flashlight."

Source: 1996 focus group transcript.

They noted that there is a thin line when deciding whether to serve someone who has already drunk a lot.

When patrons became intoxicated, commercial servers reported, they offered various forms of transportation to keep them from driving (table 7.6). When asked whether the bar had a volunteer program for driving intoxicated persons home, only about a quarter said yes. Only 56 percent said their establishments provided rides for intoxicated persons, and others reported that it is not uncommon for bar employees to drive a patron home. Most (78.5 percent) said that servers called taxis for intoxicated persons. Almost all reported asking them for car keys, encouraging them to accept a ride from a friend, or giving them a ride themselves. Fewer (30.2 percent) said they had encouraged an intoxicated patron to spend the night in a nearby hotel.

Some participants believed the most effective laws for controlling alcohol consumption have been criminal drunk driving laws rather than those imposing tort liability on the bar. One owner said, "I think highway fatalities are down, but I think it's through education; better enforcement of existing laws would be more effective as well as changing social values." Most participants felt it was too much to ask bar owners to police and control their customers' consumption.

An additional, yet more indirect, form of monitoring is for managers to hire employees who are likely to implement responsible serving practices and to train these employees carefully. Over 90 percent of employers said they routinely check employment references for servers (table 7.7). Over 70 percent said they required references. Over half had written procedures describing appropriate serving practices and the consequences of irre-

Table 7.6 Alternative Transportation

Practice	% Yes
Volunteer program to drive intoxicated persons home	26.2
Provides rides for intoxicated persons	56.3
Servers have ever asked intoxicated persons for car keys	91.4
Servers have ever encouraged intoxicated persons to accept ride from friend	94.1
Servers get cabs for intoxicated persons	78.5
Servers have ever encouraged persons to sleep in hotel	30.2
Servers have ever given ride to intoxicated persons	85.3

Source: 1996 Survey of Commercial Servers.

Table 7.7 Hiring and Employment Practices

Practice	% Yes
Routinely require references for servers	71.9
Routinely checks employment references for servers	92.6
Reimburses employees for lost tips	6.1
Has written procedures for employees about appropriate selling practices	60.6
Has form describing consequences to employees of irresponsible server behavior	51.2
Uses decoys to ascertain whether employees follow procedures	30.7

Source: 1996 Survey of Commercial Servers.

sponsible server behavior. Three-fifths of establishments had written procedures describing appropriate practices for selling alcoholic beverages. Almost a third used decoys to ascertain that these procedures were followed. Very few establishments reimbursed servers for tips they lost for refusing to serve people who were obviously drunk.

Alcohol consumption may be best monitored by bar employees who have been instructed in effective techniques. Recognizing this, almost all establishments required some sort of server training before the employee began serving alcoholic beverages (table 7.8). However, most of such training was "informal": only 19 percent of respondents said they had a formal training program. Employees generally were paid for their time in training. Only very rarely (2.4 percent) did the establishment receive outside financial support for training.

In most establishments, training described the criminal and administrative penalties for inappropriate or illegal server behavior. Detecting fake identification was almost always discussed. Approximately three-fifths of the training programs discussed the threat of tort liability and jail terms that may result from illegal serving practices. More frequently (82.3 percent of cases) they discussed potential fines. Most commonly, training included a discussion of acceptable forms of patron identification.

Almost always, follow-up server training took the form of informal discussions or of meeting to discuss incidents or problems (table 7.9). Many bars organized refresher courses (70.3 percent). Only about half the establishments that did some follow-up training held regular discussion groups. Participants in our focus groups said bars adopted server training when they began to recognize the potential for litigation (box 7.5), but most were skeptical that it actually helped their defense in litigation.

The vast majority of establishments (84.6 percent) said they had a

Table 7.8 Server Training

Practice	% Yes
Establishment trains new employees	91.6
Formal training period	18.8
Training required before beginning to serve	82.6
Server training emphasizes alternative transportation over monitoring intake	5.2
Server training discusses possibility of server involvement in dram shop claim	61.4
Server training discusses potential server involvement in depositions, lawsuits, and administrative hearings	61.7
Server training discusses	
Potential fines	82.3
Jail terms	60.5
Criminal punishment for serving minors	69.8
Types of acceptable identification	97.9
How identification can be forged	91.4
Pacing consumption of patrons	53.0
Employees paid for time in training	81.8
Establishment receives financial support for training	2.4
Establishment provides follow-up training	66.8

Source: 1996 Survey of Commercial Servers.

Table 7.9 Follow-up Training

Practice	% Yes
Provide refresher courses	70.3
Meetings to discuss incidents and problems	92.5
Regularly scheduled discussion groups	49.2
Informal discussions	97.1
One-on-one consultations	95.9

Source: 1996 Survey of Commercial Servers.

Box 7.5 Owners' or managers' perceptions on server training and tort suits.

Owner 1

We took the position of a more aggressive, defensive position. We said, okay let's do this right. And then we looked at the cost to do it versus exposures, our liability issues, we restructured some of our corporate layering to take a defensive position against it. And then we began a formalized process to educate our people. It was initially more out of a litigation defense as opposed to we felt we weren't doing a good enough job. We felt we were. And now the question of putting under the light of scrutiny, you've got to think like lawyers. And that's changed our process. That's when we introduced Training Alcohol Management, we required the employees to go through it. Now they sign off that they've been educated on it. When they have the staff meetings, they all sign that we covered alcohol awareness problem issues.

Owner 2

And as we go through the process of the litigation experience, we realize that no matter what we do, we're dead. So then you say, the hell with you, we'll just go the other way. We'll just layer ourselves out and we'll do as much as we can. But then the economics starts squeezing you. To spend the dollars per employee. Now we're finding is that we are in no better position before than after spending the money for the training.

Owner 3

For me to spend x amount of dollars per employee to train, okay. Again you've got to look at it a couple of different ways. One being the social business value of what you're doing and then you have the economic realities of what you're doing. And you've got to balance those two things through. Well, when we start running the numbers, at some point, we just say, you know, so forth, so on, and we're saying to ourselves, we're not winning here, from the economic format. We're doing the right thing consciously, as a person in our society, as a business providing a service, but we're screwed. So we start pulling the budget back a bit and said, okay, instead of $14 an employee, we're going to budget down to $10 now. Because that's $4 we might as well save anyway because

Source: 1996 focus group transcript.

competitor in the immediate area (table 7.10). Most reported that they and their competitor monitored to approximately the same extent. However, one-third stated that the competitor monitored drinking patterns of adults less closely than they did. Only about 1 percent said the competitor monitored more closely. Clearly the difference was in the owner's perception or was colored by an attempt to look good in the eyes of the interviewer. Interestingly, only 15.7 percent said they would lose patrons if they monitored more closely than their competitor did. This response suggests that patrons are not attentive to monitoring, which perhaps applies only to a small minority of patrons in any event. And 17.3 percent said they would increase monitoring of adult drinking patterns if their competitor did.

Our focus group meetings revealed that large establishment owners were more concerned about competition than were owners of small establishments. Some participants admitted to checking their competitors' prices and food selection. One claimed, "We always steal each other's menus. I've got stacks of them at home." Clearly, prices and products are easier to follow than are monitoring practices.

Other Characteristics of Establishments

Characteristics of establishments obtained from our Survey of Commercial Servers are presented in table 7.11. On average, respondents had been in business for twenty years. The range of establishment ages was substantial: one had been in business ninety-seven years. Slightly over half (53 percent) were incorporated, and one in twenty was part of a chain; 88 percent were licensed to serve mixed drinks. On average, 89 percent of patrons arrived by car or truck. The modal patron was in the age range twenty-five to forty. Most patrons were men. Fewer than 10 percent on average were students; far more common was a blue-collar clientele. Most patrons were regulars, and fewer than two-fifths came alone. Most establishments offered some type of entertainment: almost all had a television set, and most had a jukebox, a pool table, or video games. On average, they had six employees during peak hours. Only 2 percent of bars were unionized.

Effects of Administrative, Criminal, and Dram Shop Liability on Pricing

To test the first part of hypothesis 1, that imposing administrative, criminal, and dram shop liability on commercial servers raises the price they charge

Table 7.10 Competition and Influence of Competition

Item	% Yes
Establishment has competition in area	84.6
Competition monitors drinking patterns of adults less closely than respondent	33.3
Competition monitors drinking more closely than respondent	1.4
If respondent monitored more closely would lose appreciable number of patrons to competitor	15.7
Competitor would increase monitoring if respondent did	17.3

Source: 1996 Survey of Commercial Servers.

Table 7.11 Characteristics of Commercial
Establishments

Characteristics	Mean
Age of establishment (years)	20.3
Incorporated (%)	52.8
Part of chain (%)	4.9
Number of bars in chain	23.7
Percentage of	
Customers under 21	2.0
Customers aged 21–24	18.4
Customers aged 25–40	50.1
Customers aged 40+	29.5
Students	9.7
Blue-collar workers	58.0
Regular customers	65.7
Men	67.2
Customers who come alone	37.2
Customers who come with one other person	34.2
Customers who come in groups	28.7
Customers who come by car	89.0
Percentage of sales from	
Package sales of alcoholic beverages	7.2
Alcohol on premise	72.1
Food	20.8
Bar unionized	1.9
Number of employees during peak hours	5.7
Licensed to serve mixed drinks (%)	88.3

Source: 1996 Survey of Commercial Servers.

for alcoholic beverages, we regressed four measures of price as alternative dependent variables: lowest price of draft beer during regular hours; glass of house wine during regular hours; shot of Jack Daniels; and the first principal component of all the products above. Overall, the empirical results were similar across equations (table 7.12).

As we discussed in previous chapters, our Survey of Commercial Servers asked respondents to estimate the likelihood of being cited or sued for various types of infractions, such as serving a minor or an obviously intoxicated adult. We defined the threat variables on a scale of one to five, with one being "very likely" and five being "not at all likely" (see fig. 5.1). In the price regressions shown in table 7.12, we used the threat variables that apply to serving obviously intoxicated adults.

According to the regression results, when owners or managers of bars believed they were more likely to be cited by the ABC if they served obviously intoxicated adults, prices of drinks were higher, holding other factors constant. None of the other threat variables had a statistically significant effect on prices. The result for the probability of being cited by the ABC may mean that the additional cost of coping with the threat is shifted to consumers as higher prices. Another possibility is that the threat of sanctions is related to entry barriers imposed by ABCs. However, we did not find any effect on entry in the analysis of entry barriers described in chapter 2.

Also, our analysis accounted for the effect of competition on beverage prices. Establishments that identified a principal competitor charged less for drinks. The parameter estimate on the competition variable was negative and statistically significant at conventional levels in three of four regressions (all except the price regression for a shot of Jack Daniels).

Other factors affecting price were establishment incorporated (+); establishment part of chain (+); fraction of customers over age forty (−); fraction of customers who were blue-collar workers (−); fraction of customers who were regulars (−); fraction of customers who were men (only in two of the four regressions [+]); fraction of sales from food (+); and population density (+).

All the results above are plausible. Regular customers save more by frequenting a lower-priced establishment. Thus their demand for alcohol is likely to be more price sensitive. Patrons who go to a bar for food probably drink less on average and hence are less sensitive to the price charged for alcoholic beverages. In any case, the bar tab is less than the total bill, so the price elasticity of demand for alcohol is likely to be lower in establishments oriented toward food. Older patrons and blue-collar workers may be less willing to pay for ambiance; our survey could capture only certain aspects of ambiance. Input prices, such as rent, tend to be higher in larger cities, holding other factors constant.

Effects of Administrative, Criminal, and Tort Liability on Monitoring by Servers

To test whether administrative, criminal, and tort liability deterred irresponsible server behavior, we studied the effects of these policies on various dimensions of server monitoring. Our Survey of Commercial Servers requested information on a variety of monitoring practices, which we used to test our hypotheses and to estimate the effects of dram shop liability insurance in blunting the deterrent effect of tort.

Definitions of the thirteen monitoring variables, the questions they were based on, and the means, standard deviations, and minimums and maximums of variables are shown in table 7.13. Nine of the variables were

Table 7.12 Determinants of Price

Explanatory Variables	Regular Domestic Draft Beer during Regular Hours		Glass of House Wine during Regular Hours		Shot of Jack Daniels		Principal Component	
	Coeff.	Std. Err.	Coeff.	Std. Err.	Coeff.	Std. Err.	Coeff.	Std. Err.
Threat variables								
Suit	0.022	0.017	0.0024	0.022	0.036	0.023	0.046	0.043
Police	−0.026	0.020	−0.034	0.027	−0.030	0.028	−0.056	0.053
ABC	0.035	0.021	0.068[b]	0.027	0.072[a]	0.029	0.13[b]	0.053
ALE	0.018	0.022	0.0007	0.0029	0.0006	0.031	0.025	0.057
Competition	−0.14[b]	0.059	−0.20[b]	0.080	−0.053	0.081	−0.34[b]	0.16
Establishment characteristics								
Incorporated	0.044	0.047	0.18[a]	0.062	0.16[a]	0.063	0.29[b]	0.12
Part of chain	0.31[a]	0.11	0.20	0.14	0.42[a]	0.14	0.63[b]	0.26
Age of establishment	−0.0004	0.0012	−0.0020	0.0015	−0.0030	0.0016	−0.0038	0.0031
Fraction of sales from food	0.24[b]	0.11	0.42[a]	0.14	0.18	0.15	0.51	0.28
Clientele characteristics								

Fraction of	Coeff.	Std. Err.	Coeff.	Std. Err.	Coeff.	Std. Err.	Coeff.	Std. Err.
Customers aged 25–40	−0.16	0.19	0.041	0.24	−0.30	0.26	−0.48	0.51
Customers aged 40+	−0.35	0.18	−0.40	0.24	−0.51[b]	0.26	−1.08[b]	0.49
Students	0.063	0.23	0.099	0.30	0.070	0.31	0.17	0.59
Blue-collar workers	−0.41[a]	0.085	−0.54[a]	0.11	−0.49[a]	0.12	−1.19[a]	0.23
Regular customers	−0.40[a]	0.10	−0.35[b]	0.14	−0.40[a]	0.14	−0.88[a]	0.27
Men	0.36[b]	0.16	0.19	0.22	0.36	0.22	0.79	0.44
Customers who come alone	−0.16	0.15	−0.14	0.20	0.084	0.20	−0.38	0.40
Customers who come in groups	−0.034	0.17	−0.011	0.22	0.27	0.22	0.038	0.43
Customers who come by car	0.080	0.077	0.16	0.11	0.034	0.11	0.18	0.21
Population density	0.0039[a]	0.0004	0.0032[a]	0.0005	0.0031[a]	0.0005	0.0080[a]	0.0010
Constant	1.65[a]	0.25	2.44[a]	0.33	2.76[a]	0.34	0.69	0.66
R^2	0.29		0.26		0.25		0.34	
Adjusted R^2	0.27		0.23		0.23		0.31	
	$N = 643$		$N = 572$		$N = 574$		$N = 524$	

[a]Statistically significant at the 1 percent level (two-tailed t-test).
[b]Statistically significant at the 5 percent level (two-tailed t-test)..
Coeff. = coefficient; Std. Err. = standard error.
Table reports nonstandardized regression coefficients.

Table 7.13 Monitoring Variables

Explanatory Variables	Questions	Mean	Std. Dev.	Min.	Max.
1. Not drinking on job	In certain circumstances, are employees allowed to drink on the job?	0.81	0.39	0	1
2. Patron education	Number answering yes to following questions: Does bar use any of the following to educate patrons about the danger of drinking and driving? Button worn by employees? Menu messages? Nonalcoholic selections? Advertised designated driver programs or "safe ride" programs? Signs posted at bar?	2.16	1.27	0	5
3. Providing rides	Does bar have service that provides rides for patrons who have had too much to drink?	0.57	0.50	0	1
4. Services provided for drunk drivers	Number answering yes to following questions: Have servers ever tried to get a drunk patron to Give up car keys? Accept ride from friend? Accept ride from employee? Accept ride in cab? Sleep it off at nearby hotel?	3.83	0.98	0	5
5. Employee responsibility form	Does bar distribute employee responsibility form describing full implications for employee of irresponsible and careless server behavior?	0.52	0.50	0	1
6. Checking references when hiring	Does bar routinely require references for servers and check them?	0.63	0.48	0	1
7. Content of server training	Number answering yes to following questions: Does bar's server training discuss	4.96	2.30	0	7

	Question	Mean	S.D.	Min	Max
	Possibility of server's being named as defendant in dram shop suit?				
	Potential server involvement in depositions, lawsuits, or administrative hearings?				
	Potential fines?				
	Potential jail terms for servers?				
	Potential criminal records for service to minors?				
	Which type of IDs are acceptable?				
	How particular IDs can be altered, forged, or illegally obtained?				
8. Written procedures for employee regarding serving	Does bar provide written procedures for employees regarding appropriate serving practices?	0.61	0.49	0	1
9. Monitor for minor	Does bar designate specific employee to monitor drinking by minors?	0.63	0.48	0	1
10. Pat down	Does the bar use "pat down" for situations when chance of minors' bringing in their own alcohol may be higher than normal?	0.11	0.32	0	1
11. Check ID	Is there a door person whose chief responsibility is to check patron IDs?	0.39	0.49	0	1
12. Use own decoy	Does bar hire its own decoys to determine whether employees are adhering to establishment's rules?	0.31	0.46	0	1
13. Employment of security guard	Do you employ a security guard?	0.73	1.30	0	4
	No				
	Less than one night per week.				
	1–3 nights per week.				
	4–6 nights per week.				
	7 nights per week.				

Source: 1996 Survey of Commercial Servers.

binary, including whether employees were allowed to drink on the job; the bar provided rides for patrons who had too much to drink; the employee had a responsibility form describing the full implications of irresponsible and careless server behavior; the bar routinely required references for servers and checked them; the bar provided written procedures for employees regarding appropriate serving practices; the bar designated specific employees to monitor drinking behavior by minors; the bar used pat downs (checks for concealed alcohol brought into the bar); the bar had a door person whose chief responsibility was to check patron identifications; and the bar employed its own decoys to determine whether employees adhered to the establishment's rules. When the dependent variable was a binary, we used logit analysis.

Four of the thirteen monitoring variables were count variables of the establishment's policies related to a specific monitoring component, such as patron education and server training. Within the survey, our measure of patron education had up to five possible affirmative responses: buttons worn by employees; menu messages warning about excessive drinking; nonalcoholic selections on the menu; advertisements for "safe ride" programs in the bar; and warnings posted in the bar. The vast majority of establishments did some monitoring, although few carried out all the monitoring components (fig. 7.1).

To analyze the implementation of bar policies to prevent drunk driving, we compiled a measure of services provided to drunk drivers that varied from zero to five. These five services included getting drunk persons to give up their car keys; accept a ride from a friend; accept a ride from an employee; accept a ride in a cab; and sleep it off at a nearby hotel. Many bars took several of these actions (see fig. 7.1).

Our measure of server training asked whether or not seven items were discussed in the bar's server training program, including the possibility of a server's being named as a defendant in a dram shop suit; potential server involvement in depositions, lawsuits, or administrative hearings; potential fines; potential jail terms for servers; potential criminal records for serving minors; acceptable types of identification; and how particular identifications can be altered, forged, or illegally obtained. For the 7.6 percent of bars with no server training, this variable took the value of zero. A substantial number of server training programs included a discussion of all seven topics (fig. 7.1).

Finally, we included a variable for the number of days per week the bar employed a security guard. Possible responses ranged from zero to every night (fig. 7.2). Most respondents said they did not employ security guards.

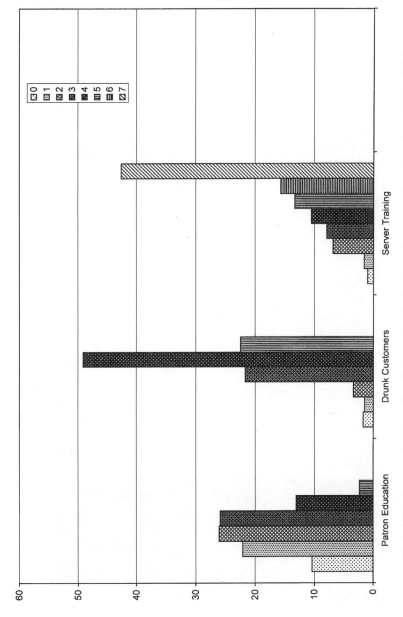

Fig. 7.1 Total count of patron education, services to drunk customers, and contents for server training.

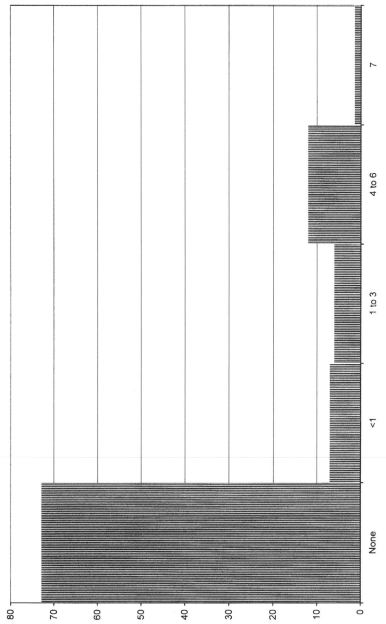

Fig. 7.2 Number of times per week bar employs security guards.

Interestingly, insurers sometimes considered employing guards a reason for surcharging dram shop liability premiums.

When the dependent variable was a count variable, we estimated the equations with ordered logit regression. For these variables the marginal effect shown is for the highest possible category (highest level of precaution).

To investigate the effect of the threat of administrative, criminal, and tort sanctions on the bar's precaution level, we regressed the thirteen measures of server monitoring practices on the probability of being sued and of being cited by the police, ABC, and ALE. Other explanatory variables were the binary variable indicating that the bar identified a specific competitor and the other covariates included in the pricing analysis discussed above (table 7.14). In this analysis of the bars' precaution levels, we matched the threat variable to the type of monitoring performed. For example, if the monitoring applied to minors, we used the variable for the probability of being sued or cited for serving minors. For dependent variables that did not apply exclusively to a particular type of infraction, we used the threat variables for serving obviously intoxicated adults as a default. Since the purpose of this analysis was to test the chapter's first hypothesis about the effects of various sanctions on the bar's precaution level and the third hypothesis concerning the effect of competition on monitoring, we present only parameter estimates and associated marginal effects for the threat and competition variables.

A higher perceived probability of being sued for "bad" serving practices led to increased monitoring in eight of the thirteen regressions. More specifically, the probability of a suit had positive and nearly statistically significant effects—that is, below the 5 percent level but at the 10 percent level or better—for not drinking on the job ($p = 0.080$) and for providing more services for drunk drivers ($p = 0.067$). The probability of a tort suit had positive and statistically significant effects at the 5 percent level or better for providing rides to intoxicated persons; having a form detailing employees' responsibilities; checking references of prospective employees; having more varied content in server training; providing employees with written procedures for serving; and monitoring minors. Among the statistically significant effects of tort, several of the marginal effects were approximately 0.04.

Far fewer of the coefficients for the perceived probability of citation by local police, ABC, and ALE were positive and statistically significant at conventional levels. For police, only one parameter estimate on these variables was positive and statistically significant at even the 10 percent level—the effect of frequency of employment of security personnel ($p = 0.086$).

Table 7.14 Commercial Server Precautions

Dependent Variables	Perceived Probability of Threat from					
	Suit	Police	ABC	ALE	Competition	Discount
1. Bar prohibits employees from drinking on job (N = 618)	0.15 (0.086) [0.020]	−0.097 (0.10) [−0.013]	0.08 (0.11) [0.011]	0.14 (0.11) [0.018]	0.48 (0.28) [0.064]	
2. Number of components of patron education provided by bar (N = 642)	0.045 (0.055) [0.0010]	0.021 (0.067) [0.0005]	−0.044 (0.068) [−0.0010]	0.13 (0.070) [0.0028]	0.40 (0.21) [0.0089]	
3. Bar provides rides for intoxicated patrons (N = 646)	0.16[a] (0.065) [0.039]	−0.18[b] (0.078) [−0.44]	0.028 (0.079) [0.0067]	0.069 (0.084) [0.017]	−0.028 (0.22) [−0.0068]	
4. Number of other services bar provides for intoxicated patrons (N = 628)	0.11 (0.060) [0.018]	−0.022 (0.071) [−0.0037]	0.061 (0.084) [0.010]	0.0074 (0.082) [0.0012]	0.48[a] (0.20) [0.080]	
5. Bar has employee responsibility form detailing server liability (N = 604)	0.18[a] (0.068) [0.047]	0.11 (0.082) [−0.027]	0.016 (0.083) [0.0041]	−0.012 (0.089) [0.0030]	0.13 (0.24) [0.031]	0.56[b] (0.23) [0.14]
6. Bar checks references of potential employees (N = 649)	0.18[a] (0.069) [0.042]	−0.040 (0.084) [−0.0090]	−0.17 (0.092) [−0.037]	0.31[a] (0.094) [0.070]	0.44 (0.23) [0.098]	
7. Number of components included in server training program (N = 536)	0.22[a] (0.063) [0.052]	−0.062 (0.078) [−0.014]	0.0048 (0.082) [0.0011]	0.19[b] (0.084) [0.043]	0.31 (0.23) [0.072]	0.79[a] (0.21) [0.18]

Dependent variable					
8. Bar provides employees with written serving procedures ($N = 605$)	0.20[a] (0.071) [0.036]	0.14 (0.085) [0.025]	−0.12 (0.091) [−0.021]	0.070 (0.096) [0.013]	0.15 (0.25) [0.028]	0.54[b] (0.25) [0.099]
9. Bar designates employee to monitor for drinkng by minors ($N = 619$)	0.16[a] (0.061) [0.037]	−0.12 (0.082) [−0.028]	−0.10 (0.071) [−0.024]	0.16[b] (0.076) [0.037]	−0.011 (0.24) [−0.0026]	
10. Bar uses pat down to check minors for concealed alcohol ($N = 507$)	0.027 (0.11) [0.0020]	−0.33[b] (0.15) [−0.024]	0.16 (0.15) [0.012]	0.29 (0.17) [0.021]	−0.73[b] (0.37) [−0.054]	
11. Bar checks patron identification at door ($N = 649$)	0.099 (0.063) [0.023]	−0.035 (0.086) [−0.0084]	0.15[b] (0.077) [0.036]	−0.37 (0.082) [−0.0087]	−0.03 (0.25) [−0.0076]	
12. Bar uses own decoy to monitor serving practices of employees ($N = 603$)	0.065 (0.063) [0.014]	(−0.021) (0.085) [−0.0044]	−0.021 (0.089) [0.019]	−0.057 (0.079) [−0.012]	−0.22 (0.24) [−0.046]	
13. Number of evenings bar employs security guard ($N = 646$)	−0.13 (0.084) [−0.0050]	0.16 (0.093) [0.0062]	0.31[b] (0.13) [0.012]	0.15 (0.13) [0.0077]	−0.21 (0.26) [−0.0083]	

[a]Statistically significant at 1 percent level.
[b]Statistically significant at 5 percent level.
Full regression sare not shown for the thirteen dependent variables.
Standard errors in parentheses; marginal effects in brackets.
Table reports nonstandardized regression coefficients.

The associated marginal effect of this variable was very small. For the ABC, the only positive and statistically significant effects were for frequency of employment of security personnel and for checking patrons' identification. For the ALE, the coefficients on checking references of prospective employees, content of server training, and monitoring to prevent minors' drinking were statistically significant. Two of the variables in the ALE regression, patron education ($p = 0.070$) and pat down of minors ($p = 0.085$), were positive and nearly significant. From this it appears that if nontort sanctions improve monitoring, their main effect is on service to minors rather than to obviously intoxicated adults.

Our analysis also showed that having a competitor tended to increase monitoring. Most of the parameter estimates on measures of precautionary behaviors aimed toward serving obviously intoxicated adults were positive, and several were statistically significant at conventional levels. How having a competitor affects the precaution level cannot be determined a priori, yet there is an explanation that is consistent with a comment made in one of our focus groups. The likelihood that an intoxicated person will enter one's establishment rises when there are other commercial servers nearby. Thus there is a private benefit to the bar, as well as a social benefit, from implementing various approaches to monitoring. Subsequently, monitoring may increase in such circumstances.

The competition variable tended to have negative effects on precautions affecting service to minors. Perhaps the bars feared they would lose young patrons if they were too stringent in screening minors at the entrance. It might be easier for crowds of youths to go to a competitor. We included an explanatory variable for population density in the county where the bar was located. The results on the competition variable therefore probably did not reflect degree of urbanization.

Liability insurance may reduce the effect of tort insofar as premiums are not experience rated or insurers refuse to write coverage for establishments with adverse tort claims records. However, monitoring may actually increase when establishments have purchased insurance through firms that engage in loss prevention. In an alternative specification, we added two explanatory variables. The first was a binary variable that took the value one if the establishment had liability insurance. The second was the establishment's perceived probability of suit multiplied by the binary variable for dram shop liability insurance. With this specification, we could determine whether having liability insurance directly affected an establishment's precautionary levels and whether it blunted the effect of tort on precautions.

We present results only for the suit, insurance, and insurance-suit interaction variables. The general conclusion to be drawn from this analysis is that neither insurance nor insurance in interaction with the perceived probability of a suit influences precaution taking by bars (table 7.15). Only one coefficient on the insurance variable attained statistical significance at even the 10 percent level: the coefficient on services provided to drunk drivers ($p = 0.10$). This coefficient was positive, implying that insurance makes establishments more cautious in handling intoxicated adults. But insurance decreased the deterrent effect of tort in this case, judging from the negative coefficient on the interaction variable. Only one of the coefficients on the interaction term was statistically significant even at the 10 percent level—the coefficient for having an employee responsibility form ($p = 0.057$). Here, however, the result seems to reflect multicollinearity with the suit variable, so little weight should be attached to this finding.

Effects of Administrative, Criminal, and Tort Liability on Server Product Mix and Ambiance

To determine the effect of the threat of tort liability and oversight by the police, ABC, and ALE on the establishments' product mix and ambiance, we regressed the fraction of sales from food, a count of types of entertainment, and the individual types of entertainment offered on the perceived probability of being sued or cited and on characteristics of the establishment. The types of entertainment were pool, video games, television, jukebox, live entertainment, dancing, and Internet access. An assumption of responsible server practice is that an occupied patron, or one who eats, will be less likely to drink excessively and leave the bar intoxicated. We estimated the equation for the fraction of sales from food with ordinary least squares, the equations for individual types of entertainment with logit, and the measure of the count of types of entertainment with ordered logit.

Regressions for the first two dependent variables are shown (table 7.16). The regression results for the individual types of entertainment were similar to the one for the count of entertainment types. None of the variables for the perceived probability of being sued or cited were statistically significant at conventional levels. In fact, signs on the coefficients varied, and they were very imprecisely estimated.

In the analysis of determinants of the fraction of sales from food, some variables had statistically significant effects at the 5 percent level or better. The variables that resulted in lower sales of food (and correspondingly higher alcohol sales) included the fraction of patrons aged twenty-five to forty, the fraction of students, the fraction of men, and the fraction of cus-

Table 7.15 Effects of Dram Shop Liability Insurance
on Commercial Server Precautions

Dependent Variables	Threat from Suit	Insurance	Insurance and Suit
1. Bar prohibits employees from drinking on job (N = 618)	0.13 (0.23) [0.017]	0.22 (0.74) [0.030]	0.033 (0.24) [0.0044]
2. Number of components of patron education provided by bar (N = 642)	−0.13 (0.16) [−0.0028]	−0.066 (0.53) [−0.0014]	0.20 (0.17) [0.0043]
3. Bar provides rides for intoxicated patrons (N = 646)	0.40[b] (0.19) [0.098]	0.57 (0.59) [−0.14]	−0.27 (−0.16) [−0.066]
4. Number of other services bar provides for intoxicated patrons (N = 628)	0.32[b] (0.16) [0.054]	0.89 (0.54) [0.15]	−0.24 (0.16) [−0.039]
5. Bar has employee responsibility form detailing server liability (N = 604)	−0.17 (0.20) [−0.043]	−0.83 (0.67) [−0.21]	0.40 (0.21) [0.10]
6. Bar checks references of potential employees (N = 649)	0.15 (0.18) [0.034]	0.069 (0.60) [0.0015]	0.043 (0.19) [0.0095]
7. Number of components included in server training program (N = 536)	0.25 (0.19) [0.057]	0.14 (0.68) [0.032]	−0.026 (0.20) [−0.0061]
8. Bar provides employees with written serving procedures (N = 605)	−0.076 (0.21) [−0.014]	0.36 (0.69) [0.067]	0.31 (0.22) [0.057]
9. Bar designates employee to monitor for drinkng by minors (N = 619)	0.13 (0.20) [0.029]	0.025 (0.74) [0.0056]	0.041 (0.21) [0.0093]
10. Bar uses pat down to check minors for concealed alcohol (N = 507)	−0.080 (0.37) [−0.0059]	0.077 (1.31) [0.0057]	0.12 (0.38) [0.089]
11. Bar checks patron identification at door (N = 649)	−0.14 (0.20) [−0.034]	−0.52 (0.75) [−0.12]	0.27 (0.21) [0.064]
12. Bar uses own decoy to monitor serving practices of employees (N = 603)	−0.27 (0.24) [−0.058]	−0.71 (0.83) [−0.15]	0.37 (0.24) [0.077]
13. Number of evenings bar employs security guard (N = 646)	0.0015 (0.34) [0.0001]	0.96 (1.32) [0.037]	0.064 (0.34) [0.0025]

[a]Statistically significant at 1 percent level.
[b]Statistically significant at 5 percent level.
Full regressions are not shown for the thirteen dependent variables.
Standard errors in parentheses; marginal effects in brackets.
Table reports nonstandardized regression coefficients.

tomers who arrive alone. In contrast, incorporation was associated with increased food sales.

In the analysis of the count of entertainment types, a statistically significant effect was found at the 1 percent or better level for establishments with more blue-collar patrons. This variable's coefficient was positive, showing that these establishments offered more types of entertainment. Those variables with statistically significant negative effects, reflecting fewer forms of entertainment (and correspondingly higher alcohol sales), were fraction of patrons aged forty or over $(-)$; and the presence of food $(-)$. Age of establishment $(p = 0.053)$ and fraction of customers aged twenty-five to forty $(p = 0.084)$ had negative effects and were almost sta-

Table 7.16 Ambiance

Explanatory Variables	Fraction of Sales from Food		Number of Entertainments Provided		
	Coeff.	Std. Err.	Coeff.	Std. Err.	M.E.
Threat variable					
Suit	0.0040	0.0061	−0.015	0.057	−0.0022
Police	0.0066	0.0073	−0.080	0.066	−0.012
ABC	−0.0073	0.0075	0.042	0.066	0.0060
ALE	0.0092	0.0080	−0.011	0.071	−0.0016
Competition	0.0042	0.021	−0.075	0.20	−0.011
Establishment characteristics					
Incorporated	0.058[a]	0.016	0.13	0.15	−0.018
Part of chain	0.060	0.039	−0.049	0.36	−0.0071
Age of establishment	0.0001	0.0004	−0.0072	0.0037	0.0010
Fraction of sales from food			−2.10[a]	0.37	−0.31
Clientele characteristics					
Fraction of					
Customers aged 25–40	−0.14[b]	0.066	−1.09	0.63	−0.16
Customers aged 40+	−0.092	0.064	−1.99[a]	0.60	−0.29
Students	−0.27[a]	0.081	−0.93	0.75	−0.13
Blue-collar workers	−0.0051	0.030	0.78[a]	0.28	0.11
Regular customers	−0.039	0.037	−0.085	0.35	−0.012
Men	−0.12[b]	0.057	0.24	0.56	0.034
Customers who come alone	−0.29[a]	0.052	0.15	0.52	0.022
Customers who come in groups	0.066	0.059	−0.010	0.55	−0.0015
Customers who come by car	0.035	0.027	0.26	0.24	0.038
Population density	−0.0000	0.0001	−0.0024	0.0017	−0.0003
Constant	0.41[a]	0.086			
	$N = 646$		$N = 646$		

[a]Statistically significant at 1 percent level.
[b]Statistically significant at 5 percent level.
Coeff. = coefficient; Std. Err. = standard error; M.E. = marginal effect.
Table reports nonstandardized regression coefficients.

tistically significant. Apparently, food and entertainment are substitutes for each other, since those establishments having a larger percentage of sales from food offer fewer forms of entertainment.

We also estimated regressions for the mix of clientele—age distribution, students versus nonstudents, and blue-collar customers versus others—that are not presented. We found no evidence that threat of suit or citations influenced the mix of patrons.

CONCLUSION

The key finding of this chapter is that the increased probability of a suit, as perceived by the management, raised the bar's level of precaution in serving obviously intoxicated adults. However, the probability of a suit had no effect on precautions undertaken to avoid serving alcohol to minors. Overall, perceived probability of citations from local police, ABC, and ALE had less of an effect on precaution levels. If there was an effect of the latter types of oversight, it was on service to minors.

In this chapter we focused on the perceived, rather than actual, threat of sanctions. This focus is valid, since we were able to illustrate in earlier chapters that management's perceptions are related to actual threats.

As we reported in chapter 6, most of the establishments had some liability insurance. Here we studied how such insurance influences the precautions they take. We found no effect. Perhaps the hassle and psychological costs of being sued are a sufficient deterrent. From what we heard in our focus groups and learned from the survey, there appears to be little if any loss prevention in this sector. The lack of loss prevention by insurers is reflected in our lack of findings on insurance in our analysis of the establishments' level of precautions.

The effect of competition is complex. As we anticipated, the establishments lowered prices in response to competition. We found some evidence that management was more cautious in handling obviously intoxicated adults and in providing server training when it faced a competitor. However, if anything the bars seemed to be less cautious about serving minors when they faced competition.

In the next chapter we will reexamine the deterrent effects of various sanctions by asking employees, rather than owners or managers, to answer questions about the precautions taken by employees. The perceptions of the probability of being sued or cited will be the same ones used here.

8

Monitoring by Bartenders and Servers

INTRODUCTION

It is bartenders and servers who translate alcohol policies (or lack of them) into action. Because they do not bear the ultimate responsibility for the establishments where they work, they may be more likely than their owners and managers to "tell it like it is" rather than coloring their responses to reflect the "correct" policies they think interviewers want to hear. For these reasons, understanding the issues at hand from the perspective of these employees is a key point of this study.

This chapter has several objectives. First, we describe the characteristics of the 862 bartenders and servers who were interviewed. Second, we examine monitoring practices from their viewpoint and compare their responses with those of the owners and managers. Third, we report bartenders' and servers' perceptions of server training. Fourth, we investigate how far liability threats of various types, as perceived by the owners and managers, affect monitoring by bartenders and servers. Fifth, we investigate the determinants of employees' earnings to learn whether they have financial incentives to take precautions or if they tend to earn more when they encourage excessive drinking.

SURVEY OF EMPLOYEES

In addition to bar owners and managers, we interviewed two employees from each establishment included in our Survey of Commercial Servers. A total of 545 establishments supplied lists of employees, which provided a sample of 1,133 employees. Of these, 942 agreed to be interviewed: 80 of them were ineligible, leaving 862 employee respondents. When possible, we selected one bartender and one member of the wait staff. They were interviewed by phone for about fifteen minutes about their actual serving practices rather than establishment policies.

CHARACTERISTICS OF BARTENDERS AND SERVERS

Most of the survey respondents were bartenders or worked as both bartenders and servers (table 8.1). In fact, only 13 percent described themselves solely as servers: that is, they served food and drinks but did not pour or mix drinks. When providing names of potential interviewees, the owners and managers may have thought bartenders would be more knowledgeable about the bar's practices and procedures than servers and therefore listed mainly bartenders.

Three-quarters of survey respondents reported that their work shifts

Table 8.1 Employee Characteristics

Characteristics	%
Employee works as	
Bartender	71.1
Server	12.5
Both	16.4
Works until bar closes	74.9
Number of years at current job	
<1	9.7
1–5	29.5
6–10	24.2
10+	36.5
Paid hourly wage	83.4
Earns money from tip pool	16.0
Age of server	
<25	13.7
25–34	35.8
35–44	29.2
45+	21.4
Highest level of school completed	
No high school diploma	11.4
High school graduate	40.1
Some college	34.8
College graduate	12.0
Graduate school	1.6
Married	28.4
Performs other work for pay	31.6
Total household income (1995)	
$<\$15,000$	39.4
\$15,000–\$29,999	32.9
\$30,000–\$44,999	13.5
\$45,000+	7.3

Source: 1996 Survey of Employees.

lasted until the bar closed. Much of the activity pertinent to drinking and driving occurs near closing, placing them in a prime position to monitor their patrons' drinking. About half of the respondents were under age thirty-five; only about one-fifth were over forty-five. About 10 percent had worked at their current job for less than a year; nearly 40 percent had worked there more than ten years. The median respondent was a high school graduate; only about one-tenth did not graduate from high school.

Fewer than a third of respondents were currently married, probably reflecting this occupation's late-night lifestyle and lack of steady, dependable income. An approximately equal number had never been married. Almost a third also worked at other jobs for pay. Nearly 40 percent had 1995 family income below $15,000; the median was under $30,000.

SERVING PRACTICES

A number of serving practices are known to encourage drinking and may increase patrons' likelihood of leaving the bar intoxicated. One such practice is issuing a "last call" for drinks, alerting patrons to the final opportunity to purchase alcohol before the bar is legally required to stop serving. Those who reported working until the bar closed were asked how often a last call for drinks was given. Three-quarters said "always" (table 8.2). Only 4 percent said "never." From the servers' perspective, the last call provides not only a chance to boost sales and tips but also time to clean up the bar before closing. In this sense it may be unrealistic to expect them not to announce it.

Similarly, selling drinks by the pitcher encourages patrons to drink

Table 8.2 Serving Practices: Last Call for Drinks and Serving by the Pitcher

Practice	% Yes
Last call for drinks	
Always	74.6
Sometimes	21.8
Never	3.6
Don't know/refused	0.0
Sell drinks by pitcher	66.5
Percentage of orders by pitcher	
5 percent	54.5
6–10 percent	18.2
11–25 percent	17.1
25+ percent	10.1
Don't know/refused	0.2

Source: 1996 Survey of Employees.

more. Two-thirds of respondents said they served drinks by the pitcher, but they reported that such orders constituted fewer than 5 percent of total alcohol transactions. Only about 10 percent said orders by the pitcher were more than 25 percent of all orders.

Virtually all respondents said they served adults who came into the bar with minors (table 8.3). Only a minority said an employee was assigned to check the identification of those wanting to enter. Very few establishments (5.2 percent) used "pat downs" to detect bottles of alcohol brought in by minors.

Although approximately half of all bartenders or servers would allow an intoxicated person to enter, almost all (95.3 percent) said they would not serve a patron who was obviously drunk (table 8.4). About four-fifths said cabs were available to pick up patrons late at night. A small minority (10.7 percent) said the bar had a volunteer program for driving intoxicated patrons home.

Among procedures for ensuring that obviously intoxicated persons do not drive home, the most common practice was to encourage accepting a ride with a friend, followed by calling a taxi (table 8.5). In a minority of cases the bartender or server encouraged the patron to spend the night in a hotel. However, hotels within walking distance may not be common.

Table 8.3 Serving Practices: Monitoring Drinking by Minors

Practice	% Yes
Person at door has chief responsibility to check IDs	31.1
If group includes parent or spouse and minor, alcohol is served to adults	96.8
If group includes peers, minors, and adults, alcohol is served to adults	81.7
"Pat downs" used when chances of minors' bringing in alcohol are greater than normal	5.2

Source: 1996 Survey of Employees.

Table 8.4 Serving Practices: Monitoring of Obviously Intoxicated Adults

Practice	% Yes
Obviously intoxicated patrons are allowed to enter	51.9
If obviously intoxicated patron enters, manager is called to front station	44.5
Obviously intoxicated patrons are refused alcohol	95.3
Obviously intoxicated patrons are refused alcohol for a certain period	38.0
Establishment has volunteer program for driving obviously intoxicated patrons home	10.7
Establishment provides rides for obviously intoxicated patrons	26.3
Cabs available to pick up patrons from bar late at night	81.1

Source: 1996 Survey of Employees.

Table 8.5 Procedures Used to Deal
with Obviously Intoxicated Person

Encourage Patron to	% Yes
Give up car keys	69.3
Accept ride from friend	82.9
Accept ride from employee	64.0
Accept ride in cab	76.7
Sleep it off at hotel	29.4

Source: 1996 Survey of Employees.

Table 8.6 Server Has Been Reprimanded
by Management for Serving or Not
Serving a Patron (%)

Yes, for serving	5.8
Yes, for not serving	4.4
Yes, for both serving and not serving	3.6
No	86.0
Don't know	0.2

Source: 1996 Survey of Employees.

We asked employees whether management had reprimanded them for serving or not serving a patron for an alcohol-related reason such as appearing to already be drunk. The vast majority of respondents (86 percent) said no (table 8.6). However, 4.4 percent said they had been reprimanded for *not* serving a patron, and 3.6 percent said they had been reprimanded both for serving and for not serving. Only 5.8 percent of employees said they had been reprimanded only for serving a patron.

On many of the survey questions about bar policies, there was almost complete agreement between owners or managers and the employees we interviewed (table 8.7). For example, there was virtually total agreement about whether alcohol was served to adults in the presence of minors, about employee instruction concerning the types of acceptable identification, and about the availability of cabs late at night. Although the employers often gave a more favorable answer than the employees, this was not always so. When there was a large discrepancy, the employers' responses tended to be more favorable. For example, they were much more likely to state that the bar had procedures for getting car keys from drunk patrons and arranging rides for them or had a volunteer program to provide rides. Perhaps to the employers the term "procedures" meant a general understanding but the employees interpreted the term more literally—for ex-

Table 8.7 Questions about the Establishment's Policies Asked
of Employers and Employees (%)

Question	Agree	Employer More Favorable	Employee More Favorable
Alcohol is served to parents/relatives when minors/parents/relatives mixed	95.8	1.1	3.2
Bar teaches acceptable types of IDs	95.8	2.6	1.6
Cabs available late at night to come to bar	90.8	4.1	5.1
Bar uses "pat down" to detect hidden alcohol	87.5	7.8	4.6
Bar has procedure for getting drunk persons to accept ride in cab	85.7	8.9	5.4
Bar teaches employee how to tell if ID forged, altered, illegal	82.5	9.8	7.7
Bar has procedures for getting drunk persons rides from friends	82.2	15.7	2.0
Bar has person at door to check IDs	82.0	13.2	4.8
Alcohol served to adults when minors and adults mixed	79.5	9.5	11.1
Bar's training discusses threat of fines for servers	78.3	13.8	7.9
Bar has procedures for getting car keys from drunk persons	69.2	27.4	3.5
Bar associated with volunteer program to provide rides for drunk persons	69.2	23.6	7.2
Alcohol served when some peers legal age and some not	68.2	14.3	17.6
Bar's training discusses criminal consequences for serving minors	66.1	16.5	17.4
Bar has procedure to arrange for hotel	65.5	19.8	14.7
Bar has procedure for getting drunk persons to accept ride from employee	64.6	29.8	5.6
Bar's training discusses threat of			
Server being named in dram shop suit	63.1	23.5	13.4
Depositions, hearings, etc.	59.9	20.4	19.7
Jail terms for servers	59.7	21.6	18.6
Bar gives rides as service for patrons who drink too much	52.4	40.3	7.3

Source: 1996 Survey of Employees.

ample, as written procedures—or perhaps the employers volunteered their employees to provide rides.

For further analysis, we asked each employee a set of questions concerning possible server behaviors (table 8.8). For each, we asked how frequently within the past month the employee had acted this way: "often," "sometimes," or "never." Respondents almost always answered; the highest rate of nonresponse for any of the questions was 2.1 percent. The list began with two inquiries about serving practices deemed "irresponsible" and designated in table 8.8 by the letter I: serving more than one drink at a time, and replacing a drink before the patron's glass is empty.

These two were followed by nine questions about "responsible" practices for dealing both with adults who are intoxicated and with minors, designated in table 8.8 by the letter R, and finally a question about drinking on the job, which was considered irresponsible. Overall, to use a saying strikingly applicable in this context, the glass is half empty or half full depending on one's perspective. On one hand, the employees engaged in some safe serving practices and eschewed some unsafe ones. On the other hand, the survey found a number of self-acknowledged instances of irresponsible behavior.

Concerning the three irresponsible serving practices, 40.1 percent of bartenders or servers said they never served patrons more than one drink at a time, and 27.5 percent said they had often done so during the past

Table 8.8 Situations That Occurred between Server and Patron during Past Month

Situation	Often	Sometimes	Never	Refused to Answer
Served patron more than one drink at time (I)	27.5	32.1	40.1	0.0
Replaced drink before patron's glass empty (I)	16.8	49.7	33.5	0.0
Provided glass of water with second drink (R)	22.5	50.9	26.3	0.2
Provided additional drinks with normal amount of alcohol but more mixer (R)	17.7	48.5	31.7	2.1
Actively paced patron's drinking from beginning of service (R)	44.9	38.9	14.8	1.4
Cut off obviously intoxicated person (R)	30.6	52.8	16.5	0.1
Cut off persons who refused to slow down when they had "enough," that is, before they had too much (R)	23.5	48.4	27.7	0.3
Referred problem of obviously intoxicated person to manager (R)	16.1	37.6	45.8	0.5
Referred problem of obviously intoxicated person to another employee (R)	20.3	35.3	44.3	0.1
Arranged for intoxicated person to be taken home (R)	33.3	48.5	18.1	0.1
Checked patron's identification (R)	70.1	23.4	6.5	0.0
Consumed alcohol on job (I)	2.3	24.8	72.9	0.0

Source: 1996 Survey of Employees.
(I) = Irresponsible behavior.
(R) = Responsible behavior.

month, while 32.1 percent admitted they did this sometimes. Nearly half of employees said they sometimes replaced a drink before the previous drink was finished. Only one-third said they never did this.

The percentage of servers who reported drinking on the job was significantly lower, since only 2.3 percent said they had done so often during the past month and 24.8 percent said they did this sometimes. The rest, 72.9 percent, said they had not drunk on the job during the past month on any occasion. Given that these three "irresponsible" serving practices are widely viewed as unacceptable, especially by those outside the industry, it is likely that they are actually more prevalent than the data in table 8.8 suggest.

Among the safe practices that servers used during the month preceding the survey interview, "often" was answered most frequently for "checked patron's identification," but 6.5 percent of employees said they never checked identifications. Possibly they had no patrons who appeared to be minors or another employee was responsible for checking IDs. Fewer than half the respondents said they often actively paced a patron's drinking from the beginning of service. About 15 percent said they never did. Only about half of the employees referred obviously intoxicated persons to another employee or to the manager; perhaps the other respondents took care of intoxicated patrons themselves. About a third said they often arranged for someone to be taken home. This may not be such a low fraction, because servers may not have encountered many obviously intoxicated patrons within the month before the survey.

To obtain further information about servers' propensity to monitor, we gave respondents three scenarios and asked an open-ended question about how they would act in each situation. We then asked whether this behavior was what management expected.

The first scenario was: "A table of four young adults has ordered two rounds of beer, and they are becoming dangerously rowdy. They order another round. What would you do?" Most said "cut them off," followed by "tell them to quiet down" and "tell them 'that's enough' and ask them to leave" (box 8.1). No respondent gave a clearly inappropriate answer. Almost all (95.6 percent) said this is what management would expect them to do (not shown in box).

The second scenario was: "A patron comes in and immediately orders a shot of whiskey with a beer chaser. This patron appears to have been drinking before arriving. What would you do?" Responses were much more varied for this scenario (box 8.2). The most frequent single answer was "do not serve customer," but 106 respondents said "serve if not intox-

Box 8.1 Server scenario 1.

"A table of four young adults has ordered two rounds of beer, and they are becoming dangerously rowdy. They order another round. What would you do?"

Cut them off	492	Serve one pitcher, then cut off	13
Tell them to quiet down	135	Find out who is driving	12
Tell them "that's enough" and ask them to leave	87	Encourage them not to have another	9
		Call cab	8
Talk to owner or manager about situation	65	Offer food	8
		Call police	4
Switch to water or soda	31	Direct to alternative activity (e.g., billiards)	3
Serve them	23		
Slow them down	20	Never serve more than one pitcher	3
Talk to them and give them a warning	17	Would serve them if I knew them	2
Serve third pitcher with a warning	17	Check IDs	2
Take pitchers away	16	Those who are rowdy have to give up their mugs	1
Serve and monitor	14		
Monitor situation	14	Serve individual drinks to those who seem okay	1
Have bouncer take charge	13		

Source: 1996 Survey of Employees. Numbers are number of responses.

icated" and 96 said "serve customer." Almost as many (82) said "give beer, refuse shot," followed by "serve if not too drunk" (38) and "give coffee" (19). Several of the less frequent responses were clearly appropriate to the scenario: "ask to leave" (10), "offer food" (8), "ask him to hold off" (6), "call cab" (6), and so on. The ambiguity of the question led to very different answers and made it more difficult to give an "acceptable" response, although responses such as "serve and hope he leaves" (1) are clearly inappropriate.

The third scenario was: "One of your patrons is slurring words and stumbling a bit while paying the bill and walking toward the exit. Earlier, this person ordered two drinks from you. What would you do?" In response to this, most said they would arrange for some sort of alternative transportation (box 8.3). The top five responses were all appropriate: "call a cab" (272), "make sure he has a ride" (186), "detain" (146), "ask if he needs a ride" (139), and "take keys" (116). Ninety-three respondents said they would "serve him coffee," an inappropriate answer if the server reasoned that coffee would ameliorate the effects of alcohol. However, servers may have offered coffee to buy time both to evaluate the level of intoxication and to allow the patron to become sober. There was only one clearly inappropriate response: "tell him to be careful" (7).

Box 8.2 Server scenario 2.

"A patron comes in and immediately orders a shot of whiskey with a beer chaser. This patron appears to have been drinking before arriving. What would you do?"

Do not serve customer	168	Ask him to hold off	6
Serve if not intoxicated	106	Ask customer to pick either beer or	
Serve customer	96	liquor	6
Give beer, refuse shot	82	Call cab	6
Refuse if I think they are drunk, otherwise		Send to bar	5
serve	82	Talk to customer and see how drunk he is	5
Monitor to determine level of intoxication		Find out how much was consumed	
before serving	74	at last bar	4
Serve if not too drink	38	Suggest one drink, then cut off	4
Serve first round, then monitor	32	Give shot, refuse beer	3
Don't have hard liquor	27	Don't know	3
Give coffee	19	Don't serve, see if they need a ride	2
Would serve if I knew the customer	18	Not serve unless he was with someone	2
Encourage beer over liquor	17	Serve if not out of hand	2
Serve first round, then cut off	14	Serve and check with manager	2
Find out how much he has consumed	13	Ask to leave if drunk	2
Notify manager	12	Depends on the person	2
Encourage soda or water	12	Serve nonalcoholic beer	2
Can only serve one drink at a time	12	Ask for ID, then serve if OK	2
Serve if they are not driving	10	Don't allow straight shots	1
Depends on his condition (e.g., glassy		Give it to him and then try to get him to	
eyes)	10	slow down	1
Find out who is driving	10	Might not serve if drink	1
Ask to leave	10	Serve one half of a shot	1
Serve soda or water	8	Would cut off if he knew the person	1
Offer food	8	Serve and hope he leaves	1

Source: 1996 Survey of Employees. Numbers are number of responses.

BARTENDERS' AND SERVERS' PERCEPTIONS OF SERVER TRAINING

As we discussed earlier, server training may be a means for a bar to lower its risk of liability and to establish procedures that could form the basis for a responsible business practice defense in the event of a suit. Most the employees surveyed had received server training at a previous job or at their current job, or both (table 8.9). Slightly over half received some server training at their present job. Only 23.4 percent never received server training at any job (not shown). Almost a third (29.6 percent) received some form of follow-up training on their current job.

According to the employees, most server training programs (58.7 percent) discussed the possibility of employees' being named in a lawsuit and their potential involvement in specific aspects of the legal process such as depositions and administrative hearings (64.3 percent) (table 8.10). Fines were discussed most frequently (81.0 percent). Virtually all programs taught methods for recognizing intoxication (94.5 percent), how to handle intoxicated persons (95.9 percent), how to keep minors from drinking (93.9 percent), and acceptable types of identification (97.1 percent). Approaches for monitoring drinking were emphasized more frequently (60.7 percent) than were alternative modes of transportation (18.4 percent), with both covered in about one-fifth of the training programs.

We asked respondents to evaluate the training they received. Two-thirds said it was "very practical" (table 8.11). Almost all of the remaining

Box 8.3 Server scenario 3.

"One of your patrons is slurring words and stumbling a bit while paying the bill and walking toward the exit. Earlier, this person ordered two drinks from you. What would you do?"

Call a cab	272	Ask him to find a safe way home	13
Make sure he has a ride	186	See if capable of driving	8
Detain	146	Collect their money, then let them go	7
Ask if he needs a ride	139	Will offer a ride if I know them	7
Take keys	116	Tell him to be careful	7
Serve him coffee	93	Call police	5
Get a friend to take them home	91	Arrange hotel room	4
Offer ride from self or employee	75	Walk them to their car safely	4
See if he is driving	61	Ask them to leave or cut them off	4
Serve water or soda	41	Depends on how drunk they are	1
Talk to owner or manager	30	Take them home with me	1
Call someone to pick them up	28	We evaluate customers after every drink	1
Wouldn't serve in the first place	20	Direct to bus	1
Serve food	17	Call police for ride service	1
Let him go	17	Let him go if help refused	1
Have one of the other customers take them home	14		

Source: 1996 Survey Employees. Numbers are number of responses.

Table 8.9 Servers Reporting Server Training

	% Yes
Received server training at previous job	52.4
Received server training at current job	56.0
Received follow-up server training at current job	29.6

Source: 1996 Survey of Employees.

Table 8.10 Content of Server Training

Content	% Yes
Server training discussed	
Possibility of server being named in dram shop suit	58.7
Potential server involvement in depositions, lawsuits, and administrative hearings	64.3
Potential fines	81.0
Potential jail terms	61.8
Criminal records for serving minors	72.2
Server taught to	
Promote sales of alcoholic beverages	49.9
Keep people from becoming intoxicated	84.2
Recognize person is intoxicated	94.5
Handle people who are intoxicated	95.9
Keep minors from drinking	93.9
Reduce liquor liability risk exposure at point of sale	71.5
Taught about types of acceptable identifications	97.1
Taught how IDs can be altered, forged, or illegally obtained	89.1
Taught how to pace patrons' drinking	78.0
Taught to refuse service or told to leave this to manager	
Refuse service	86.0
Leave to manager	10.6
No instruction	2.6
Don't know/refuse to answer	0.8
Emphasis in training: providing alternative transportation or monitoring consumption	
Promoting alternative transportation	18.4
Monitoring consumption	60.7
Both	19.6
Neither	1.1
Don't know/refuse to answer	0.3
Training provides instruction on motivations for excessive drinking	58.1

Source: 1996 Survey of Employees.

respondents said their training was "somewhat practical." Only 2.3 percent said their server training program was "not at all practical."

EFFECTS OF THE THREAT OF LIABILITY AND OTHER FACTORS ON "RESPONSIBLE" AND "IRRESPONSIBLE" SERVER BEHAVIOR

Earlier in this chapter we described our procedure for asking servers and bartenders how they would handle a list of hypothetical situations that involve drinking alcohol. As stated earlier, we classified their responses (see table 8.8) into nine "responsible" (R) and three "irresponsible" (I) behaviors. For the analysis of server behaviors in this section, we used only questions about serving adults, excluding those relating to minors. For this reason we did not include the response "check patron's identification" in this analysis. In order to use the server responses given in the survey, we converted "often" and "sometimes" to "yes" and "never" to "no." We dropped the very few cases in which the bartender or server gave no answer.

Using ordered logit analysis, we assessed how the number of "responsible" and "irresponsible" responses an employee gave were influenced by the following: the probability of being sued or being cited by the local police, ABC, and ALE; competition; the characteristics of the responding bartender or server (age, education, total experience, and experience on this job); the characteristics of the workplace—whether the bar was part of a chain, its age, and whether it was incorporated; the mix of clientele; the fraction of sales from food; and the population density of the county where the bar was located.

The perceived probabilities used in this analysis came from questions directed to bar owners and managers (discussed in chapters 2, 3, 5, and 7) concerning the likelihood of a tort suit, an administrative citation, and a criminal citation after serving alcohol to an obviously intoxicated person. These probabilities were taken from the bar owners and managers rather than employees, since the latter may justify their failure to engage in responsible server practices by saying they did not know the laws. In addition, the perceptions of the owners or managers were more likely to be accurate than those of employees, since they act in the interest of maintaining their business. The marginal effects shown are for the highest number category: nine "responsible" or three "irresponsible" responses (including zero values in both R and I).

Holding many other factors constant, a higher perceived probability of a tort suit decreased the number of irresponsible behaviors by bartenders and servers (i.e., serving more than one drink at a time, replacing a drink before the patron's glass was empty, and consuming alcoholic beverages on the job) (table 8.12). For this particular equation, the coefficient on the tort variable was negative and statistically significant at the 1 percent level. However, tort had no effect on the number of responsible behaviors. The

Table 8.11 Server Training
Evaluation by Server

Rating	% Yes
Very practical	66.9
Somewhat practical	30.3
Not at all practical	2.3
Don't know/refused to answer	0.5

Source: 1996 Survey of Employees.

Table 8.12 Effects of Liability and Other Factors on "Responsible" and "Irresponsible" Server Behavior

Explanatory Variables	Number of "Responsible" Responses			Number of "Irresponsible" Responses		
	Coeff.	Std. Err.	M.E.	Coeff.	Std. Err.	M.E.
Perceived probabilities						
Probability of suit	0.0024	0.058	0.0003	−0.29[a]	0.061	−0.031
Probability of citation by police	−0.073	0.071	−0.0096	−0.018	0.07	−0.0019
Probability of citation by ABC	0.015	0.086	0.0019	0.14	0.082	0.015
Probability of citation by ALE	0.057	0.095	0.0074	−0.086	0.087	−0.0091
Competition	−0.20	0.20	−0.027	−0.37	0.20	−0.039
Server characteristics						
Bartender	0.60[a]	0.22	0.079	0.034	0.27	0.0036
Bartender and server	0.43	0.25	0.056	−0.14	0.31	−0.015
Part time	−0.42[b]	0.17	−0.056	−0.30	0.18	−0.032
Aged <25	0.34	0.31	0.045	0.95[a]	0.32	0.10
Aged 25–34	0.25	0.24	0.033	0.79[a]	0.24	0.084
Aged 35–44	0.43	0.22	0.056	0.45[b]	0.22	0.048
Education	0.87	0.44	0.11	−0.012	0.44	−0.0013
Experience: total years	−0.042	0.10	−0.0055	−0.14	0.10	−0.014
Experience: at present job	−0.34	0.18	−0.044	0.40[b]	0.17	0.042

	Coeff.	Std. Err.	M.E.	Coeff.	Std. Err.	M.E.
Establishment characteristics						
Incorporated	0.26	0.16	0.035	0.20	0.17	0.021
Part of chain	0.030	0.30	0.0039	0.26	0.33	0.027
Age of establishment	−0.072	0.41	−0.0095	0.25	0.42	0.026
Fraction of sales from food	−0.76[b]	0.39	−0.10	−0.24	0.42	−0.026
Clientele characteristics						
Fraction of						
Customers aged 25–40	−0.40	0.58	−0.052	−0.17	0.66	−0.018
Customers aged 40+	−1.39[b]	0.59	−0.18	−0.27	0.66	−0.028
Students	0.85	0.71	0.11	2.08[b]	0.87	0.22
Blue-collar workers	0.27	0.30	0.036	−0.14	0.31	−0.015
Regular	−0.58	0.35	−0.076	0.26	0.37	0.027
Men	0.0013	0.61	−0.0002	−1.03	0.61	−0.11
Customers who come alone	0.27	0.55	0.035	1.40[b]	0.59	0.15
Customers who come in groups	−0.84	0.58	−0.11	−0.021	0.59	−0.0022
Customers who come by car	−0.58	0.32	−0.077	0.075	0.28	0.0079
Population density	0.061	0.044	0.008	−0.046	0.047	−0.0048
	N = 668			*N* = 668		

[a]Statistically significant at 1 percent level.
[b]Statistically significant at 5 percent level.
Coeff. = coefficient; Std. Err. = standard error; M.E. = marginal effect.
Table reports nonstandardized regression coefficients.

perceived probability of citation by the ABC was positive and nearly significant ($p = 0.093$) for irresponsible behaviors. None of the local police or ALE variables were statistically significant at conventional levels in either regression, indicating they had no effect on server behavior.

As in chapter 7, we measured competition with a binary variable that equaled one if the owner or manager identified a competitor. This same binary variable was used in this section to measure its effect on server behavior. Having a competitor decreased the number of irresponsible behaviors, suggesting that most customers, when given a choice, prefer to drink where order is maintained. The coefficient on this variable was negative and almost statistically significant ($p = 0.062$).

Several characteristics of bartenders or servers had statistically significant effects on the number of either responsible or irresponsible behaviors. Working as a bartender or a bartender and server rather than only a server increased the number of responsible behaviors. The same was true for years of schooling completed. Years of total experience did not affect the number of responsible behaviors, but those with more years at their present job ($p = 0.057$) and those working part time ($p = 0.050$) reported significantly fewer responsible behaviors. Servers over thirty-five reported more responsible behaviors than their younger counterparts ($p = 0.055$).

Personal characteristics affected the number of irresponsible behaviors. Servers under forty-five reported more irresponsible behaviors than the omitted reference group, those forty-five or over. Furthermore, neither education nor total years of experience influenced the number of irresponsible behaviors. However, those with more years at the present job reported significantly more irresponsible behaviors. Perhaps either they felt more confident in reporting such behavior or such behavior is rewarded in this industry.

Only two of the establishment characteristics, fraction of sales from food and incorporation, had a statistically significant effect on the number of responsible behaviors. Employees who worked in establishments that were more dependent on revenue from food reported fewer responsible behaviors. Perhaps they did less monitoring because there was less drinking and therefore they saw less reason to monitor. Establishments that were incorporated reported significantly more responsible behaviors by servers, possibly because corporate level policies mandate more detailed server training or closer supervision of employees.

Three clientele characteristics influenced the number of irresponsible behaviors. Not surprisingly, employees in establishments oriented toward students exhibited more. Bars with more people coming alone ("singles" bars) also engaged in more irresponsible behaviors. Additionally, employees in bars with a higher proportion of men reported fewer irresponsible behaviors at almost statistically significant levels ($p = 0.094$).

To further investigate the effects of precautionary behavior, we replicated the analysis of the perceived threat of tort liability and administrative and criminal sanctions reported in chapter 7. In this analysis, however, we used data from employees rather from than owners or managers, and we included covariates describing characteristics of the respondent. Because the employees were not asked all the same questions as owners or managers (see table 8.12), we could replicate the analysis for only five types of precautions, including not drinking on the job, a count of measures taken to deal with intoxicated patrons, whether the employee checked identifications, the use of pat downs for minors, and a count of subjects covered by the server training program. We used the owners' or managers' responses for the probability of being sued or cited for serving an obviously intoxicated adult in equations for the first, second, and fifth dependent variables and their responses for the probability of serving a minor in the equations for the third and fourth variables. Only results for the threat and competition variables are presented (table 8.13).

Table 8.13 Commercial Server Precaution Levels

| Dependent Variables | Perceived Probability of Threat from | | | | |
	Tort	Police	ABC	ALE	Competition
1. Not drinking on job	0.30[a]	0.10	−0.041	0.043	0.61[b]
($N = 668$)	(0.078)	(0.092)	(0.10)	(0.11)	(0.25)
	[0.055]	[0.019]	[−0.0074]	[0.0079]	[0.11]
2. Services provided	0.083	−0.052	0.067	−0.039	0.13
for drunk customers	(0.058)	(0.066)	(0.074)	(0.079)	(0.21)
($N = 668$)	[0.011]	[−0.0070]	[0.0090]	[−0.0053]	[0.017]
3. Check identification	0.17[b]	0.017	−0.024	0.097	−0.17
($N = 658$)	(0.075)	(0.11)	(0.092)	(0.11)	(0.28)
	[0.034]	[0.0034]	[−0.0048]	[0.019]	[−0.033]
4. Pat down	0.046	−0.20	−0.16	0.35	−0.24
($N = 658$)	(0.13)	(0.17)	(0.15)	(0.19)	(0.46)
	[0.0020]	[−0.0087]	[−0.0070]	[0.015]	[−0.010]
5. Content of server	0.13	0.023	0.026	0.003	0.11
training	(0.071)	(0.077)	(0.091)	(0.096)	(0.20)
($N = 641$)	[0.026]	[0.0046]	[0.0053]	[0.0006]	[0.022]

[a]Statistically significant at 1 percent level.
[b]Statistically significant at 5 percent level.
Full regressions are not shown for the thirteen dependent variables.
Standard errors in parentheses; marginal effects in brackets.
Table reports nonstandardized regression coefficients.

The perceived probability of being sued had positive effects on responsible server behavior in all five regressions, again indicating that dram shop liability is an effective deterrent. In two of the five, the coefficient on the tort variable was statistically significant. Having more subjects covered in server training had nearly significant positive effects on the perceived probability of a tort suit ($p = 0.070$). In the measure of services provided for intoxicated adults and "pat downs" for minors, the coefficients were positive but not statistically significant at conventional levels.

By contrast, the perceived probability of being cited by the local police or the ABC was not a factor in responsible server behaviors, since none of the coefficients attained statistical significance at conventional levels. Only one ALE coefficient was positive and statistically significant at even the 10 percent level—the coefficient in the regression for pat downs ($p = 0.063$).

The binary variable for having a competitor was positive and statistically significant at the 1 percent level in one regression—for not drinking on the job. Otherwise the coefficients varied in sign and were uniformly not significant at conventional levels.

COMPENSATION

The mean basic hourly wage of bartenders or servers was $7.40 (table 8.14). In addition, they received $4.17 an hour in individual tips. Including payments from tip pools, on average the total amount of tips received was $4.75 per hour. The employees surveyed reported working at their jobs for an average of 30.9 hours a week and having worked serving alcohol for a mean of ten years. Most (65.0 percent) said they had lost tips for refusing to serve an obviously intoxicated person (table 8.15), a frequent occurrence according to respondents. Although only 18 percent said they had had no such losses in the month before the survey, 63 percent had lost tips one to five times during the previous month and 7 percent had done so more than ten times. Only 2 percent of employees said the establishment reimbursed them for lost tips when they refused to serve an obviously intoxicated patron.

Are employees financially rewarded for "irresponsible" or "responsible" behavior? To address this issue, we regressed various measures of employee compensation, all defined in terms of compensation per hour, on counts of the behaviors from the list reported in table 8.8. The dependent variables were hourly earnings based on the employee's report of monthly compensation divided by the number of hours worked per week multiplied by an assumed number of weeks; an alternative measure of hourly earnings

Table 8.14 Employee Work Characteristics

Characteristic	Mean
Earnings per hour	$7.40
Individual tips per hour	$4.17
Tips and tip pools per hour	$4.75
Hours worked per week	30.9
Total number of months employed serving alcohol	120.2

Source: 1996 Survey of Employees.

Table 8.15 Tips

Item	% Yes
Have ever lost tips for refusing to serve obviously intoxicated person	65.0
Number of times this happened during past month	
None	17.9
1–5	62.8
6–10	9.2
11+	7.5
Don't know/refused	2.9
Establishment reimburses employees for lost tips	2.1

Source: 1996 Survey of Employees.

based on the employee's estimate of earnings during the week before the survey; earnings from tips (both including and excluding money from the bar's tip pool); and hourly pay exclusive of tips. The dependent compensation variables were expressed as natural logarithms.

We considered the possibility that behavior might be determined jointly with compensation by considering behavior to be endogenous in some variants and estimating the compensation and behavior equations with two-stage least squares. The compensation relationship was identified by including the variables for the probability of being sued and the probability of being cited by the local police, ABC, and ALE as determinants of behavior but not of compensation.

To determine whether server practices were endogenous, we performed specification (Hausman) tests. In all cases the null hypothesis of exogeneity was not rejected. Therefore we present only ordinary least squares results.

According to this analysis, the number of irresponsible behaviors had a positive effect on hourly earnings; the coefficient on this variable was statistically significant at the 1 percent level (table 8.16). The number of responsible behaviors and having a competitor had no effect on earnings.

Among the personal characteristics variables, workers under forty-five and those with more education had higher earnings. Among the establish-

Table 8.16 Determinants of Servers' Hourly Earnings

Dependent Variables	Hourly Earnings	
	Coeff.	Std. Err.
Number of responsible behaviors	0.0010	0.015
Number of irresponsible behaviors	0.088[a]	0.030
Competition	0.054	0.073
Server characteristics		
Bartender	−0.013	0.081
Bartender and server	−0.11	0.096
Part time	−0.095	0.064
Age <25	0.25[b]	0.11
Age 25–34	0.33[a]	0.088
Age 35–44	0.21[b]	0.080
Education	0.70[a]	0.15
Experience: total number of years	0.072[b]	0.035
Experience: at current job	−0.0078	0.060
Establishment characteristics		
Incorporated	0.16[a]	0.056
Part of chain	−0.088	0.11
Age of establishment	0.063	0.15
Fraction of sales from food	0.012	0.13
Clientele characteristics		
Fraction of		
Customers aged 25–40	0.26	0.22
Customers aged 40+	0.0045	0.22
Students	0.33	0.28
Blue-collar workers	−0.31[a]	0.10
Regulars	−0.11	0.13
Men	0.36	0.21
Customers who come alone	−0.50[a]	0.19
Customers who come in groups	−0.55[a]	0.20
Customers who come by car	0.011	0.098
Population density	0.051[a]	0.014
Constant	0.44	0.37
R^2	0.21	
Adjusted R^2	0.17	
	$(N = 624)$	

[a]Statistically significant at 1 percent level (two-tailed t-test)
[b]Statistically significant at 5 percent level (two-tailed t-test)
Coeff. = coefficient; Std. Err. = standard error.
Table reports nonstandardized regression coefficients.

ment characteristics, incorporated bars and those with higher proportions of male patrons ($p = 0.088$) paid servers more. Bars oriented toward a blue-collar clientele and those with high proportions of patrons who came alone or in groups rather than in couples ("singles" bars) paid less on average. Workers in establishments in more densely populated counties were paid more.

Rather than showing all the results for the alternative specifications, we present only those for the number of responsible and irresponsible behaviors (table 8.17). Coefficients on the other variables were similar to those presented in table 8.16. Again, the number of irresponsible behaviors correlated with increased server earnings for all measures of earnings, although the parameter estimates were not always statistically significant at conventional levels. Limiting the analysis to single components of hourly earnings in alternative specifications—hourly earnings from tips and compensation from tip pools—the number of responsible behaviors increased server earnings. By contrast, irresponsible behaviors had no effect on earnings.

With the alternative measure of hourly earnings, the number of responsible behaviors had a positive and statistically significant effect on the dependent variable at better than the 5 percent level. The number of irresponsible behaviors also had a positive and almost significant effect ($p = 0.058$), suggesting that irresponsible behavior was also rewarded by tips. Interestingly, patrons rewarded servers, but the establishments themselves did not provide a financial incentive for employees either to engage in responsible serving practices or to avoid irresponsible ones.

Table 8.17 Alternative Estimates of Effects of "Responsible" and "Irresponsible" Server Behavior on Earnings

Dependent Variables		Good		Bad	
Hourly earnings (from table 8.16)	($N = 624$)	0.0010	(0.015)	0.088[a]	(0.030)
Hourly earnings from tips other than tip pool	($N = 697$)	0.048	(0.025)	0.073	(0.051)
Hourly earnings from tips and tip pool	($N = 717$)	0.054[b]	(0.025)	0.081	(0.050)
Hourly earnings: alternative measure	($N = 729$)	0.049[b]	(0.022)	0.084	(0.044)
Basic hourly wage	($N = 560$)	0.0062	(0.0077)	0.0071	(0.016)

[a]Statistically significant at 1 percent level.
[b]Statistically significant at 5 percent level.
Full regressions are not shown for the thirteen dependent variables.
Standard errors in parentheses.
Table reports nonstandardized regression coefficients.

CONCLUSION

The main finding in this chapter, as in chapter 7, is that tort is an effective deterrent. The employees we surveyed were more likely to take certain precautions when the perceived threat of a lawsuit was relatively high; bear in mind that the perceptions used in this analysis were those of the owners or managers rather than the employees surveyed. Also relevant is the significant relation between these perceptions and the actual probability of a suit, as illustrated in chapter 5.

That tort encourages bartenders and servers to be more careful about some aspects of their jobs is the good news. Not so favorable were the findings that tort affected only some forms of preventive behavior; that the employees admitted to some behaviors that could be classified as "irresponsible"; and that administrative law and criminal law (i.e., local police, ABC, ALE) appear to be ineffective deterrents, as least for server behavior. The next chapter will report the results of our study of the effects of tort, administrative, and criminal law and other factors on motor vehicle mortality, drinking, binge drinking, and drinking and driving.

In this chapter we also investigated whether employees of bars benefit financially when they engage in responsible behaviors, such as arranging rides for obviously intoxicated patrons, or avoid irresponsible behaviors such as drinking on the job. On this issue, there is also good and bad news. Unfortunately we found some evidence that employees earned more when they engaged in bad behaviors. An encouraging finding is that responsible behavior appears to be rewarded with higher tips, although not in terms of overall hourly compensation. Most employees we surveyed reported losing tips through what is called "responsible serving practice." Clearly, behavior in the "real" world is indeed more complex than in scholars' models. Competition in the product market had little effect on either precautions or earnings.

9

Effects of Regulation on Drinking and on Alcohol-Related Auto Accident Death Rates

CHAPTER OVERVIEW

Approximately 41 percent of all deaths from traffic accidents are associated with alcohol, and approximately one-third of deaths among persons aged fifteen to twenty-four result from motor vehicle crashes (National Highway Traffic Safety Administration 1994; U.S. Department of Transportation 1991; Goodman et al. 1991; Escobedo, Chorba, and Waxweiler 1995). In 1995 more than 1.4 million people were arrested for driving while intoxicated, 10 percent of all arrests made that year (Hingson 1996). These statistics illustrate the high emotional and monetary costs of fatalities on the road, prompting federal, state, and local agencies to attempt to control the sale and consumption of alcohol (Rice 1993; Runge 1993). The resulting policies are designed to influence drinking practices and regulate the supply of alcohol (Gordis 1996).

In chapters 2 and 3 we examined the direct effect of imposing administrative regulations and criminal liability on establishments and individuals serving alcohol. In chapter 5 we discovered the effectiveness of imposing civil liability on bars for irresponsible server behavior. As established in these chapters, in states or counties where the threat of punishment is greater, alcohol servers may be more attentive to how much clients drink. More conservative server practices may indirectly curb excessive drinking and thereby reduce rates of drinking and driving.

Additionally, alcohol policies aimed at drinkers may reduce the likelihood that individuals will consume large amounts of alcohol and behave in ways they may be punished for. Those who choose to engage in criminal behaviors such as drunk driving may to some extent first assess the risks of being caught by the police and of causing an accident. At least when sober, someone who considers driving under the influence of alcohol may think about the consequences of detection: not only court-ordered punishment, but also the stigma of being labeled a "drunk driver." Such a label could bring negative reactions by friends and family, adverse effects on employment, and—important in some states—higher insurance premiums (Sloan and Githens 1994). A potential drunk driver may also make judgments about police effectiveness, police resources, and the severity of expected punishment. Other policies, such as imposing high taxes on alcohol, are primarily designed for other reasons, such as revenue generation, and are likely to affect light as well as heavy drinking.

In this chapter we hypothesize that states with a higher expected penalty for drunk driving and a greater likelihood of being caught have lower accident rates. Examples of penalties that differ by state include whether a driver's license is immediately revoked on being cited for drinking and driving and whether states ban open containers of alcohol in motor vehicles. Assessing the effectiveness of alcohol polices in reducing motor vehicle fatalities is a difficult task requiring the use of multiple databases. This chapter examines the association between alcohol-related motor vehicle deaths, the price and availability of alcohol, administrative and legal deterrents, and state driving characteristics. We disentangle the effect of state-level alcohol policies and prices using longitudinal data for the years 1984 through 1995.

The empirical analysis of this chapter is in two parts. First we studied individual behavior using data from the Behavioral Risk Factor Surveys (BRFS), 1984–95. The behaviors studied related to several decisions: whether to drink at all, whether to consume five or more alcoholic beverages on a single occasion (termed "binge drinking"), and whether to drive after drinking too much. We analyzed how each of these decisions was affected by many variables, including price, individual state policies (see chapters 2 through 5), personal characteristics, and state characteristics. The second part of the chapter focuses on the effects of heavy drinking. We report the results of our analysis of motor vehicle fatality rates for 1984–95 using data from the Fatal Accident Reporting System (FARS) database and secondary sources for state level policies.

ANALYSIS OF DRINKING BEHAVIOR: DATA

We obtained data on individuals from the BRFS, conducted by state health departments under the direction of the United States Centers for Disease Control each year from 1984 to 1995. Eighteen states participated in 1984; by 1990 the number had risen to forty-five. By 1995, all fifty states participated. On average there were 938 interviews per state in 1984, and by 1995 there were 2,279. The BRFS is the only annual national survey of alcohol use and related behavior, such as patterns of drinking and driving.

For each year we took a random 25 percent sample of the observations of people over age twenty-one, yielding 199,358 observations. This household survey, conducted annually by telephone, obtains information from persons over eighteen on demographic characteristics such as age, gender, schooling, marital status, family income, and lifestyle. The BRFS is the only annual national survey of alcohol use and related behavior, such as patterns of drinking and driving. Lifestyle and behavioral characteristics include diet, smoking, exercise, and use of seat belts. The BRFS asked whether in the past month the person had consumed any alcoholic beverage, had binge drunk, or had driven after drinking too much.

Using data from the 1995 BRFS, the probability of drinking and driving by someone who had not drunk five or more alcoholic beverages on one occasion during the past month was only 0.01. In contrast, the probability was 0.17 if the respondent reported at least one binge episode (fig. 9.1). Nearly half of respondents (49.3 percent) had drunk alcohol at least once during the past month. Of those who drank, 26.0 percent reported at least one binge episode. Five percent of all adults surveyed reported drinking and driving at least once during the past month. All told, these figures translate into a total of 13.9 million persons drinking and driving each month in 1998.

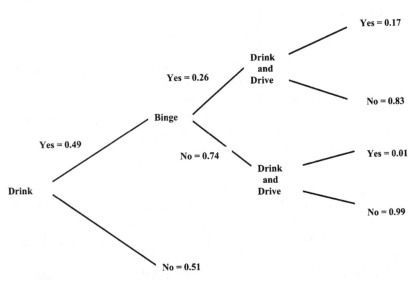

Fig. 9.1 Decision tree: drinking, binge drinking, and drinking and driving, 1995.

Since the BRFS obtained information on adults' driving under the influence of alcohol from self-reports, if anything our estimates should be too low, and perhaps substantially so.

We obtained information on criminal sanctions from the U.S. Department of Transportation (1985–96) for use throughout this chapter. In addition, we performed our own search on LEXIS to obtain information on states' adoption of dram shop laws and their enforcement, as well as to determine whether a state had contributory or comparative negligence in a given year. Tort laws may have been established by statute or may have resulted from a judicial decision. Data on the number of full-time police per thousand population and on public expenditures for police protection per thousand population came from the *Statistical Abstract of the United States*. We obtained data on bars and liquor stores in machine-readable form from the U.S. Census Bureau's *County Business Patterns*.

ANALYSIS OF DRINKING BEHAVIOR: EMPIRICAL SPECIFICATION
Dependent Variables

From the BRFS 25 percent sample, we obtained a subsample of those who reported drinking at all in the past month, which we used in the analyses of binge drinking ($N = 86,273$) and of drinking and driving ($N = 87,087$). To analyze drinking and driving among binge drinkers, we used an even smaller sample of those who reported a binge drinking episode in the month before the survey ($N = 22,261$). Because each of the dependent variables was a binary, we used logit analysis to estimate equations for the probability that someone engaged in binge drinking and in drinking and driving at least once, given that the person drank alcohol at all and, alternatively, binge drank at all. We analyzed how each of these decisions was affected by several categories of variables, including price, administrative, criminal, and tort law and insurance, individual demographics and health behaviors, state characteristics, and a time trend. To account for unobserved correlation between individual observations in the same state, we calculated Huber-White robust standard errors.

Explanatory Variables

Explanatory variables included personal characteristics of the respondent, price, civil liability and insurance, criminal liability, measures of the availability of alcoholic beverages, measures of religiousness, and a time trend.

For personal characteristics, we controlled for age, sex, race, and marital status and defined binary variables for high school, some college, and college degree or more than college. We defined having less than a high school education as the omitted reference group. We measured family income in thousands (1995 dollars). In some instances family income was missing, in which case we set that variable to zero and set another binary variable for income missing equal to one. We also included a binary variable for whether the person was unemployed at the time of the survey.

For health behaviors, we included a binary variable for whether the person smoked and a count variable for how often the person had exercised during the past month. All the remaining variables were the same as those used in the analysis of motor vehicle death rates described below.

We developed an index of alcohol prices based on estimates by city provided by the American Chamber of Commerce Researchers Association (ACCRA), a quarterly publication. ACCRA data have been used successfully to explain both alcohol and cigarette use (see, e.g., Chaloupka 1991). ACCRA provided separate estimates of prices per bottle of beer, wine, and distilled spirits. To obtain an overall price index for alcohol, we converted the quantities in bottles to gallons and then weighted the various prices by the shares of beer, wine, and distilled spirits in total consumption, measured in gallons. The ACCRA price data were for consumption at home (rather than in bars and restaurants), and the cities included in ACCRA's survey varied over time.

To construct a state- and time-specific measure of price, we took a simple average of the price in all cities in the state included in the survey for a given year. We set the alcohol price in California in 1990 equal to one and then deflated the price in each state by the relevant component of the consumer price index (CPI). We used an alcohol price index rather than measures of state alcoholic beverage taxes, which may not systematically affect prices paid by consumers in states that operate their own retail outlets. To state all monetarily expressed variables in real terms, such variables were divided by the national CPI for all goods and services.

For administrative liability, we included as explanatory variables the number of bars and the number of liquor stores per thousand population over age fifteen. We also included binary variables for whether grocery stores were permitted to sell alcoholic beverages and whether there were restrictions on liquor store advertising.

To measure the effect of criminal liability on drinking behavior, we included variables for mandatory minimum penalties for a first offense—fines (1995 dollars), jail (days), and license suspension or revocation (months); fines for not wearing a seat belt (1995 dollars); whether the state prohibited open containers of alcohol in vehicles; whether it prohibited al-cohol consumption by anyone in the vehicle or only by the driver; whether by state law a person implicitly consents to an alcohol test if detained for a DUI offense; whether police could suspend or revoke a driver's license based on a specific alcohol level or other signs of drunk driving ("adminis-trative per se"); whether a preliminary breath test could be used as proba-ble cause for a DUI arrest; and the number of police per thousand state population.

To analyze the effect of tort law and insurance on individual decisions, we included variables for whether the state had a dram shop law; whether injured adult drinkers were allowed to bring suit; whether a bar could use a responsible business practice defense to escape liability; whether social hosts could be held liable for an accident caused by someone drinking in their homes; and whether a state uses a contributory negligence standard in applying tort law.

To the extent that tort law in general deters harmful behavior, dram shop and social host laws should have the same effect. When adults have standing to sue, however, this may provide an incentive for careless drink-ing behavior, since individuals could sue a bar for allegedly not having con-trolled their drinking, presumably at a time when they were not well positioned to manage their own behavior.

The responsible business practice defense clarifies the legal standard of care by allowing defendant bar owners or managers to claim they ad-hered to the community's standard of care by implementing good server practices. The effect of such a provision on individuals' drinking behav-ior is difficult to predict. From the standpoint of the bar, the business practices defense may increase certainty about the legal negligence stan-dard. Perhaps bars will be more willing to carry out good server practices if the standard is clear. On the other hand, owners or managers who rea-son that implementing a few practices may take the bar "off the hook" in the event of a dram shop suit may consequently be more careless. Also, in general, it may be more difficult for a bar to prove it adhered to good serving practices than to show it was careful in the specific case under consideration by the court. How far this rule prompts bars to monitor ex-cess drinking should be more or less reflected in the self-reports of binge drinking and driving under the influence of alcohol that the BRFS ob-tained.

As we explained in chapter 5, the switch from the standard of contrib-utory negligence to that of comparative negligence may make drinkers less careful, since they will not be completely barred from recovery if found to be partially at fault. The effect of compulsory bodily injury insurance cannot be determined in advance. On the one hand, if drivers purchase more liability insurance that is not experience rated, they will be less careful (moral hazard). On the other hand, if insurers impose surcharges on drivers with bad records, requiring insurance may reduce careless behavior.

A time trend was included in this analysis to account for time-varying aggregate factors common to all states. The preliminary analysis included state binary variables that were highly collinear with the policy variables. Many of the policies had been in effect for several years, making it difficult to disentangle state policies from time-invariant state effects.

Rather than including state binaries, we used variables for state residents' religiousness to represent variations in the taste for drinking versus not drinking. The variables included were a binary for adoption of state-level prohibition before national prohibition and the percentage of the state population who belonged to churches, synagogues, or mosques. The religions included in our analysis were Catholic, Mormon, Jewish, Muslim, Baptist, and other Protestants. The omitted reference group was the percentage of state residents who were not members of an organized religion. Our measures of religious affiliations did not vary over time (Bradley et al. 1992).

Finally, we included variables for miles driven in the state per year and the fraction of highway miles that were rural. The miles driven variables varied by state and year.

CONCEPTUAL FRAMEWORK

We assume that the individual derives positive utility from alcohol but can take certain precautions to prevent loss caused by heavy drinking. The net utility from drinking L is given by

$$L = u(s,y) - (x + p)s - sl(x;R;I), \qquad (9.1)$$

where u = utility; s = number of drinking episodes per time period; y = exogenous variables affecting taste for drinking; x = per episode cost of preventing loss; p = money price per episode; l = expected loss to the individual caused by excessive alcohol consumption per episode; R = strictness of liability regime; and I = index of individual's liability coverage.

Drinking increases the individual's utility, but not without a cost. The cost might be walking home, ordering a taxi, or obtaining a ride from an acquaintance, thereby incurring an obligation to return the favor. Increasing x decreases the expected loss per drinking episode, whereas increasing p

makes the "full price" per drinking episode "$x + p$" higher. An individual maximizes L over s and x. The first-order conditions are

$$L_x = s_s - sl_x = 0 \qquad (9.2)$$

and

$$L_s = u_s - (x + p) - l = 0. \qquad (9.3)$$

According to equation 9.2, the individual purchases prevention up to the amount at which a dollar's worth of expenditure yields a dollar's worth of averted loss $(1 + l_x = 0)$. In equation 9.3, the number of drinking episodes per time period is set at the level where the marginal utility of an episode equals the marginal cost of an episode.

We performed comparative statics analysis to evaluate the effects of changes in R, I, p, and y on x and s, imposing the restriction that l_{xR} is negative and l_{xI} is positive. The results from this pooled time-series cross-section regression are presented in table 9.1. An increase in the strictness of the liability rule increases individuals' care level while decreasing their drinking episodes. Conversely, an increase in insurance coverage decreases the care level and increases alcohol consumption. Individual consumption of alcohol responds negatively to price and positively to an exogenous rise in taste for alcohol, and price and taste have no effect on x.

Analysis of Drinking Behavior: Results
Price

The price of alcohol had no significant effect on the probability of drinking at all, binge drinking, or drinking and driving (table 9.2). The mean value of

Table 9.1 Comparative Statics Analysis

Change in Exogenous Variables	Effect	Sign
Effects on optimal level of x		
R	$sl_{xR}u_{ss}/D$	+
I	$sl_{xI}u_{ss}/D$	−
p	0	0
y	0	0
Effects on optimal level of s		
R	$-sl_{xx}l_R/D$	−
I	$-sl_{xx}lI/D$	+
p	$-sl_{xx}/D$	−
y	$sl_{xx}u_{sy}/D$	+

Note: R = strictness of liability regime; I = index of individual's liability coverage; p = money price per episode; y = exogenous variables affecting taste for drinking.

the index was 0.71, implying an elasticity at the observational means of −0.068. Mean own price elasticities using data from several foreign countries were −0.35 for beer, −0.68 for wine, and −0.98 for liquor (Clements, Yang, and Zheng 1997).

State Policies

Overall, administrative regulation affected the use and abuse of alcohol, as anticipated by advocates of such regulation. The one exception is discussed below. As anticipated, when bar density increased, so did the probability of binge drinking and of drinking and driving, given that one drank at all and given that one binge drank. All these results were statistically significant at the 1 percent level. Allowing grocery stores to sell beer and wine increased the probability of general drinking, binge drinking, and drinking and driving, conditional on general drinking. Restrictions on liquor store advertising decreased the probability of drinking ($p = 0.086$) and drinking and driving, conditional on drinking at all.

The one unanticipated result of this analysis pertained to liquor store density. As density increased, the probability of binge drinking fell significantly. Liquor store customers may drink most alcohol at home, an environment that may be less exciting than a bar but that does not require people to drive. Drinking at home may also be less conducive to drinking large amounts.

The results for criminal law were conflicting. The mandatory minimum fine for the first offense had a significant negative effect on the probability of drinking and driving among all drinkers. A mandatory minimum jail term also was a deterrent for drinking and driving among all drinkers. This variable was nearly significant in the regressions for binge drinking ($p = 0.090$) and drinking and driving among binge drinkers ($p = 0.10$). For each day of additional jail sentence, the probability of binge drinking fell by approximately 0.12. For the remaining variables, the parameter estimate was statistically insignificant. Open container laws were a significant deterrent to drinking and driving among all drinkers and among binge drinkers. Only one other variable in this category—administrative per se—was statistically significant at conventional levels and implied deterrent effects on general drinking. The explanatory variable for mandatory minimum first offense—license sanction—had positive effects on the probability of drinking and was statistically significant at the 5 percent level or better.

Several of the civil liability and insurance variables had statistically significant effects, suggesting that tort liability deters careless drinking and driving. Dram shop laws reduced the probability of engaging in all of the

Table 9.2 Probability of Alcohol Consumption, Binge Drinking, and Drinking and Driving

| | Drink At All | | | Binge Drinking | | | Drinking and Driving | | | | | |
| | | | | | | | Drinkers | | | Binge Drinkers | | |
Variable	Coeff.	Std. Err.	M.E.	Coeff.	Std. Err.	M.E.	Coeff.	Std. Err.	M.E.	Coeff.	Std. Err.	M.E.
Alcohol price	−0.38	0.25	−0.095	−0.31	0.37	−0.054	0.032	0.48	0.0011	−0.094	0.46	−0.012
Alcohol price missing	−0.47[b]	0.23	−0.12	−0.38	0.32	−0.066	−0.15	0.41	−0.0051	−0.21	0.39	−0.028
Administrative law												
Number of bars per 1000 population over 15	0.29	0.19	0.073	0.55[a]	0.14	0.095	0.70[a]	0.17	0.023	0.55[a]	0.14	0.072
Number of liquor stores per 1,000 population over 15	−0.20	0.32	−0.051	−0.74[b]	0.32	−0.13	−0.55	0.37	−0.018	−0.033	0.36	−0.0044
Grocery stores can sell alcohol	0.19[a]	0.072	0.046	0.23[b]	0.091	0.040	0.28[a]	0.11	0.0092	0.0982	0.083	0.011
Restrictions on advertising	−0.11	0.067	−0.029	−0.082	0.056	−0.014	−0.12[b]	0.062	−0.0041	−0.096	0.069	−0.013
Criminal law												
Mandatory minimum first offense:												
Fine	−0.20	0.13	−0.049	−0.15	0.11	−0.027	−0.25[b]	0.13	−0.0082	−0.096	0.14	−0.013
Jail	−0.48	3.19	−0.12	−3.91	2.31	−0.67	−6.59[b]	2.73	−0.22	−3.51	2.14	−0.46
License sanction	0.088[a]	0.027	0.022	−0.016	0.028	−0.0028	−0.014	0.031	−0.0005	0.0085	0.029	0.0011
Seat belt fine	0.43	0.26	0.11	0.24	0.31	0.042	−0.69	0.44	−0.023	−0.71	0.37	−0.093
Open container fine	0.020	0.048	0.0050	−0.081	0.059	−0.014	−0.12[b]	0.049	−0.0040	−0.13[a]	0.040	−0.017
Anticonsumption law: anyone	0.037	0.052	0.0092	−0.0042	0.056	0.0007	0.036	0.046	0.0012	0.035	0.045	0.0046
Anticonsumption law: driver only	0.066	0.065	0.016	0.012	0.062	0.0021	−0.027	0.077	−0.0009	−0.045	0.070	−0.0060
Implied consent	0.076	0.062	0.019	−0.048	0.063	−0.0082	−0.040	0.069	−0.0013	−0.048	0.063	−0.0063
Administrative per se	−0.12[b]	0.052	−0.030	0.049	0.048	0.0085	0.038	0.069	0.0013	−0.021	0.074	−0.0027
Preliminary breath test	0.018	0.052	0.0045	−0.012	0.058	−0.0020	0.0096	0.074	0.0003	−0.022	0.061	−0.0029
Police per 1,000 population	−0.058	0.034	−0.014	0.015	0.026	0.0025	0.057	0.047	0.0019	0.011	0.062	0.0014
Tort law and insurance												
Dram shop law	−0.11[a]	0.018	−0.028	−0.013	0.016	−0.0022	−0.039[b]	0.019	−0.0013	−0.039	0.021	−0.0052
Drinker has standing to sue	0.047	0.061	0.012	0.13[a]	0.047	0.022	0.098[b]	0.048	0.0033	−0.015	0.061	−0.0020
Social host law	0.018	0.051	0.0044	−0.19[a]	0.065	−0.032	−0.24[a]	0.086	−0.0081	−0.13	0.070	−0.017
Responsible business practice	0.031	0.057	0.0077	0.013	0.059	0.0022	−0.042	0.050	−0.0014	−0.047	0.054	−0.0062
Contributory negligence	−0.14[a]	0.054	−0.036	−0.16[a]	0.058	−0.028	−0.18[a]	0.062	−0.0062	−0.11[a]	0.040	−0.014

	Coeff.	Std. Err.	M.E.	Coeff.	Std. Err.	M.E.	Coeff.	Std. Err.	M.E.	Coeff.	Std. Err.	M.E.
Compulsory bodily injury insurance	−0.035	0.059	−0.0087	0.14	0.070	0.023	0.046	0.089	0.0015	−0.066	0.063	−0.0087
Demographic variables												
Age	−0.022[a]	0.0007	−0.0054	−0.041[a]	0.0014	−0.0071	−0.044[a]	0.0022	−0.0015	−0.020[a]	0.0022	−0.0026
Male	0.54[a]	0.018	0.14	1.09[a]	0.028	0.19	0.85[a]	0.044	0.028	0.37[a]	0.052	0.048
Single	0.31[a]	0.021	0.078	0.44[a]	0.031	0.075	0.55[a]	0.047	0.018	0.38[a]	0.052	0.050
High school	0.41[a]	0.020	0.10	−0.24[a]	0.037	−0.041	0.085	0.067	0.0028	0.21[a]	0.067	0.028
Some college	0.63[a]	0.038	0.16	−0.42[a]	0.040	−0.072	0.018	0.070	0.0006	0.24[a]	0.068	0.031
College	0.84[a]	0.038	0.21	−0.61[a]	0.038	−0.11	−0.084	0.069	−0.0028	0.22[a]	0.075	0.029
Caucasian	0.33[a]	0.046	0.082	0.18[a]	0.045	0.031	0.20[a]	0.064	0.0068	0.12	0.068	0.0157
Family income (in 1,000 1995 dollars)	0.011[a]	0.0003	0.0027	−0.0009[b]	0.0004	−0.0001	−0.0002	0.0007	0.0000	0.0006	0.0008	0.0001
Income missing	0.25[a]	0.030	0.063	−0.21[a]	0.034	−0.036	−0.35[a]	0.072	−0.012	−0.23[a]	0.084	−0.030
Unemployed	−0.19[a]	0.034	−0.048	0.15[a]	0.037	0.026	−0.017	0.066	−0.0006	−0.12	0.073	−0.016
Health behaviors												
Smoking	0.56[a]	0.039	0.14	0.75[a]	0.020	0.13	0.39[a]	0.037	0.013	−0.0087	0.043	−0.0011
Exercise sessions per month	0.0050[a]	0.0006	0.0012	−0.0005	0.0008	−0.0009	−0.056[a]	0.0016	−0.0002	−0.0070[a]	0.0015	−0.0009
State characteristics												
Miles driven	0.0090	0.0016	0.0022	0.013	0.013	0.0023	0.032	0.018	0.0011	0.0010	0.016	0.0013
Fraction of miles rural	−0.0011	0.0026	−0.0003	−0.0035	0.0018	−0.0006	−0.0086[a]	0.0025	−0.0003	−0.0072[a]	0.0027	−0.0009
Early adoption of prohibition	−0.12	0.064	−0.031	−0.16[b]	0.062	−0.027	−0.017	0.057	−0.0006	0.040	0.042	0.0053
Percentage Catholic	0.0015	0.0028	0.0004	−0.0025	0.0026	−0.0004	−0.0023	0.0026	−0.0001	−0.0013	0.0024	−0.0002
Percentage Mormon	−0.016[a]	0.0015	−0.0040	0.0011	0.0016	0.0019	−0.0035[b]	0.0016	−0.0001	−0.0022	0.0013	−0.0003
Percentage Jewish	−0.0061	0.016	0.0015	−0.056[a]	0.013	−0.0096	−0.092[a]	0.013	−0.0031	−0.060[a]	0.015	−0.0079
Percentage Baptist	−0.019[a]	0.0028	−0.0046	−0.0050	0.0030	−0.0009	−0.0019	0.0030	−0.0001	0.0009	0.0026	0.0001
Percent other Protestant	−0.0046	0.0037	−0.0012	−0.0006	0.0038	−0.0001	0.0040	0.0039	0.0001	0.073[b]	0.0035	0.0009
Trend	−0.0075	0.0076	−0.0019	0.032[a]	0.0087	0.0055	−0.015	0.0098	−0.0005	−0.025[a]	0.0077	−0.0033
Constant	0.16	0.36	0.041	0.089	0.40	0.015	−2.09[a]	0.59	−0.070	−0.97	0.62	−0.13
Chi-square$_{(44)}$	41373.99			20781.78			33531.64			8103.07		
$p >$ chi-square	0.0000			0.0000			0.0000			0.0000		
		$N = 175{,}990$			$N = 86{,}273$			$N = 87{,}087$			$N = 22{,}261$	

[a]Statistically significant at 1 percent level.
[b]Statistically significant at 5 percent level.
Coeff. = coefficient; Std. Err. = standard error; M.E. = marginal effect.
Table reports nonstandardized regression coefficients.

negative behaviors. The results were significant for drinking at all and for drinking and driving among all drinkers and were almost significant ($p = 0.056$) for drinking and driving among binge drinkers. The results on whether adult drinkers could sue bars suggest that allowing adult patrons to sue for their own negative behavior encourages binge drinking and drinking and driving for persons who said they had drunk some during the last month. These results were statistically significant at the 5 percent or 1 percent level in each regression.

Social host liability decreased the probability of binge drinking and of drinking and driving among all drinkers and was nearly significant for drinking and driving among binge drinkers ($p = 0.061$). However, it had a positive effect on the probability of drinking at all, suggesting that hosts still serve alcohol in states with social host liability but may serve less to guests who are likely to drive home.

Employing the contributory negligence standard reduced the probability of drinking at all, binge drinking, and drinking and driving, conditional on both drinking at all and binge drinking, at statistically significant levels of 1 percent or better. Compulsory motor vehicle insurance increased binge drinking. As noted above, compulsory insurance lowers the precautionary level in that the loss resulting from an injury is covered (moral hazard). But if the premium is experience rated, careless individuals are made to pay for the harm they cause, or for violations of laws, through higher liability premiums in future years. Our result suggests that moral hazard dominates, as it would under weak experience rating of liability insurance premiums.

Personal Characteristics

Analyzing the effects of personal characteristics on the decisions to drink, binge drink, and drink and drive revealed that younger people were more likely to engage in all these bad behaviors at statistically significant levels of 1 percent or better. Males and single persons were much more likely to do so at the 1 percent level or better.

Those with at least a high school diploma were more likely to drink at all but less likely to binge drink. However, those with a high school education or more who binge drank were more likely to drink and drive than those with less education. These variables were all statistically significant at the 1 percent level or better. Those with higher family incomes were also more likely to drink but less likely to binge drink. This effect was also statistically significant at the 1 percent level or better. Unemployed people were less likely to drink but more likely to binge drink.

Smokers were more likely to drink and to binge drink and drink and drive, conditional on drinking. In these three regressions, the coefficient on the smoking variable was statistically significant at the 1 percent level. Those who exercised were more likely to drink but were less likely to drink and drive in both drinking and driving regressions.

Driving patterns also appear to have some effect on drinking behavior. Those who drove more total miles were more likely to drink and drive at an almost statistically significant level ($p = 0.067$). Those driving more rural miles, however, were significantly less likely to drink and drive in both regressions and were almost significantly less likely to binge drink ($p = 0.053$).

State Characteristics

Persons living in a state that adopted prohibition before national prohibition were significantly less likely to binge drink and were almost significantly less likely to drink at all ($p = 0.056$). This finding implies that preferences for drinking or not drinking prevalent in particular geographic areas change very slowly. Many of the state prohibition laws were enacted a century before the BRFS data were collected.

Residents of states with more Mormons were less likely to drink at all (significant at the 1 percent level) and were significantly less likely to drink and drive, contingent on drinking. In states with a high percentage of Mormons, binge drinkers were also less likely to drink and drive at a nearly significant level ($p = 0.077$). Residents of states with higher percentages of Baptists were also significantly less likely to drink. High percentages of Jewish people significantly decreased the probability of binge drinking and drunk driving for all drinkers and for binge drinkers.

Trend

We found a trend toward a decline in drinking and driving among binge drinkers, significant at the 1 percent level. However, the coefficient on the trend variable in the analysis of binge drinking was positive and statistically significant at the 1 percent level, implying a secular trend in the direction of heavier drinking among those who drink. This trend controlled for other factors affecting heavy drinking.

ANALYSIS OF MOTOR VEHICLE FATALITIES: DATA AND EMPIRICAL SPECIFICATIONS

Data on state-level prices and criminal and civil sanctions were assembled and merged with state rates of traffic fatalities from the Fatal Analysis Reporting System (FARS) database. All variables, except state-specific dummy variables, were state- and year-specific from 1984 to 1995. Local police departments are required by federal law to submit detailed information on each motor vehicle crash leading to a fatality. Among the variables collected by FARS is information on time and location of the accident and whether the drivers involved were under the influence of alcohol. FARS collects two measures of alcohol involvement. One is the police officer's evaluation of whether the driver had been drinking before the accident. This evaluation may be based on formal breath, blood, or urine test results or on other evidence concerning the driver's behavior or alcohol on the driver's breath. The other measure is the blood alcohol content (BAC). Although the latter variable is conceptually superior to the former measure of drinking by drivers, especially in the years before 1990 or so, there were many missing values because police failed to conduct BAC tests in spite of federal law mandating such testing.

Dependent Variables

We examined three state motor vehicle death rates separately for those under the legal drinking age (fifteen to twenty) and for those aged twenty-one to sixty-four: total motor vehicle death rate; total alcohol-related death rate as defined by a police report; and single-car night driving death rate, which accounts for a high proportion of alcohol-related deaths. The last variable is useful because police reporting of alcohol use is not universal or systematic.

To analyze the relation between highway mortality rates and the various policy variables, we first used the standard minimum logit chi-square method (Maddala 1983). The dependent variables were logit transformations of the six mortality rate categories (three types of mortality and two age groups) for each state. Weighted least squares regressions were used to account for the variance structure. The weights were given by $[n_{ijt}p_{ijt}(1 - p_{ijt})]^{1/2}$ where n = state population for the i age group in j state in year t. The corresponding mortality rate is represented by p. To explore the panel structure of our data, we also estimated the model above, assuming a first-order autoregressive process in the error terms. The generalized estimating equation method for panel data (Liang and Zeger 1986) was used in the estimation. We calculated Huber-White robust variance estimates to control for heteroscedasticity or misspecified correlation structure.

Explanatory Variables

For measures of administrative regulation, we included measures of bar and liquor density as defined above in the analysis of drinking behavior. State-level criminal policies included in the analyses were preliminary breath test; zero tolerance for minors whereby driving with blood alcohol content levels over 0.0 is considered "drunk driving"; implied consent; administrative per se; fine for not wearing a seat belt; DUI first-offense fine; mandatory minimum jail sentence for first offense; mandatory minimum first-offense license sanction; open alcohol container law; anticonsumption laws, both for any vehicle occupant and for drivers only; and police per thousand state population.

We included three dram shop variables in each of the death rate analyses: for minors, whether the state had a dram shop law for minors, whether minor drinkers were allowed to sue, and liability for social hosts serving minors; for adults, whether the state had a dram shop law for adult drinkers, whether adult drinkers could sue a commercial server of alcohol, and liability for social hosts serving intoxicated adults. In addition, we included variables for states allowing a responsible business practice defense, contributory negligence, and compulsory bodily injury insurance.

Other covariates described state characteristics that may influence the motor vehicle fatality rates: the state index of alcohol prices, mean miles driven annually, the percentage of miles driven on rural roads, per capita income, and the unemployment rate. A trend variable accounted for variation by year and state binary variables (not shown in the table with the regressions) for unaccountable differences by state.

ANALYSIS OF MOTOR VEHICLE FATALITIES: RESULTS
Effects of Tort Liability on Minors

Imposing tort liability on commercial servers for serving underage drinkers reduced motor vehicle fatality rates, irrespective of the dependent variable used (table 9.3). Implementing a responsible business practice defense had a negative effect on alcohol-related deaths that was almost statistically significant at conventional levels ($p = 0.072$). For total deaths, imposing compulsory liability insurance increased the fatality rate. Although positive, only one of the coefficients on this variable was statistically significant at conventional levels. Social host liability had unanticipated positive coefficients in the total death and single-car nighttime death regressions. For total deaths, the standard error was small relative to its coefficient.

Effects of Tort Liability on Adults

As in the minor fatality rate regressions, imposing liability on bars for serving obviously intoxicated adults reduced motor vehicle fatalities for all three dependent variables (table 9.4). None of the other tort variables were statistically significant in the adult regressions.

Table 9.3 Motor Vehicle Fatality Rates for Minors

Variable	Minor Total Deaths		Minor Alcohol-Related Deaths		Minor Single-Car Night Driving Deaths	
	Coeff.	Std. Err.	Coeff.	Std. Err.	Coeff.	Std. Err.
Alcohol price index	−0.20	0.14	−0.67[b]	0.33	−0.13	0.25
Alcohol price index missing	−0.14	0.11	−0.46	0.27	−0.070	0.20
Administrative law						
Number of bars per 1,000 population over 15	0.26	0.20	−0.13	0.30	−0.12	0.36
Number of liquor stores per 1,000 population over 15	0.17	0.28	−0.27	0.38	0.16	0.57
Criminal law						
Mandatory minimum first offense:						
Fine	−0.18	0.094	−0.31	0.18	−0.37[b]	0.17
Jail	0.88	0.69	3.43[a]	1.24	0.64	1.69
License sanction	−0.073	0.046	−0.24[b]	0.094	−0.038	0.084
Seat belt fine	0.10	0.24	0.10	0.56	−0.73	0.83
Open container law	0.034	0.058	−0.028	0.13	0.096	0.067
Anticonsumption law: anyone	−0.12	0.061	−0.88	0.13	−0.13	0.10
Anticonsumption law: driver only	0.14[a]	0.054	0.14	0.10	0.076	0.092
Implied consent	0.019	0.029	0.27	0.063	−0.049	0.045
Administrative per se	−0.050	0.026	−0.059	0.042	−0.068	0.046

	Coeff.	Std. Err.	Coeff.	Std. Err.	Coeff.	Std. Err.
Preliminary breath test	0.099[b]	0.047	0.13	0.081	0.13	0.070
Zero tolerance	0.035	0.031	−0.11	0.075	0.010	0.068
Police per 1,000 population	0.072[a]	0.026	0.038	0.079	0.11[a]	0.040
Tort law and insurance						
Dram shop law	−0.37[a]	0.096	−0.34[b]	0.16	−0.48[a]	0.16
Drinker has standing to sue	0.029	0.030	0.045	0.059	−0.045	0.047
Social host law	0.076[a]	0.022	−0.0019	0.047	0.072	0.047
Responsible business practice	−0.018	0.042	−0.12	0.066	0.009	0.082
Contributory negligence	−0.031	0.042	0.069	0.057	−0.015	0.067
Compulsory bodily injury insurance	0.10[a]	0.032	0.062	0.047	0.047	0.047
Demographic variables						
Per capita income	−0.016[b]	0.0070	−0.032[b]	0.014	−0.039[a]	0.012
Unemployed	−5.36[a]	0.96	−6.45[a]	1.37	−4.75[a]	1.42
State characteristics						
Miles driven	0.011	0.0085	0.030	0.041	−0.011	0.017
Fraction of miles rural	0.0055[b]	0.0024	0.011	0.0064	0.0015	0.0034
Trend	−0.023[a]	0.0087	−0.048[a]	0.018	−0.0006	0.016
Chi-square$_{(26)}$	5342.59		27264.73		7794.23	
$p >$ chi-square	0.0000		0.0000		0.0000	
	$N = 595$		$N = 595$		$N = 595$	

[a]Statistically significant at the 1 percent level (two-tailed t-test).
[b]Statistically significant at the 5 percent level (two-tailed t-test).
Coeff. = coefficient; Std. Err. = robust standard error.
Table reports nonstandardized regression coefficients.

Table 9.4 Motor Vehicle Fatality Rates for Adults

Variable	Adult Total Deaths		Adult Alcohol-Related Deaths		Adult Single-Car Night Driving Deaths	
	Coeff.	Std. Err.	Coeff.	Std. Err.	Coeff.	Std. Err.
Alcohol price index	−0.10	0.12	−0.12	0.22	0.011	0.16
Alcohol prince index missing	−0.086	0.092	−0.071	0.16	0.018	0.14
Administrative law						
Number of bars per 1,000 population over age 15	0.24[a]	0.082	0.20	0.18	0.24[b]	0.12
Number of liquor stores per 1,000 population over age 15	0.040	0.12	0.21	0.25	0.20	0.23
Criminal law						
Mandatory minimum first offense:						
Fine	−0.0018	0.074	−0.088	0.12	−0.0021	0.083
Jail	0.46	0.78	1.99	2.00	−0.098	1.15
License sanction	0.0080	0.019	−0.14	0.087	−0.017	0.020
Seat belt fine	0.080	0.094	−0.18	0.25	0.12	0.18
Open container law	−0.053	0.031	−0.13[a]	0.044	−0.028	0.041
Anticonsumption law: anyone	−0.0006	0.040	−0.039	0.069	−0.0099	0.040
Anticonsumption law: driver only	0.0052	0.040	0.081	0.073	−0.019	0.037
Implied consent	0.031	0.021	0.022	0.048	0.038	0.023
Administrative per se	−0.042[a]	0.015	−0.058[b]	0.027	−0.046	0.025
Preliminary breath test	−0.0055	0.015	0.0060	0.035	0.0031	0.029

	Coeff.	Std. Err.	Coeff.	Std. Err.	Coeff.	Std. Err.
Police per 1,000 population	0.017	0.020	-0.11	0.067	0.0013	0.030
Tort law and insurance						
Dram shop law	-0.40[a]	0.044	-0.31[a]	0.13	-0.24[a]	0.060
Drinker has standing to sue	0.0005	0.024	0.041	0.036	-0.011	0.029
Social host law	-0.025	0.021	-0.044	0.046	-0.0038	0.027
Responsible business practice	-0.0096	0.020	-0.052	0.044	-0.040	0.031
Contributory negligence	-0.029	0.046	0.050	0.084	0.025	0.034
Compulsory bodily injury insurance	0.012	0.022	0.0071	0.034	0.017	0.027
Demographic variables						
Per capita income	-0.0009	0.0050	-0.013	0.010	-0.0098	0.0064
Unemployed	-3.94[a]	0.38	-5.01[a]	0.98	-4.04[a]	0.61
State characteristics						
Miles driven	0.011	0.0074	0.028	0.031	0.0094	0.0081
Fraction of miles rural	0.0020	0.0014	0.0045[b]	0.0040	0.0012	0.0018
Trend	-0.027[a]	0.0060	-0.030[b]	0.012	-0.020[a]	0.0078
Chi-square$_{(26)}$	68758.30		7316.59		46362.75	
p > chi-square	0.0000		0.0000		0.0000	
	$N = 595$		$N = 595$		$N = 595$	

[a]Statistically significant at the 1 percent level (two-tailed t-test).
[b]Statistically significant at the 5 percent level (two-tailed t-test).
Coeff. = coefficient; Std. Err. = robust standard error.
Table reports nonstandardized regression coefficients.

Effects of Criminal Law on Minors

For single-car nighttime accidents, imposing mandatory minimum first-offense fines reduced fatalities. For the other two dependent variables this policy also had a deterrent effect, but the results were not quite statistically significant at conventional levels ($p = 0.056$ for total deaths and $p = 0.081$ for alcohol-related deaths). Implementing mandatory minimum first-offense license sanctions reduced alcohol-related deaths. Other results with almost significant coefficients were administrative per se license revocation, which reduced total deaths ($p = 0.052$), and anticonsumption law for all vehicle occupants, which also reduced total deaths ($p = 0.054$).

Some policies had statistically significant effects, but the coefficients implied implausible and certainly unintended influences. These were preliminary breath tests for total deaths; mandatory minimum first-offense jail term for alcohol-related deaths; and anticonsumption law, driver only, for total deaths.

Effects of Criminal Law on Adults

Administrative per se license revocation reduced total deaths and alcohol-related deaths. In the single-car analysis, the deterrent effect of this policy was almost statistically significant ($p = 0.068$). A ban on open containers reduced alcohol-related deaths. Mandatory minimum first-offense license sanctions also reduced alcohol-related deaths; the coefficient on this variable was almost statistically significant at conventional levels ($p = 0.099$). As in the corresponding analysis for minors, anticonsumption laws for drivers had only an implausibly positive impact on total deaths.

Effects of Alcohol Price on Minors and Adults

Although the coefficients were all negative, alcohol price had a statistically significant effect only on alcohol-related deaths in the analysis of minors. For adults, the price coefficient was negative in two of the three regressions but never statistically significant at conventional levels.

Effects of State Characteristics on Minors

State per capita income consistently had a negative effect on fatality rates, as did unemployment. The trend variable had a negative effect on deaths and was statistically significant in two of the three regressions. In the analysis of total deaths, the percentage of miles driven on rural roads had a positive effect. Police per thousand population had an implausible positive effect on fatality rates.

Effects of State Characteristics on Adults

Consistent with the analysis of minors, unemployment and trend had negative effects. A higher number of bars per thousand population over age fifteen increased total deaths and single-car nighttime deaths.

CONCLUSION

Several studies have used state-year panel data to examine the influence of various potential deterrents, including price, minimum drinking age, and various criminal sanctions on motor vehicle mortality and on mortality from other causes often related to heavy alcohol consumption (Cook and Tauchen 1984; Males 1986; DuMouchel, Williams, and Zador 1987; Saffer and Grossman 1987; Chaloupka, Saffer, and Grossman 1993; and Sloan, Reilly, and Schenzler 1994a, 1994b). The observational periods and details of empirical specification differed for each, but these studies used essentially the same method. Among variables associated with the threat of criminal liability were mandatory jail terms for DUI, mandatory license revocations, fines for not using a seat belt, and police per thousand state population. Although an increase in alcohol price reduced mortality fairly consistently, results on the criminal sanction variables were mixed. No single sanction uniformly had a statistically significant effect on death rates. Of these variables, police staffing was perhaps the criminal deterrent with the most consistent effect on alcohol-related mortality.

Effects of Tort Law and Insurance on Individual Choices

Dram shop laws allow parties injured by alcohol-impaired individuals to sue those who served them alcohol. Such laws are civil deterrents, implemented either legislatively or judicially, that make the server potentially liable for actual damage caused by an intoxicated customer or guest. Commercial alcohol servers have long opposed dram shop laws, arguing that drinkers should be responsible for their own actions (Jacobs 1989). Advocates argue that the threat of civil liability encourages servers to monitor drinking behavior. Empirical analyses have consistently demonstrated the effectiveness of dram shop liability in reducing mortality (Chaloupka, Saffer, and Grossman 1993; Kenkel 1993; Sloan, Reilly, and Schenzler 1994a, 1994b; Ruhm 1996).

Our study confirms these prior findings on the effectiveness of tort liability both in deterring heavy drinking and in reducing fatalities from alcohol-related motor vehicle accidents. Other than unemployment rate increases, minor and adult dram shop laws have the strongest impact on fatality rates. Dram shop liability was effective in reducing the number of people who chose to drink at all and who chose to binge drink. Among the people who drank at all and who binge drank, however, dram shop liability did not have significant deterrent effects on those who self-reported episodes of drunk driving.

To our knowledge, this is the first empirical study of the effectiveness of social host liability. In our analysis, a higher fraction of persons who drank lived in states that recognize such liability. Social host liability, however, was highly effective in curbing binge drinking and self-reported episodes of drunk driving both among those choosing to drink and among binge drinkers. It lowered the adult death rate from alcohol-related motor vehicle accidents somewhat but had no effect on the fatality rate for minors. Adults may be more responsible in naming a designated driver or finding other ways to get home after drinking in someone's home.

There is always a question of cause and effect. Social host liability may have been adopted in states with a particular type of drinking behavior. To deal with this issue, we included state binary variables in the analysis of motor vehicle mortality to detect state effects, such as drinking preferences, that we did not directly measure. In the analysis of drinking behaviors, we included explanatory variables for religion and state adoption of prohibition before national prohibition. These variables are plausibly correlated with drinking preferences or tastes for drinking that we could not measure directly.

Imposing third-party liability is very unpopular both among commercial servers of alcoholic beverages and among people giving parties. The public is not uniformly devoted to such measures to deter individual drunk drivers (Applegate et al. 1995). Extending responsibility to people other than the drunk driver is an unpopular alternative: 82 percent of citizens oppose making it possible for victims of drunk drivers to sue bar owners for accidents caused by those who drink at their bars. Citizens are reluctant to support policies that intrude on their own rights or conveniences (Applegate et al. 1995). But imposing this type of liability has proved an effective method of deterring heavy drinking and drunk driving.

Effects of Criminal Sanctions

Most available evidence suggests that administrative per se laws reduce motor vehicle fatalities (Chaloupka, Saffer, and Grossman 1993; Kenkel 1993), but there is also some evidence that such laws are ineffective (e.g., Ruhm 1996). Mandatory jail terms for DUI showed deterrent effects in some studies (Kenkel 1993; Sloan and Githens 1994) but had no effect in others (Wilkinson 1987; Chaloupka, Saffer, and Grossman 1993; Evans, Neville, and Graham 1991; and Ruhm 1996).

Criminal sanctions such as jail sentences, fines, and license revocation for DUI convictions also focus on the behavioral consequences of excessive drinking. Subsequently, many states have imposed mandatory minimum jail terms, minimum fines, and minimum periods of license revocation or suspension for DUI conviction. The rationale of these sanctions is to increase the certainty of punishment, thereby deterring driving under the influence. All states except New Hampshire and Wisconsin allow jail sentences for first offenders, with most states allowing judges considerable discretion in sentencing. Seventeen states (1995) have mandatory sentencing or community service after the first DUI conviction. Ross concluded that laws that increase the perceived certainty of punishment have short-term effectiveness (Ross 1987), but have little deterrent effect in the long run owing to a decline in the public's perception that the laws will be enforced (Chaloupka, Saffer, and Grossman 1993).

Various criminal sanctions focus directly on abusive behavior resulting from excessive use of alcohol. For example, before mandatory sentencing laws for drinking and driving, only 5.5 percent of county prison admissions were DUI offenders, compared with almost 40 percent in the early 1990s when these became prevalent (U.S. Federal Bureau of Investigation 1992). The combined effects of increased DUI news coverage and DUI law enforcement have been found to increase the public's perception of the risk of arrest and to decrease drinking and driving (Voas, Holder, and Gruenewald 1997; Deshapriya and Iwase 1996).

As of the mid-1990s, most states defined legal intoxication by a specific blood alcohol content. In all states except South Carolina and Massachusetts, driving with a BAC greater than 0.10 is considered a crime (Blank 1994). In sixteen states the legal BAC level has been lowered to 0.08. Lowering the BAC level was reportedly related to recent declines in the proportion of fatal crashes involving fatally injured drivers whose blood alcohol levels were 0.08 or higher and 0.15 or higher (Hingson 1996). However, the reporting of BAC is not standardized across states. For example, in Pennsylvania the police must have probable cause to believe the driver is intoxicated in order to request a BAC test (Blank 1994). The person in question must act intoxicated. Therefore a police officer would not request a BAC test for someone found unconscious at the site of a motor vehicle accident because the unconscious state may have been caused by the crash. A North Carolina study found that alcohol-impaired drivers who require emergency room treatment for injuries are infrequently charged with drinking while impaired (Runge et al. 1996). As Ruhm (1996) showed, the empirical findings on the deterrent effects of alcohol policies, including criminal laws, are highly dependent on equation specification. In general, models used in past work have been too lean. In our research we included many more policy variables, including a broader set of tort and administrative regulation variables.

With our larger set of explanatory variables, on balance, we found that most of the criminal laws studied were not effective. Exceptions were mandatory fines and jail terms for drinking and driving among all drinkers, which were also effective in reducing motor vehicle mortality for minors. As in some previous studies, administrative per se laws reduced fatalities for adults but according to self-reports had no deterrent effect on binge drinking or on drinking and driving. Unlike some previous research, states with more police staffing had higher fatality rates for minors in the total death and single-car nighttime driving regressions. In contrast to Chaloupka, Saffer, and Grossman (1993), we found evidence in both the drinking and adult fatality analyses that open container laws are effective deterrents.

On balance, we are left with a pessimistic view about the influence of criminal laws in this context. It would probably be fruitless to keep reestimating equations like ours with different specifications in an attempt to "rescue" these policies.

Effects of Administrative Regulation

Not surprisingly, more deaths among adults, more binge drinking, and more drunk driving occurred in areas with high concentrations of bars. These results emphasize the need for careful planning and for making zoning laws available to administrative agencies responsible for issuing alcohol licenses. We obtained a counterintuitive result on liquor stores, namely that binge drinking decreased with an increased density of liquor stores. Perhaps, in contrast to bars, liquor from retail stores is bought mainly for home use and for persons who drink moderately.

Results from our analysis of motor vehicle fatality rates were consistent with those for drinking and for drinking and driving. Increased bar density raised fatalities for adults but not for minors. The drinking and the drinking and driving data used in the behavioral risk analysis were only for persons aged eighteen and over. Thus we could not perform a parallel analysis for minors with these dependent variables. Liquor store density had no statistically significant effect on any of the fatality rates we analyzed.

Previous research on the effects of administrative regulation and the availability of retail alcoholic beverage outlets in general has been far more limited than has research on criminal sanctions. Wilkinson (1987) found that allowing outlets to close later than 2:00 A.M. had a negligible influence on consumption. The number of outlets had a small but significant effect on alcohol demand. Restrictions on advertising reduced consumption by 7 percent. Persons living in monopoly states drank 5 percent less alcohol than those in license states.

Raising Price to Deter Excess Use of Alcohol and Its Adverse Effects

Previous research has also demonstrated that raising prices deters alcohol use. This is generally accomplished by imposing taxes on alcohol, which in turn are reflected in higher consumer prices. Various empirical studies suggest that alcohol use is negatively related to price and positively related to family income (see, e.g., Manning et al. 1991). Chaloupka, Saffer, and Grossman (1993) found that beer taxes have a negative effect on drunk driving, greater for young drivers than for older drivers. According to this study, the most effective policies are the beer tax and the relatively severe one-year administrative license action. Raising the beer tax to its 1951 real value would lower fatalities by 11.5 percent. In relative terms, Chaloupka rated the next most effective policies as having a minimum drinking age of twenty-one, having dram shop laws, and having a high mandatory minimum fine of $500.

Kenkel (1993) found that price had a negative and statistically significant effect on heavy drinking. He also found that drinking by young adults was more sensitive to price than drinking by other age groups. Young adults were more likely to experience a substantial income effect owing to price change and were more likely to be influenced by peers or bandwagon effects that increase the price elasticity of demand. Additionally, young adults' demand for drunk driving is more responsive to changes in the price of alcoholic beverages than that of adults of legal drinking age. Alcohol price has been shown to reduce traffic accident fatalities (e.g., Saffer and Grossman 1987). According to Wilkinson (1987), one fatality can be prevented by increasing DUI fines by $148.90 or by increasing the price of a gallon of ethanol by $6.78 (1995 dollars).

With the large number of explanatory variables, including state binary variables, we did not obtain a statistically significant alcohol price on motor vehicle fatalities either for adults or for minors.

Secular Trends in Heavy Drinking and Its Adverse Effects

Snortum and Berger (1989) found that in 1983 and in 1986 drivers in the United States exhibited increasing control and restraint in drinking and driving. They also documented a reduction in alcohol-related fatalities over the same period. These are also examples of long-term behavioral changes influenced by stricter drinking and driving legislation.

Holding the many covariates in our regressions constant, we too found secular trends in drinking and driving and in motor vehicle fatality rates. The reasons underlying these trends are necessarily speculative. It is plausible to expect that the same publicity about drinking and driving as a social problem that resulted in the enactment of many new criminal laws and the expansion of tort liability also influenced social norms about excessive drinking and driving. However, there is one notable exception to our findings. We found a positive trend in self-reported binge drinking, holding the other determinants of binge drinking constant. This suggests that a trend toward less alcohol use may be obscuring the change in the distribution of drinking. That is, there may be an increase in drinking by a minority of adults while at the same time moderate drinkers are reducing their consumption. This pattern is worth watching.

10

Conclusions and Policy Implications

In this book we have both presented new empirical evidence and summarized the literature on alcohol use, drinking and driving, more general issues of regulation, and the laws relevant to our analysis. Much of the new empirical evidence was based on our surveys of commercial servers of alcohol, their employees, and agencies that regulate alcohol establishments and servers.

This research is important for at least two reasons. First, on a general level, the deterrent effect of tort liability has not been well documented in any field. There is also a lack of understanding regarding how tort relates to other forms of law and regulation. However, the theoretical analyses of tort as a deterrent are optimistic about its effects (e.g., Brown 1973; Shavell 1980).

Although tort law has several goals—compensating victims, providing retribution, and furnishing information for injury victims—its main goal is to create incentives for taking care and thereby reduce the rate of accidents. Conceptually, the negligence standard of care is to be set at the point where the marginal cost of prevention and the marginal benefit of loss averted meet. Once this standard is set, under a well-functioning system there should be no negligence and no need for liability insurance.

Reality clearly conflicts with this prediction. Measured against this tough standard of eliminating the need for liability insurance and for lawsuits, tort law is clearly a failure. Motor vehicle accidents are frequent, and intoxicated drivers cause many of them. Tort is under attack from many quarters, ranging from firms in danger of being named in lawsuits to legal scholars who base their arguments in large part on the high cost of litigation, how slowly the system operates, the comparatively few injury victims who are compensated, and the variable results from the judicial system both in determining liability—enforcing the negligence standard—and in setting damages (see, e.g., Bovbjerg, Sloan, and Blumstein 1989; Huber 1988; O'Connell and Partlett 1988; Schwartz 1997; Sugarman 1989). Variability in results not only is unfair but may interfere with the signals tort transmits to a party in a position to take precautions.

Given that these weaknesses of tort are well accepted, its main rationale is deterrence. It is inappropriate to hold tort to the absolute standard of eliminating negligence, and to the extent that imposing tort reduces careless behavior and accidents, it should be possible to tolerate many of its other deficiencies.

Although the effectiveness of tort as a deterrent in any one area may not generalize to others, the accumulation of evidence on its success in a number of fields may ultimately help societies decide whether to enhance or, alternatively, curb its use. Favorable findings from earlier studies on tort as a deterrent of motor vehicle fatalities in general (DeWees, Duff, and Trebilcock 1996; Schwartz 1994), and of dram shop liability in particular, encouraged us to undertake this more detailed investigation. To our knowledge, our study is the first to conduct a national survey of commercial servers of alcohol about the actions they take (or do not take) to deter alcohol abuse.

Tort may be effective in deterring some types of injuries but not others. Shavell (1984) developed a framework for identifying those situations in which either tort liability or government regulations might be more appropriate for reducing injury. He argued that tort is advantageous when private parties are well informed about the underlying risks and the cost of avoiding accidents; when harm is concentrated in a few injury victims, which increases their incentives to file tort claims; and when causation is relatively easy to prove. Conversely, he concluded that regulation is preferred when the optimal degree of precaution is not individualized to particular circumstances; when the regulatory agency has better information than private persons; when injurers are unlikely to have the wealth to cover the losses they cause; and when lawsuits are rare because losses are highly dispersed and causation is difficult to prove. For these reasons, automobile accidents and some product-related accidents tend to be more appropriate for tort, whereas environmental and occupational injuries are more appropriate for regulation.

Dram shop liability arguably falls in the former category. Monitoring excess consumption of patrons is obviously feasible; the losses drunk drivers generate are borne by a few victims; fault is relatively easy to determine; and regulatory agencies cannot possibly oversee the myriad situations in which alcohol is consumed. The police and the alcohol law enforcement agencies are monitors, but in a more passive way. Monitoring by ABCs is more indirect, such as by regulating entry.

Tort suits resulting from motor vehicle accidents are among the most numerous types of lawsuits. Yet because payments per case tend to be far lower than for other types of injury, particularly medical malpractice and products liability, auto torts receive much less emphasis in discussions of public policy (see, e.g., Schuck 1991). This is probably less a reflection of their importance than the result of a lack of a sufficiently well-organized and motivated constituency—such as physicians against medical malpractice and manufacturers against products liability—to argue how "terrible" tort suits are.

If the policy target is deterrence, at least conceptually, employing so many forms of regulatory control seems superfluous. Yet not only in the United States but throughout the world, other instruments of control are utilized to promote roadway safety. In fact, as we explained in previous chapters, far more reliance is placed on administrative regulation and criminal law than on tort. A quick explanation is that potential tort-feasors do not have the resources to fully pay for the losses they may cause, and therefore tort cannot suffice as a deterrent. The roots of these alternative forms of control go back too far for us to believe that they were based on a rational cost versus benefit calculation, even if such calculations are integral to the political process of today.

Not only have we examined the role of tort as a deterrent, but we have also compared tort with other major forms of regulation. As a method for curbing excessive alcohol abuse, tort has not been the main policy instrument. Rather, control has been the responsibility of public alcohol agencies and the state and local police. Taxing alcoholic beverages has been a source of revenue for federal, state, and local governments as well as a deterrent to drinking and driving and other socially harmful behavior.

We are among several groups of scholars who have examined the effects of the various forms of regulation on motor vehicle fatalities and the prevalence of drinking and driving. We have extended previous work, both expanding the variables considered and updating empirical research to the mid-1990s. To our knowledge this is the first quantitative comparison of the regulation of commercial servers of alcohol, although such regulation dates back centuries. Because we collected our own data, we were able to make direct comparisons of behavioral responses of bar owners and employees to alternative forms of control.

Specific institutions surround the regulation of alcohol use. We cannot know for sure that our results on the relative performance of alternative instruments are generalizable. At the end of the day, only by accumulating evidence from a number of sources can one come to a general conclusion about the relative effectiveness of various deterrents and develop a more general theory about the circumstances in which specific ones are effective or ineffective. The study should be viewed as part of a larger effort to understand their performance.

A second purpose was to better understand a major cause of mortality, morbidity, job loss, and individual and family dysfunction—drinking too much alcohol. Alcohol is a major killer, far more than many causes of deaths that receive more widespread attention in the media. Yet most often alcohol use does not achieve this level of recognition. Moderate, responsible drinking generally does not have harmful effects. Also, the adverse outcomes from heavy drinking seem largely to accrue to the individual, and in contrast to some other major diseases, such as some forms of cancer, adverse outcomes are largely under the control of the individual drinker.

As we discussed in chapter 1, both the moral considerations and the high social costs of heavy drinking, including the external costs (see, e.g., Manning et al. 1989), have provided a rationale for public intervention in private consumption decisions. Even if this study did not provide scientific evidence on general questions of economics and the law, it would be important for what it implies about a major public health issue. Insofar as measures aimed at preventing heavy drinking and associated behaviors succeed, a direct consequence will be a much healthier public. Whether people are happier—better off in the sense of higher social utility—is another matter. Concerns about the adverse welfare effects of restricting consumer choice have been at the heart of political opposition to strict control measures, although the arguments have not used this exact terminology.

Major Findings

The conclusion sections have reviewed the findings of each chapter, and we will not repeat them all here. Rather, we focus on what we see as our major findings.

Behavior of Regulatory Systems

Various public enforcement systems are involved in alcohol control. The most important are alcoholic beverage commissions (ABCs), alcohol law enforcement agencies (ALEs), police departments, and the courts.

By design, alcohol control regulation is engineered to limit the entry of commercial sellers of alcohol. In most industries, such barriers are considered bad in that they confer de facto franchises on firms that do gain entry, but reducing heavy consumption of alcohol is desirable given the costs imposed by such behavior. However, because there was only one state without a licensing system (Nevada), we could not compare entry patterns in states with and without such controls. The lack of regulation in Nevada may reflect preference differences between its residents and those of other states, but we could not explicitly measure such differences. (See, for example, Fuchs's "A Tale of Two States": Nevada and Utah [1974, 52–54].)

Instead, we identified differences in the structures of state alcohol control schemes that we later found to be correlated with the stringency of regulation. For example, we found fewer bars per thousand population in states with advertising restrictions. We also found that a history of alcohol prohibition at the state level played a part in the way ABC agencies are structured today. We found that other policies, such as banning the sale of beer and wine in drugstores and grocery stores, increased the number of bars, reflecting a substitution effect.

We also found, not surprisingly, that certain demographic characteristics affected the number of bars. Religious preference had some effect: there were fewer bars in counties with high populations of religious groups that characteristically oppose drinking alcohol.

Clearly, entry patterns are affected by state alcohol regulations; however, each state agency controls alcohol through a unique combination of policies that partly reflect the social norms of the community. It is therefore difficult to draw conclusions about the effectiveness of any single administrative policy in isolation.

We found substantial variation in police resources, regardless of how such resources were measured; we measured full-time equivalent personnel employed, as well as other indicators such as citations per bar in the police department's jurisdiction. The resulting variation in activity is to be expected, since police departments plausibly attach different priorities to alcohol control, and jurisdictions differ greatly in population characteristics associated with the heavy use of alcohol. In general, police were passive in enforcing alcohol laws. Most reported entering bars when they were called to deal with fights or other disturbances, and they issued few citations for alcohol-related offenses on a typical weekend evening. Police may view such offenses as minor compared with more serious crimes. Also, commercial interests, such as the tourist and restaurant industries, often oppose stringent enforcement of criminal laws. Police campaigns against heavy drinking may adversely affect the tourist trade and make local residents reluctant to spend evenings in public places. To a certain extent, the goals of public safety and profits from entertainment conflict.

States also differed in civil liability and liability insurance practices affecting both drivers and commercial sellers of alcohol. According to our findings, these civil liability practices, including having a responsible business practice defense, a comparative versus contributory negligence standard, and other procedural rules, affected the actual number of suits against a bar. Bars in states with stricter civil liability laws, from the bar's standpoint, were more likely to have experienced a dram shop suit than bars in less restrictive states.

Perceptions and Effects

From our surveys of bar owners or managers and bar employees, it is evident that all the alcohol regulatory systems (i.e., administrative, criminal and civil) have some influence on behavior. The extent of this influence, as reflected in attempts to comply with alcohol regulations and behave acceptably, varied with the perceived risks of detection of bad server behavior. We obtained many statistically significant relationships between laws and regulations and owners', managers', or employees' perceptions of the risk of being cited or sued for serving minors and obviously intoxicated adults.

These correlations are reassuring in two respects. First, they illustrate that decision makers are clearly aware of the legal and regulatory environment in which they operate. Second, since we used the perceptions as explanatory variables in our empirical analysis of servers' behavior, they demonstrate that perceptions are systematically related to laws and regulations.

Judging from the two focus group meetings we held with bar owners and from comments made by respondents in our national survey of bar owners or managers, there appears to be widespread resentment of the regulations these businesses operate under. The bar owners and managers viewed many of the rules as cost-increasing nuisances. Even though the rules may increase costs, we did not find that, where implemented, they increased alcohol prices. Although bars did not necessarily agree with these policies, they generally abided by the rules and relied on public agencies in emergencies, such as when dealing with fights on their premises. When police sat outside in their patrol cars and waited for infractions to occur, bar management often considered them a nuisance. As another indicator of business opposition to public intervention, a few respondents complained when they learned that the federal government sponsored our study. Using tax revenue to finance an academic study of server regulation seemed to add insult to injury.

Effects of Administrative Regulation

Bar owners and managers were on the whole influenced by the work of the alcoholic beverage commission. Those ABC boards that actively followed up on illegal alcohol-related conduct such as fights in bars, DUI violations, and illegal consumption or trade were viewed as more likely to cite a bar for serving minors and intoxicated adults.

The relation between the ABC and the enforcement methods used also influenced bar owners' and managers' perceptions of the likelihood of citation. When alcohol enforcement was located outside the jurisdiction of the ABC, that is, within local or state police departments or a state department of revenue, they perceived a citation by the ABC as less likely. This perception could be attributed to their recognizing that no ABC personnel were dedicated solely to looking for alcohol violations. In reality, however, when enforcement was located outside the ABC, the likelihood of being cited was much higher. This may be because ABC agents were more concerned with monitoring entry regulation and license administration than with catching wrongdoers.

The number of liquor stores per thousand population had no effect on the number of alcohol-related traffic deaths, but increases in the number of bars raised the death rate for adults. This suggests that ABCs should pay close attention to the number of on-site permits granted, in addition to the location and clustering of on-site establishments. Where bar density was higher, the propensity to binge drink (drink five or more alcoholic beverages on a single occasion) was higher, as was the self-reported propensity to drink and drive. By contrast, the increased density of off-site establishments had a negative effect on binge drinking and no effect on drinking and driving, implying that there was less heavy drinking and less drinking and driving when alcohol was more accessible from stores. In part this unanticipated result may mean that people who buy from stores go home to drink, or at least that drinking episodes tend to be somewhat postponed from the time alcohol is purchased. From this it appears that policies designed to discourage drunk driving should target on-site, rather than off-site, establishments.

Effects of Criminal Law and Its Enforcement

As discussed in the literature review, drunk drivers perceive a low risk of detection owing to the few police resources dedicated to detecting drunk drivers. For alcohol-related offenses by the bar, we could detect no effect of enforcement on the likelihood of serving a minor or an intoxicated adult. This is also due to the limited police budget and lack of alcohol-focused employees.

Alcohol-related traffic deaths continued to decline in the 1990s. This may be attributable to a combination of many factors, including stricter laws, more awareness about drunk driving and designated drivers, changes in social norms about heavy drinking, and improved safety equipment on automobiles. For the variables we tested, mandatory fines and driver's license sanctions for a first drunk driving arrest lowered fatalities among minors. The fine variable did not have the same effect for adults, but the adult fatality rate was significantly improved by mandatory revocation of the driver's license at the time of arrest. Imposing mandatory minimum jail terms did not reduce fatalities for either group. Mandatory fines and mandatory jail sentences for first offenders reduced drunk driving among all drinkers in our analysis of behavioral risks. Although we found that criminal laws had some statistically significant deterrent effects on individual consumers' behavior, it is important to recognize that results from previous alcohol-related research on criminal laws have been conflicting and have often implied that such laws had no effect.

As in our focus groups, for the most part we found that bar owners and managers felt that the police, as the enforcers of criminal law, were burdensome and harmful to their businesses. Owners reported that the police almost always patrolled around the bar. They were helpful, however, when called to respond to fights. The bar owners reported that when they perceived the likelihood of citation to be high, they were more likely to employ private security guards. This evidence is inconsistent with the Philipson and Posner (1996) model discussed earlier (chapter 3), which hypothesized that when public enforcement is high, private enforcement is low. We could detect no effect of the police on the behavior of bartenders and wait staff at the bars we surveyed.

We found that criminal law had little influence on serving practices. We detected almost no effect of the perceived certainty of punishment on servers' behavior. Criminal laws may not be effective unless accompanied by social norms that discourage illegal service. Additionally, criminal punishments may not be large enough relative to the risk of detection. The effects of criminal laws may also be affected by the plea bargaining system that lets offenders escape full punishment by pleading guilty to a lesser offense. We also found that police resources had no effect on binge drinking.

Effects of Tort

Based on the new research presented in this book and on previous research, dram shop laws appear to be the most effective means of encouraging good server behavior and reducing alcohol-related traffic deaths. Although these laws have been in force in most states for only about fifteen years, they have had significant effects in reducing the social costs of alcohol use. In states with strict tort laws (from the viewpoint of the bar), contributory negligence, no responsible business practice defense, no damage limits, no statute of limitations, and no receipt of notice provisions, the perceived threat of being sued for serving a minor was higher.

Bar owners who perceived a higher risk of tort suit tended to monitor their employees more closely. They were significantly less likely to allow employees to drink on the job and were more likely to provide services for intoxicated customers, check the references of job applicants, cover more subjects in server training programs, and provide employees with procedures for serving alcohol. We also noted more monitoring for minors in bars where the perceived threat of suit for serving a minor was higher.

Bar owners generally felt threatened by dram shop liability, leading them to supervise their servers more closely and to spend more money on liability insurance. They generally believed it was unfair to hold them responsible for other people's actions. Although most bars had never had a tort claim brought against them, most owners were aware of the potential and said they monitored both customers and employees closely for this reason. Most server training programs included an educational component detailing the risk of lawsuits and the potential liability of both employees and the establishment for serving minors and obviously intoxicated adults.

From our interviews of bartenders and other employees, it is clear that servers, for the most part, have been instructed about proper alcohol service. Despite this, employees admitted to occasional bad serving practices, such as running up tabs and serving intoxicated patrons in order to get higher tips. These bad server behaviors were less frequent in bars where owners perceived a higher probability of a dram shop suit, which also suggests that owners are training their employees in order to reduce the risk of a suit. Employees in establishments serving food reported more good server behaviors than those in establishments that served mostly alcohol. This is consistent with the view presented in our focus groups that bars were feeling pressure to "turn into restaurants," shifting the emphasis away from alcohol to reduce liability. However, in our statistical analysis based on the survey data we collected, we could find no influence of perceived liability risk on the establishment's product mix, such as the percentage of revenue from service of food. Of course, establishments that dramatically altered their food/alcohol balance in favor of the former may have been systematically excluded from our sample.

Dram shop laws were very effective in reducing alcohol-related traffic deaths for both adults and minors. Adult dram shop laws reduced drinking at all and drinking and driving among all drinkers but had no effect on binge drinking. To our knowledge, ours is the first study to assess the deterrent effects of social host liability, which reduced binge drinking and drinking and driving among all drinkers.

On balance, it might seem strange that tort is a more effective deterrent that criminal law. We suspect there are several reasons that criminal laws are not more effective. First, penalties may often not have been high enough to deter potential criminals. Second, such penalties may be uncertain, even in states with mandatory minimum fines and sentences. The minimums apply only when there is a conviction, and plea bargaining for a lighter sentence and other forms of negotiation are likely to be widespread. To be convicted, one must first be apprehended, and the probability of being apprehended after committing a criminal act seems to be low. Third, many servers do not carry liability insurance. The effect of insurance in mitigating the deterrent effect of tort is absent when the bar does not have coverage. Although this should not affect criminal liability's effectiveness, it does raise the potential deterrent effect of tort.

Role of Liability Insurance

Results from our insurance analysis proved inconclusive owing to low response rates and scarcity of information about the dram shop insurance industry. We were able to determine that dram shop insurers offer discounts for good behaviors such as server training, providing rides, having alcohol sales of less than 30 percent of total business, and not having a claim in the past two to three years. In general, where the premiums for liability insurance were high, demand for the insurance was low. Accordingly, smaller bars with assets under $150,000 were less likely to have liability insurance. Small establishments may be less inclined to insure and may simply go out of business or declare bankruptcy if they are sued.

Bartenders and Wait Staff

Although employees, like their employers, are potentially liable for infractions, their incentives may not be fully aligned with those of their employers. This may be especially true because, during the daily course of their work, employees may be either rewarded financially by patrons for bad serving practices or not rewarded for good ones. Our empirical analysis revealed that employees' behavior had no effect on the wages employers paid per hour. One reassuring observation was that servers' good behavior increased their earnings from tips. On the other hand, bad serving behavior increased total earnings. Thus the picture was mixed. It does seem somewhat ironic or unfortunate that employers did not reward employees for going out of their way, such as providing or arranging rides for intoxicated patrons.

Overall, with some notable exceptions, we found considerable agreement between the responses about bar policies we obtained from the bar owners or managers and from employees. This is reassuring in two respects: employees and employers are on the same wavelength when it comes to policies; also, they seem to have told us the truth, perhaps because employees were interviewed without their employers present. The threat of various forms of liability produced similar effects for our analyses of both employer and employee data. An important exception was for providing rides to obviously intoxicated patrons, which employees were less likely to report as a practice of the bar than were their bosses. Perhaps the bosses expected their employees to be Good Samaritans but were at home themselves when the time to do so arrived.

POLICY IMPLICATIONS

Based on our literature review, survey findings, and empirical analysis, we reached the following policy conclusions.

1. Alcohol-related loss is substantial. Not only are the external effects of private drinking of considerable magnitude, but heavy drinking imposes substantial costs on individuals and their families as well. These costs are both short and long term. This is not a new finding, but it is worth reiterating. A strong case can be made for public intervention in private decision making.

2. To be effective, public intervention in alcohol issues should focus on multiple targets. Even though the individual drinker will logically remain the main target, there is a rationale for regulating other agents, such as commercial sellers of alcohol and perhaps social hosts. Among the commercial sellers, the main target should be the on-site seller. A strong case can be made that in a democratic society adults should be responsible for their own actions. When their decisions adversely affect the well-being of other citizens measured in terms of morbidity, mortality, and financial outlays for insurance and taxes, however, the argument for individual choice is

weakened. Certainly this consideration of relying on private choices made by "responsible" persons does not apply to minors, who may not exercise reasonable care because of their immaturity.

The strongest case for regulating commercial sellers is that they are sometimes well positioned to curb heavy drinking and its secondary effects. Although this is not so in every instance, the law should be sufficiently flexible to uncover those cases when the seller could not have known the customer was intoxicated. Certainly alcoholics may not be able to judge when their drinking is excessive, so some form of oversight is appropriate. Employees of government agencies cannot efficiently monitor each occasion of heavy drinking, and a bartender or an employee may be in a better position to judge than an outsider. Also, there is the normative issue of allowing the bar to profit from the sale of alcohol when, at the same time, its business is generating negative externalities. As we learned from our survey, a lot happens in bars, such as fights, though there is considerable variation on this score. One should be careful not to tar them all with the same brush.

The argument for regulating social hosts is more controversial. Profiteering is generally not an issue. But the finding that social host laws are effective is intriguing, given the high social cost of heavy drinking. Social hosts may often be in a good position to monitor drinking, or at least not to serve too much alcohol to anyone. Here the privacy issues are stronger than for a bar, which, after all, has a government-granted license to operate as a public drinking place.

3. As there should be multiple targets, so there should be multiple policy instruments. Ordinarily, with one policy objective—in this case reducing heavy drinking and its effects—there is a rationale for one policy instrument. But here heterogeneity is a particular problem. For example, given its effectiveness as shown in this study, as well as in the work of others, there is an important role for taxing alcohol. Not only is taxation a source of revenue, but it is also a means of product restriction, since consumption is clearly affected by price. However, in this context individuals are heterogeneous. To stamp out all heavy drinking, especially drinking that is likely to yield negative externalities, it would be necessary to impose very high taxes.

3a. Generally, competition is to be preferred to monopoly. Policies that confer de facto franchises on the sellers that do gain entry under regulation are often counterproductive. Competitive pricing does not recognize the negative externalities from excessive use of alcohol. Thus allowing free entry is not likely to be socially optimal. In particular, a high density of on-site commercial servers is associated with high motor vehicle fatalities, drinking at all, binge drinking, drinking and driving among all drinkers, and driving after binge drinking.

From the standpoint of deterrence, the rationale for barriers to entry of liquor stores is substantially weaker, as is the case for public provision, a practice in a minority of states.

3b. Generally, placing alcohol enforcement under one administrative body (the state ABC) provides a more effective deterrent than placing it outside the ABC (such as with state or local police). This result seems highly plausible. States without this arrangement should consider combining these functions under a single authority.

4. States have varied in how far they have implemented tort laws for regulating drinkers, drivers, and bartenders. Yet perhaps the most consistent pattern we found was the effectiveness of tort in curbing excessive drinking, in deterring commercial servers from unsafe serving practices, and in encouraging safe drinking practices in noncommercial social environments. Given our results and those of past studies, there is a strong rationale for tort law as a method of controlling excessive alcohol use. Commercial servers of alcohol are not unique in opposing tort as another complicating factor in operating their businesses, but the public interest appears to outweigh such arguments.

In recent years there has been a shift from contributory to comparative negligence, justified by equitable division of blame with injury victims who may have been slightly at fault for the accident. It seems unfair to deny such persons all compensation from tort. A comparative negligence standard increases the bar's liability exposure. Whereas under a contributory negligence standard injured drinkers would be prevented from suing owing to their own negligence in drinking too much, they might recover under comparative negligence. The empirical evidence suggests that incentives to be careful are lower under comparative negligence. At the time such statutory changes were enacted, states did not have access to this empirical evidence. Our results, and those of some past studies, make us question the wisdom of this change.

5. On the other hand, criminal liability did not fare as well in our study as we expected. The rationale for imposing criminal liability includes the likelihood that tort-feasors may not have the resources to fully compensate injury victims. And unlike those committing tort, persons found guilty of a crime may be imprisoned, thus keeping them from harming others. However, jail terms for DUI are far too short to serve the incapacitation function, and the financial penalties may not be high enough to deter such careless behavior.

UNRESOLVED ISSUES AND AGENDA FOR FUTURE RESEARCH

Several issues are unresolved and merit further investigation. Following the lead that earlier studies found dram shop liability reduced drunk driving and motor vehicle fatalities, we focused here on commercial servers of alcohol, mainly to determine whether such laws really affected servers' behavior.

During the investigation, we also examined the effects of administrative and criminal law. We surveyed local police departments in selected jurisdictions, as well as state ABCs, which also enforce alcohol laws. However, there is much more to be learned about why criminal laws are not more effective in deterring either bad server practices or drinking and driving and its adverse effects. Is police enforcement of these laws inadequate?

In retrospect, we wish we had asked the police we surveyed more about enforcement practices as they pertain to servers, not just how often they entered bars in the areas they covered. More detailed questioning about police oversight of DUI laws is needed. Given their other priorities, is enforcing DUI laws of secondary importance? In spite of efforts by many state legislators to strengthen laws against drinking and driving and bad server practices, is the judicial system lax in punishing offenders? Are there states that really do imprison DUI offenders for long periods, essentially incapacitating chronic drinkers? And what has been the experience of such initiatives? Do courts refer many offenders to alcohol treatment as a substitute for or complement to meting out punishments? And how effective has treatment been? A substantial amount has been written on treatment, but we need to learn more about interactions between treatment and the judicial system.

We surveyed some dram shop liability insurers and state insurance departments, and we asked commercial servers about liability insurance. This was the least successful aspect of our study. In retrospect, the question we asked the commercial servers should have distinguished between dram shop insurance and other forms of liability insurance. The dram shop liability market is very small, so most state regulators could tell us little about dram shop insurer practices. Our impression is that, aside from discounts offered for server training, insurers serving the alcohol industry engage in very little loss prevention. We found that the demand for dram shop insurance is highly premium sensitive, and many of the commercial servers with few assets did not purchase it. In such cases, a firm that loses a suit may simply declare bankruptcy and exit the industry, leaving the plaintiff without compensation. It would be useful to know how many firms really leave the industry in response to tort suits. Most states have minimum levels of compulsory liability insurance for motor vehicles. Corresponding laws do not exist for commercial servers.

There is still more to be learned about loss prevention, experience rating, and underwriting practices of dram shop insurers. Our efforts to obtain information by mail and telephone did not suffice. In view of the difficulties we encountered, it would probably be advisable to visit a representative number of dram shop insurers. It would also be useful to examine rate filings at state insurance departments.

In some of our previous work, it was evident that imposing premium surcharges on drivers was an effective deterrent to drinking and driving and reduced motor vehicle deaths as well. This empirical analysis was based on a one-time survey of motor vehicle insurers; it would be useful to update this information. If such a survey is performed, it should include premium-setting practices under no-fault.

Our findings suggested that a high density of bars in an area has deleterious effects, yet we found that bars undertook certain precautions when they faced nearby competition. In particular, bars understandably were more cautious when their patrons engaged in barhopping; for example, bar employees would screen entering patrons more carefully for those who might already be drunk. Our measure of competition was very simple: we asked the bar to identify a competitor. Most (88 percent) did so. Ideally, we would have had better measures of competition among bars. Knowing the exact location of the bars we surveyed would have helped in determining the level of local competition and analyzing its effect on monitoring, pricing, and density as well as on crime and fatality rates. However, we promised confidentiality to our commercial server respondents, and accordingly our survey firm did not reveal the identity of individual respondents to us.

Also, it would be useful to know if there are circumstances in which bars compete in *not* monitoring patrons. Such "races to the bottom" would be important to document and would provide a firmer basis for limiting the entry of establishments to certain locations.

Social host laws represent an expansion of tort into a new area of third-party liability, and study results appear to support their effectiveness. This subject merits additional empirical analysis.

Most of the empirical analysis of effects of statutory changes on drinking and driving has used mortality data, but most traffic accidents do not result in death. State motor vehicle departments maintain information on driver records. If such information was analyzed, it would be important to assemble longitudinal data from several states. Only with a time series of cross sections is it possible to more conclusively evaluate how state laws affect behavior.

Other analyses might use information on closed claims collected and maintained by insurers. Although closed-claims data are available nationally for certain years, this information is not nearly as useful as longitudinal data. Without mandatory closed-claims reporting, such as exists for medical malpractice claims, it would probably not be possible to develop driver-specific accident histories. Accident-prone drivers probably switch insurers or switch in and out of coverage. Thus, as a practical matter, this type of research is more an aspiration than a reality.

With few exceptions, research on heavy drinking and drinking and driving has been limited to alcohol use. However, we know from this study and from past research that heavy drinking is related to abuse of other substances such as illicit drugs. A potentially important issue is whether policies that succeed in curbing heavy drinking trigger compensatory responses. Various forms of risky behavior may be substitutes. To the extent that this is true, alcohol control policies may win the battle but lose the war. After all, the ultimate objective is to improve the health and well-being of the population. Reducing heavy alcohol consumption and its effects is only one means for achieving this.

Appendix

Design of Our Surveys

Overview

There have been a considerable number of surveys concerning individual patterns of alcohol consumption. In addition, detailed information exists on motor vehicle mortality and other deaths caused by excessive alcohol use.[1] By contrast, there is a paucity of information on alcohol-related organizations: establishments serving alcoholic beverages, liability insurers that cover such firms, agencies that regulate insurance, and public institutions responsible for curbing heavy drinking and for mitigating its effects.

To improve our understanding of policies, rules, regulations, and laws and their effect on the behavior of drinking establishment owners and servers, we surveyed individuals and organizations involved either in serving alcohol or in regulating such service. We conducted surveys with bar owners or managers (commercial servers), employees of bars, police departments, state departments of alcohol regulation, state departments of insurance, and liquor liability insurers.

Survey of Commercial Servers

Drinking establishments were surveyed by telephone by Mathematica Policy Research (MPR) from its Princeton, New Jersey, office from September 1996 through February 1997. The survey inquired about the frequency of dram shop liability claims against establishments and the resolution of such claims, including stage of resolution and outcome; fraction of claims paid and indemnity paid; liability insurance coverage and premiums paid; discounts offered by insurers and the loss prevention programs they provided to establishments; promotions and pricing practices, such as happy hours, hungry hours, and serving portions; policies to edu-

---

1. Motor vehicle fatality information is used in the empirical analysis presented in chapter 9. For other information on alcohol-related mortality, see, e.g., Ruhn (1996); Sloan, Reilly, and Schenzler (1994b); and Thun et al. (1997).

cate patrons about the dangers of drinking and driving; policies to monitor and curb drinking of obviously intoxicated patrons; policies to stop minors from drinking on the premises; transportation arrangements for intoxicated patrons; hiring and employment practices, including employees' dependence on tips and tip pools and the responsibilities of employees versus management in dealing with intoxicated persons; server training programs, both existence and content; local ordinances, such as bans on happy hours and requirements for server training, and servers' perceptions of the extent of local law enforcement; and information about competitors and the market context in which bars operate. We obtained information on prices of specific alcoholic beverages, ambience or clientele, and product mix, and on the establishment's competitors.

At the end of the survey, respondents were asked for the name, address, and telephone number of the insurer that provided dram shop coverage, if they had such insurance. On average, the survey took twenty minutes to complete.

Focus Groups and Pretest

To develop the survey, we first conducted focus groups to determine appropriate questions and to learn more about bar owners' or managers' opinions on regulatory policies in this context and their responses to them. Focus group participants were recruited from a commercial database consisting of establishments in the area of Princeton-Trenton, New Jersey, with the standard industrial code (SIC) 5813, drinking places (alcoholic beverages). This area was chosen because the survey firm, Mathematica Policy Research (MPR), is in Princeton. Letters of invitation were mailed to 135 owners or managers of area drinking establishments, followed by recruitment telephone calls. Nine people registered for a group interview with owners and managers of small establishments (those with fewer than ten employees); eleven people registered for a group interview with owners and managers of larger establishments (those with at least ten employees). Four interviewers participated in each of the focus groups. The group interviews provided useful data about the bars' operations as well as feedback about survey questions and procedures.

The survey instruments were substantially revised after the focus groups. Participants were adamant that people in their position would not tolerate a long telephone survey. Their feedback was also useful in identifying words, phrases, and questions that were not meaningful to them and, conversely, those that were. They suggested we remove open-ended questions and questions that would require looking up information and change income questions so that answers would be ranges or ratios rather than specific dollar amounts.

In May and June 1996, MPR and Duke University did a pretest of the survey instruments and procedures. Telephone interviews were attempted with owners or managers of a sample of drinking establishments in the Philadelphia-Trenton-Newark (Pennsylvania and New Jersey) corridor and in the Raleigh-Durham-Chapel Hill (North Carolina) area. The pretest sample was limited to these areas so that we could do field observation in establishments that had completed the telephone surveys. We conducted twenty establishment interviews and twenty-five employee surveys.

Field visits to bars were used to corroborate responses to the survey about serving practices. In May 1996 five field staff members were trained to observe serving practices in the establishments that completed an interview during the pretest. Each bar was observed anonymously for the two hours just before closing time on a Friday or Saturday night, and observers completed a form for each place they visited.

Since the survey instruments tested well in both content and timing, only minor revisions were made after the pretest. We concluded, however, that paying owners did not greatly affect their willingness to participate, and that a larger payment to the employees we surveyed might encourage greater cooperation. Therefore for the main study owners did not receive payment, and employees were paid more than originally planned.

Field observation confirmed the hypothesis that there would be discrepancies between the information the respondents reported about the physical environment and serving policies of their establishments and the observations of the field staff.

Sample Selection

We randomly selected drinking establishments across the United States from the *American Yellow Pages,* 1996 edition. An establishment is a place of business that may be part of a firm with other establishments. We selected those listed as standard industrial classification (SIC) code 5813, which includes businesses labeled bars, beer gardens, beer parlors (taprooms), beer taverns, bottle clubs, cabarets, cocktail lounges, discotheques, nightclubs, saloons, taverns, and wine bars (U.S. Executive Office of the President 1987).

The sampling design was a three-stage stratified design with states forming the strata and with three stages of selection: county within state, establishment within county, and employee within establishment. The study was to be conducted in 150 locations throughout the forty-eight contiguous states (excluding Alaska, Hawaii, and the District of Columbia). This sample size of locations was proportionally allocated to states using state-level counts of establishments identified in a list compiled from the *Yellow Pages.* The state location was rounded to the nearest integer, with a minimum of one location per state (the maximum per state was thirteen). In the end, 152 selections were made.

A geographic unit was needed to cluster establishments for the next stage of sampling, and we defined the county in which the initial establishments were located as the primary sampling unit. Because establishments were randomly selected within a state (rather than by counties), a county was included in the sample only if one or more establishments there were selected. A county with many establishments had a greater chance of being included than a county with few. The sampling process was therefore equivalent to sampling counties with replacement and with the probability proportional to size, using the number of establishments within a county as the size measure. In some states two or more initial establishments identified the same county, and these were considered separate selections of the county for sampling purposes. The initial establishments were used only to identify the county for the next stage of sampling, and an initial establishment was returned to the sampling frame for the second stage. The initial establishment may or may not have been selected in the second stage. One establishment was in a town that spanned two counties, so the two counties were treated as a single unit for the selection of establishments.

Within each sampled county, we constructed a sampling frame of the establishments and selected a sample of establishments within each area. If a county had multiple selections (for example, three), then we selected three times as many establishments as in a county with a single selection. The purpose of the increased sample size for counties with multiple selections was to achieve approximately equal selection probabilities for the individual establishments within a state. For some counties, the number of establishments was less than that needed to achieve equal selection probabilities. In these counties, all establishments were selected and ultimately caused an unequal selection probability across the sample.

We wanted to include respondents for whom drinking and driving might be a problem. Thus we excluded establishments in airports, train stations, bus stations, and motels or hotels with fewer than two-thirds of the patrons coming from outside the premises. We asked that the establishment cater to patrons who frequent it primarily to drink, that it be open for business Friday and Saturday nights at least until 11:00 P.M., and that it have, on average, at least ten customers at 11:00 P.M. on a busy night. In addition, we asked that the establishment be owned or managed by an English-speaking person.

Of the 2,310 establishments initially sampled, 1,882 (81.5 percent) were screened (table A.1). The decision about how many establishments to screen was based on MPR's forecast of the size of screen needed to yield the desired number of responses. Of those screened, 1,156 establishments satisfied our eligibility criteria. Of those that were ineligible, almost half were no longer in business.

Response Rate

Many of the questions, such as those on pricing practices and insurance coverage, patron education, and server training, were straightforward. However, the questions about monitoring and intervention policies caused greater concern, starting with the survey design phase. Owners and managers may have feared that reporting failure to monitor and stop behaviors that may lead to driving under the influence might provoke litigation against them. Hence they may have refused to answer certain questions or refused to participate altogether. Alternatively, they may simply have been embarrassed or reluctant to put themselves in a bad light.

Thus we took several precautions to increase owners' or managers' participation in the survey and to enhance the accuracy of their responses to these poten-

Table A.1 Screening and Interview Responses and Eligibility
among Establishments in the Survey of Commercial Servers

	Count	Percentage	Average per Location[a]
Total establishments sampled	2,310	100	15.2
Screening response			
Yes	1,882	81.5	12.4
No	428	18.5	N/A
Eligibility			
Total screened	1,882	100	12.4
Eligible	1,156	61.4	7.6
Ineligible[b]	726	38.6	4.8
Interview response			
Total eligible	1,156	100	7.6
Yes	778	67.3	5.1
No	378	32.7	N/A

Source: Mathematica Policy Research.
[a]A total of 152 locations (counties) were selected.
[b]Ineligible establishments include 346 that were closed or out of business and 380 that were ineligible for other reasons.

tially sensitive questions. We promised respondents that MPR would submit data to the Duke University researchers without identifying information except the state, the standard metropolitan statistical area if applicable, and for states with dram shop liability established at the substate level, whether the establishment was subject to dram shop liability. Before study results were released to anyone, MPR destroyed all records of respondents' names and addresses. With information destroyed before data analysis, responses of individual establishments could not be subpoenaed. The Duke researchers supplied MPR with information by census tract or county (e.g., on racial mix, employment, housing/retail mix, and median income). After the survey was completed, MPR merged these data with the establishment surveys.

Total Commercial Server Establishments

Of the 1,156 establishments that were eligible, 778 (67.3 percent) of their owners or managers agreed to participate in this study: 22 fewer than our target of 800. As noted earlier, we surveyed drinking establishments in forty-eight states.

SURVEY OF EMPLOYEES
Rationale

At the end of the interview with the bar owner or manager, MPR asked for permission to interview two employees without the owner or manager present. To avoid having to secure a roster for the entire establishment, the interviewer selected a specific time later in the week and asked the employer for the first name and initial of the surname of all bartenders and waiters or waitresses who were to be on duty at that time. MPR drew interviewees at random from this list. The plan was to interview one bartender and one member of the wait staff.

Our main reason for interviewing employees was that the stated policies might not actually have been implemented, or they might not be implemented at certain times. The survey did not ask employees about policies, but rather asked what they actually do in particular situations when they are very busy and when they are not. Employees were asked about income from tips and from a tips pool designed to pay when a patron who was "cut off" leaves without tipping. Each employee was interviewed by telephone for about fifteen minutes either at home or at the bar. The employee interviews complement rather than substitute for the interviews with the owners or managers. Individual employees are unlikely to have a broad perspective of company policies or to be able to answer certain questions, such as those concerning previous tort claims and liability insurance. Employees were paid $15 for completing the questionnaire.

Sample Selection

For the employee sample, we requested separate lists of bartenders and of servers from each responding eligible establishment. We then selected a sample so that we could have a completed interview with one bartender and one member of the wait staff. If bartenders and servers were not differentiated, then we tried to have two completed interviews with employees who served alcohol. Where the owner was the only employee, the owner was interviewed again with new questions that would have been answered by employees.

The target population of employees included all current employees at eligible establishments who were either bartenders or servers of alcoholic beverages and who had worked for at least two months serving alcohol in any establishment.

Response Rate

When asked to provide a list of employees, 169 owners or managers refused (table A.2). In addition, 64 establishments had no employees besides the owners. A total of 545 provided lists of employees, providing a sample of 1,133 employees to interview. Of this total, 83 percent agreed to be interviewed ($N = 942$), of which 80 were ineligible, leaving 862 employee respondents.

Quality of Data

We asked an employee of the establishment questions worded identically to the those on the owner survey about monitoring or intervening except that they applied to actual employee behavior rather than to the establishment's stated policy. Although we did not expect to obtain identical responses from employees and owners or managers, we would not want to trust responses from the two groups that were completely contradictory.

One indicator of survey quality is missing data. Item nonresponse was more of a problem for the Survey of Commercial Servers than for the Survey of Employees,

Table A.2 Establishment and Employee Response in the Survey of Employees

	Count	Percentage	Average per Location[a]
Total eligible establishments	1,156	100.0	7.6
Establishment response			
Provided list or had no employees[b]	609	52.7	4.0
Refused interview or to provide list[c]	547	47.3	N/A
Establishment providing employee lists	545	N/A	3.6
Employee interview response	1,133	100.0	7.6
Yes[d]	942	83.1	6.2
No	191	16.9	N/A

Source: Mathematica Policy Research.

[a] A total of 152 locations (counties) were selected.

[b] Includes 545 establishments that had employees and provided a list and 64 that had no employees.

[c] Includes 378 owners or managers who refused to provide employee lists.

[d] Includes 862 eligible employees and 80 ineligible employees.

as shown in table A.3. The employees were asked questions they would almost certainly be able to answer. By contrast, owners or managers were asked a broad range of questions. In some cases they did not have direct knowledge, such as about dram shop liability coverage. Based on the focus group discussions before the surveys were fielded, we decided not to push for answers. People who own or operate bars often are short staffed, and the bars may lack much infrastructure.

Another measure of data quality is the extent of agreement between responses of owners or managers and their employees. Disagreement may arise because respondents do not really know the answers or because their answers are colored to suggest a more desirable situation. For many items, agreement was almost 100 percent. On some items, such as providing rides to intoxicated patrons, employers were likely to suggest a more cautious policy than the employees. On a few items, employees' answers were more favorable to the establishment than employers' (see table 8.7).

SURVEY OF STATE ALCOHOLIC BEVERAGE COMMISSIONS

The threat of administrative sanctions provides one incentive for establishments to monitor their patrons' drinking. Two dimensions of the threat are pertinent: penalties conditional on a sanction's being imposed and the probability that a sanction will be imposed, which reflects enforcement. Although some information on penalties is available from secondary sources—historical accounts of alcohol regulation and state statutes—we have found no compilations of information on entry barriers, such as licenses refused, or on enforcement. The Survey of Alcoholic Beverage Commissions collected data on entry barriers, penalties, and enforcement.

Before conducting the survey, we assembled state-level alcoholic beverage

Table A.3 Missing Data in the Surveys of Employee
and Commercial Servers (%)

Survey of Employees	
Current hourly wage	7.0
Annual family income last year (1994)	6.8
Bar associated with a volunteer program to provide ride for drunk persons	5.9
Bar has procedure to arrange for hotel for drunk persons	2.6
Bar uses "pat down" to detect hidden alcohol brought into bar by minors	2.6
Bar had procedures to get car keys from drunk persons	2.2
How often bar provides additional drinks with more mixer	2.1
Bar has procedures to get drunk persons to accept ride from employee	1.4
How often bar employee paces patron's drinking from beginning	1.4
Survey of Commercial Servers	
Decoys have been used by law enforcement agencies	33.5
Name of insurer that covers liability claims	31.3
Approximate percentage of servers' earnings that comes from tips	23.7
Approximate percentage of bartenders' earnings that comes from tips	21.6
Number of days since last ALE check	16.9
Net worth of bar	12.8
Likelihood ABC would cite bar for	
Serving rowdy patrons	10.1
Serving drunk patrons	9.7
Law enforcement agencies use decoys to uncover serving alcohol to minors	9.1
Likelihood ABC would cite bar for being overcrowded	9.1

Source: 1996 Survey of Employees and Survey of Commercial Servers.

regulations. These laws describe the administrative structure of each state's alcoholic beverage commission (ABC) boards and the local ABC boards. These regulations also contain information on the funding of the alcohol administration system. They list administrative penalties imposed for violating the ABC law, the ABC's own investigative authority, and formal relationships with law enforcement agencies, and they define types of establishments subject to regulation and types of permits.

Although the statutes are a good information source, taken alone they do not fully describe interstate variation in the incentive such regulation gives servers to exercise due care. Thus, after our analysis of the statutes we surveyed all the states to document how such regulation works in practice and to develop independent variables for our empirical analysis of server behavior.

The survey was conducted during the summer of 1996 by mail, with telephone and fax follow-ups. We obtained responses from forty-three states having ABCs or their equivalent.[2] Not all survey questions were applicable to all states, and not all states collected the data required to answer some of the questions, such as number

2. Arkansas, Florida, Hawaii, Nevada, New Mexico, Rhode Island, South Carolina, and the District of Columbia did not respond.

of establishments sanctioned. Therefore there were sometimes far fewer than forty-three responses to particular questions.[3]

As described more fully in chapter 2, where we discuss findings from this survey, much of the survey dealt with enforcement. Another set of issues involved the rules and procedures governing licensing and sanctions. We investigated resources devoted to such regulation. The statute might require a state agency to perform a particular function, but the agency will not be able to do so adequately if the state fails to appropriate sufficient resources. Finally, we asked for information on applicants and reasons for turning down license applications.

As with any survey of this type, there is the risk that respondents may try to make their organizations seem more effective than they really are. It should be more difficult to color responses to the objective questions, such as the number of full-time equivalents on the agency's staff. Responses to more qualitative questions may be colored, but we could check the consistency of these responses with more objective data. Also, since we had information from statutes, we were not totally reliant on the survey. In practice, bragging about the agency was less of a problem than lack of information.

SURVEY OF POLICE DEPARTMENTS

As we explained in chapter 3, some of our previous research and that of others used measures of public expenditures on police and, alternatively, full-time equivalent police personnel per thousand state population as explanatory variables in empirical analyses of binge drinking, drinking and driving, and motor vehicle mortality. Although the coefficients on such variables were often negative, as expected, and statistically significant at conventional levels, we needed more precise measures of police operations. A problem with previous analyses has been lack of information about the mechanisms by which police availability reduces fatalities. One strategy may be to reduce the number of intoxicated persons leaving commercial establishments. There is likely to be variation in how closely police monitor drinking by minors, in how actively they patrol around bars with bad records, and in the amount of street patrol in areas with evening recreation involving commercial drinking establishments. General patrolling of the streets and highways plausibly also affects drinking and driving, but focused measurement of this was beyond the scope of our survey. We also asked bar managers about the procedures of local police. District attorneys sometimes launch sting operations in bars, so we asked the police about district attorneys.

The specific purposes of surveying police departments were to obtain information on local criminal laws as they pertain to commercial establishments and servers; to secure data on frequency of violations and on convictions and types of penalties actually imposed; to determine if violations are concentrated in a few establishments and describe the characteristics of such establishments; and to assess the resources, if any, specifically devoted to laws as they apply to on-site licensees.

3. See the discussion in chapter 3.

MPR identified all SMSAs and counties from which it was conducting the Survey of Commercial Servers. During the summer of 1996, students and staff at Duke University interviewed 103 police department officials by telephone; the refusal rate was 30 percent. Given the standard metropolitan statistical area and county identifiers, we were able to link data obtained from police with establishment and employee data from the Survey of Commercial Servers when the observations came from SMSAs. Some police departments in SMSAs are very large, so we needed to pick a more precise jurisdiction. In such instances MPR provided more detailed information on the locations of the bars being surveyed, and we attempted to survey the police precincts in those areas. Police departments were chosen based on the jurisdiction that had the most influence on the area where we had a potential drinking establishment.

SURVEY OF STATE DEPARTMENTS OF INSURANCE

There is virtually no information on dram shop liability insurance. One source of data is state departments of insurance, recognizing that liquor liability or dram shop liability insurance is a very minor line of insurance. The objectives of our Survey of State Departments of Insurance were to obtain names of insurers that sell insurance covering dram shop liability claims; to secure information on premium volume and premiums for particular liability limits; to determine whether the state department of insurance is required by statute to submit periodic reports on dram shop liability and to obtain copies of these reports; to secure information on regulation of specific underwriting practices, such as prohibitions against refusing to write coverage for firms in certain parts of a city ("redlining") and any rules affecting premium setting for such coverage; to determine whether the state requires on-site commercial insurers to have minimum liability coverage and, if so, determine the provisions made for establishments that cannot secure the minimum coverage; to learn how premium regulation operates in the state (if applicable); and to obtain information on the existence of risk pools and data on such pools when they do exist. We were able to survey state departments of insurance in forty-eight states and the District of Columbia.[4]

SURVEY OF DRAM SHOP INSURERS

The Survey of Dram Shop Insurers obtained information from the larger insurers on their underwriting practices, premiums (including surcharges for violators and claims), and loss prevention programs. We surveyed insurers identified from secondary data sources as providing dram shop insurance.

The best way to obtain information on underwriting practices is to develop alternative scenarios and ask insurers whether those specific risks would be underwritten in the state in question (see, e.g., Sloan and Githens 1994 for a description of a survey of auto liability insurers). The scenarios depicted hypothetical, yet real-

4. Nonresponding states include New Jersey and Nevada.

istic, situations. We asked whether insurers' willingness to insure depends on specific characteristics of the bar, such as location, clientele mix, server training, and ratio of sales of alcohol to sales of nonalcoholic beverages and food. Since underwriting practices may differ between establishments not previously insured by the company and renewals, we posed separate questions for each.

We requested state-specific information on premiums for coverage with specified liability limits. We documented experience-rating practices of insurers based on administrative violations, criminal violations, and claims frequency. We also asked insurers for state-specific information on claims frequency and severity (mean paid claims size).

Finally, we asked insurers about their loss prevention practices, imposed by either primary or surplus line insurers. A certain amount of loss prevention may be bundled into the product insurers provide (see, e.g., Schlesinger and Venezian 1986).

A contact person at each firm was identified by telephone before we mailed the survey. Two to three weeks after the mailing, we called the respondent to ensure that the survey was being completed and to offer any help needed. We interviewed fourteen dram shop insurers in the spring and summer of 1996.

CONCLUSION

To our knowledge, this is the first comprehensive survey of commercial establishments, employees, insurance companies, and the various agencies involved in alcohol regulation. The data obtained from these instruments provided new information on the effectiveness of alcohol regulation and the deterrent effects of liability.

References

Adkins, M. C. 1995. "Negligence: *Busby v. Quail Greek Golf and Country Club:* A Balanced Approach to Vendor Liability and Underage Drinking." *Oklahoma Law Review* 48:779–96.

All-Industry Research Advisory Council. 1989. *Compensation for Automobile Injuries in the United States.* Oak Brook, Ill.: AIRAC.

American Law Institute. 1979. *Restatement (Second) of Torts.* Philadelphia: American Law Institute.

Andenaes, J. 1974. *Punishment and Deterrence.* Ann Arbor: University of Michigan Press.

Andreoni, J. 1995. "Criminal Deterrence in the Reduced Form: A New Perspective on Ehrlich's Seminal Study." *Economic Inquiry* 33 (3): 476–83.

Applegate, B. K., F. T. Cullen, S. M. Barton, P. J. Richards, L. Lanza-Kaducel, and B. G. Link. 1995. "Public Support for Drunk-Driving Countermeasures: Social Policy for Saving Lives." *Crime and Delinquency* 41:171–90.

Applegate, B. K., R. H. Langworthy, and E. J. Latessa. 1997. "Factors Associated with Success in Treating Chronic Drunk Drivers: The Turning Point Program." *Journal of Offender Rehabilitation* 24 (3–4): 19–34.

Argeriou, M., D. McCarty, and E. Blacker. 1985. "Criminality among Individuals Arraigned for Drinking and Driving in Massachusetts." *Journal of Studies on Alcohol* 46 (6): 525–30.

Ashley, M. J., and J. G. Rankin. 1988. "A Public Health Approach to the Prevention of Alcohol-Related Health Problems." *Annual Review of Public Health* 9:233–71.

Atkin, C. K., J. Hocking, and M. Block. 1984. "Teenage Drinking: Does Advertising Make a Difference?" *Journal of Communication* 34:157–67.

Atkin, C. K., K. Neuendorf, and S. McDermott. 1983. "The Role of Alcohol Advertising in Excessive and Hazardous Drinking." *Journal of Drug Education* 13:313–25.

Babor, T. F., J. H. Mendelson, I. Greenberg, and J. Kuehnle. 1978. "Experimental Analysis of the 'Happy Hour': Effects of Purchase Price on Alcohol Consumption." *Psychopharmacology* 58:35–41.

Babor, T. F., J. H. Mendelson, B. Uhly, and E. Souza. 1980. "Drinking Patterns in Experimental and Barroom Settings." *Journal of Studies on Alcohol* 41 (7): 633–51.

Bartley, W. A., and M. A. Cohen. 1998. "The Effect of Concealed Weapons Laws: An Extreme Bound Analysis." *Economic Inquiry* 36 (2): 258–65.

Beard, T. R. 1990. "Bankruptcy and Care Choice." *RAND Journal of Economics* 21 (4): 626–34.

Beauchamp, D. E. 1980. *Beyond Alcoholism: Alcohol and Public Health Policy.* Philadelphia: Temple University Press.

Becker, G. S. 1968. "Crime and Punishment: An Economic Approach." *Journal of Political Economy* 76 (2): 169–217.

———. 1983. "A Theory of Competition among Pressure Groups for Political Influence." *Quarterly Journal of Economics* 98:371–400.

Becker, G. S., and K. M. Murphy. 1988. "A Theory of Rational Addiction." *Journal of Political Economy* 96 (4): 675–800.

Bedard, P. 1998. "One Drink over the Line." *Car and Driver* 44 (3): 106–12.

Beha, J. A., II. 1977. "And Nobody Can Get You Out: The Impact of a Mandatory Prison Sentence for the Illegal Carrying of a Firearm on the Use of Criminal Justice in Boston." *Boston University Law Review* 57:96–146 (part 1); 289–333 (part 2).

Benson, B. L., I. Kim, and D. W. Rasmussen. 1994. "Estimating Deterrence Effects: A Public Choice Perspective on the Economics of Crime Literature." *Southern Economic Journal* 61 (1): 161–68.

Berger, D. E., and J. R. Snortum. 1985. "Alcoholic Beverage Preferences of Drinking Driving Violators." *Journal of Studies on Alcohol* 46 (3): 232–39.

Black, D. A., and D. S. Nagin. 1998. "Do Right-to-Carry Laws Deter Violent Crime?" *Journal of Legal Studies* 27:209–19.

Blank, C. 1994. "Intoxicated Drivers: Everyone's Problem." *Journal of Neuroscience Nursing* 26 (2): 107–10.

Bonnie, R. J. 1985. "Regulating Conditions of Alcohol Availability: Possible Effects on Highway Safety." *Journal of Studies on Alcohol* 10 (suppl.): 129–44.

Bovbjerg, R. R. 1995. *Medical Malpractice: Problems and Reforms.* Washington, D.C.: Urban Institute Intergovernmental Health Policy Project.

Bovbjerg, R. R., F. A. Sloan, and J. F. Blumstein. 1989. "Valuing Life and Limb in Tort: Scheduling Pain and Suffering." *Northwestern University Law Review* 83 (4): 908–76.

Bovbjerg, R. R., F. A. Sloan, A. Dor, and C. R. Hsieh. 1991. "Juries and Justice: Are Malpractice and Other Personal Injuries Created Equal?" *Law and Contemporary Problems* 54 (1): 5–42.

Bowers, W. J., and G. L. Pierce. 1975. "The Illusion of Deterrence in Isaac Ehrlich's Research on Capital Punishment." *Yale Law Journal* 85:187–208.

Bradley, M. E., N. M. Green Jr., D. E. Jones, M. Lynn, and L. McNeil. 1992. *Churches and Church Membership in the United States, 1990.* Atlanta, Ga.: Glenmary Research Center.

Breyer, S. G. 1982. *Regulation and Its Reform.* Cambridge: Harvard University Press.

Brown, C. 1985. "Deterrence in Tort and No-Fault: New Zealand Experience." *California Law Review* 73 (3): 976–1002.

Brown, J. P. 1973. "Towards an Economic Theory of Liability." *Journal of Legal Studies* 2:323–50.

———. 1998. "Economic Theory of Liability Rules." In *The New Palgrave Dictionary of Economics and the Law,* ed. Peter Newman, 2:15–19. London: Macmillan Reference.

Bruce, C. J. 1984. "The Deterrent Effects of Automobile Insurance and Tort Law: A Survey of the Empirical Literature." *Law and Policy* 6 (1): 67–100.

Brumm, H. J., and D. O. Cloninger. 1996. "Perceived Risk of Punishment and the Commission of Homicides: A Covariance Structure Analysis." *Journal of Economic Behavior and Organization* 31 (1): 1–11.

Buntain-Ricklefs, J. J., F. P. Rivara, D. M. Donovan, P. M. Salzberg, and N. L. Polissar. 1995. "Differentiating Bad Drivers with and without a DWI." *Journal of Studies on Alcohol* 56 (3): 356–60.

Calabresi, G. 1970. *The Costs of Accidents.* New Haven: Yale University Press.

Carlson, K. 1982. *Mandatory Sentencing: The Experience of Two States.* National Institute of Justice, U.S. Department of Justice. Washington, D.C.: U.S. Government Printing Office.

Carpenter, J. A. 1962. "Effects of Alcohol on Psychological Processes: A Critical Review with Special Reference to Automobile Driving Skill." *Quarterly Journal of Studies on Alcohol* 23: 274–314.

Chaloupka, F. J. 1991. "Rational Addictive Behavior and Cigarette Smoking." *Journal of Political Economy* 94 (4): 722–42.

Chaloupka, F. J., H. Saffer, and M. Grossman. 1993. "Alcohol-Control Policies and Motor-Vehicle Fatalities." *Journal of Legal Studies* 22:161–86.

Cherrington, E. H. 1920. *The Evolution of Prohibition in the United States of America.* Westerville, Ohio: American Issue Press.

Christy, C. C. 1989. "Server Intervention/Responsible Beverage Service." Dissertation, George Peabody College for Teachers of Vanderbilt University.

Chung, T.-T. 1998. "Comparative Negligence." In *The New Palgrave Dictionary of Economics and the Law,* ed. Peter Newman, 1:352–54. London: Macmillan Reference.

Clark, W. B. 1976. "Loss of Control, Heavy Drinking, and Drinking Problems in a Longitudinal Study." *Journal of Studies on Alcohol* 37 (9): 1256–90.

Clements, K. W., W. Yang, and S. W. Zheng. 1997. "Is Utility Additive? The Case of Alcohol." *Applied Economics* 29:1163–67.

Colman, V., B. E. Krell, and J. F. Mosher. 1985. "Preventing Alcohol-Related Injuries: Dram Shop Liability in a Public Health Perspective." *Washington State University Law Review* 12 (20): 417–517.

Colon, I. 1981. "Alcohol Availability and Cirrhosis Mortality by Gender and Race." *American Journal of Public Health* 71 (12): 1325–28.

Colon I., H. S. Cutter, and W. C. Jones. 1982. "Prediction of Alcoholism from Alcohol Availability, Alcohol Consumption and Demographic Data." *Journal of Studies on Alcohol* 43 (11): 1199–1213.

Cook, P. J., and J. A. Leitzel. 1996. "Perversity, Futility, Jeopardy: An Economic Analysis of the Attack on Gun Control." *Law and Contemporary Problems* 59 (1): 91–118.

Cook, P. J., and M. Moore. n.d. "Alcohol." In *Handbook of Health Economics,* ed. J. Newhouse and A. Culyer. Forthcoming.

Cook, P. J., and G. Tauchen. 1982. "The Effect of Liquor Taxes on Heavy Drinking." *Bell Journal of Economics* 13 (2): 379–90.

———. 1984. "The Effect of Minimum Drinking Age Legislation on Youthful Auto Fatalities: 1970–1977." *Journal of Legal Studies* 13:169–90.

Cooprider, V. W. 1940. "Legal Questions in the Operation of Licensing Systems." *Law and Contemporary Problems* 7 (4): 621–44.

Cooter, R. D., and D. L. Rubinfeld. 1989. "Economic Analysis of Legal Disputes and Their Resolution." *NYU Law Review* 61:1067–1110.

Cooter, R. D., and T. Ulen. 1988. *Law and Economics.* Glenview, Ill.: Scott, Foresman.

Curran, C. C. 1992. "The Spread of the Comparative Negligence Rule in the United States." *International Review of Law and Economics* 12 (3): 317–32.

Deery, H. A., and A. W. Love. 1996. "The Effect of a Moderate Dose of Alcohol on the Traffic Hazard Perception Profile of Young Drunk Drivers." *Addiction* 91 (6): 815–27.

Deshapriya, E. B., and Iwase, N. 1996. "Are Lower Legal Blood Alcohol Limits and a Combination of Sanctions Desirable in Reducing Drunken Driver–Involved Traffic Fatalities and Traffic Accidents?" *Accident Analysis and Prevention* 28 (6): 721–31.

Devlin, R. A. 1990. "Some Welfare Implications of No-Fault Automobile Insurance." *International Review of Law and Economics* 10 (2): 193–205.

Dewees, D., D. Duff, and M. Trebilcock. 1996. *Exploring the Domain of Accident Law.* New York: Oxford University Press.

Diamond, P. 1974. "Single Activity Accidents." *Journal of Legal Studies* 3:107–64.

Dixon, W., and F. Massey. 1969. *Introduction to Statistical Analysis.* 3d ed. New York: McGraw-Hill.

Donovan, D. M., G. A. Marlatt, and P. M. Salzberg. 1983. "Drinking Behavior Personality Factors and High Risk Driving: A Review and Theoretical Formulation." *Journal of Studies on Alcohol* 44 (3): 395–428.

Dorr, R. C. 1929. *Drink: Coercion or Control.* New York: Frederick A. Stokes.

Douglass, E. K. 1931. *Prohibition and Common Sense.* New York: Alcohol Information Committee.

Duffy, M. H. 1983. "The Demand for Alcohol Drink in the United Kingdom: 1963–1978." *Applied Economics* 15:125–40.

DuMouchel, W. A., A. F. Williams, and P. Zador. 1987. "Raising the Alcohol Purchase Age: Its Effect on Fatal Motor Crashes in Twenty-six States." *Journal of Legal Studies* 16:249–66.

Ehrlich, I. 1975. "The Deterrent Effect of Capital Punishment: A Question of Life and Death." *American Economic Review* 65 (3): 397–417.

———. 1998. "Criminal Justice." In *The New Palgrave Dictionary of Economics and the Law,* ed. P. Newman , 1:553–60. London: Macmillan Reference.

Ehrlich, I., and R. A. Posner. 1974. "An Economic Analysis of Legal Rulemaking." *Journal of Legal Studies* 3:257–86.

Eisley, M. 1998. "Conflict on the Corner." *Raleigh News and Observer,* May 19, 1A, 8A.

Escobedo, L. G., T. L. Chorba, and R. Waxweiler. 1995. "Patterns of Alcohol Use and the Risk of Drinking and Driving among High School Students." *American Journal of Public Health* 85 (7): 976–78.

Evans, W. N., D. Neville, and J. D. Graham. 1991. "General Deterrence of Drunk Driving: Evaluation of Recent American Policies." *Risk Analysis* 11:279–89.

Ferguson, D. G. 1982. "Protection, Real Incomes and Aggregate Factor Substitution." *International Economic Review* 23 (3): 735–43.

Ferrence, R., and L. T. Kozlowski. 1995. "Moderate Drinking and Health: Being Confounded by Confounders." *Addiction* 90 (4): 485–88.

Fisher, I. 1927. *Prohibition at Its Worst.* New York: Alcohol Information Committee.

———. 1928. *Prohibition Still at Its Worst.* New York: Alcohol Information Committee.

Flanigan, G. B., J. E. Winkler, T. Daniel, and W. Ferguson. 1989. "Experience from Early Tort Reforms: Comparative Negligence since 1974." *Journal of Risk and Insurance* 56 (3): 3525–34.

Fleming, J. G. 1988. *The American Tort Process.* Oxford: Clarendon Press.

Fontaine, R. A. 1992. "DUI Pre-arrest Alcohol Purchases: A Survey of Sonoma County Drunk Drivers." *Journal of Studies on Alcohol* 53 (4): 345–48.

Fosdick, R. B., and A. L. Scott. 1933. *Toward Liquor Control.* New York: Harper Brothers.

Friedman, D. 1987. "Law and Economics." In *The New Palgrave: A Dictionary of Economics,* ed. John Eatwell, Murray Milgate, and Peter Newman, 3:144–48. London: Macmillan.

Fuchs, V. R. 1974. *Who Shall Live? Health Economics and Social Choice.* New York: Basic Books.

Gaudry, M. 1987. "The Effects on Road Safety of the Compulsory Insurance, Flat Premium Rating and No-Fault Features of the 1978 Quebec Automobile Act." Appendix to *Report of the Inquiry into Motor Vehicle Accident Compensation in Ontario.* Ontario: Queen's Printers.

Geller, E. S., N. W. Russ, and W. A. Delfphos. 1987. "Does Server Intervention Training Make a Difference? An Empirical Field Evaluation." *Alcohol Health and Research World* 11 (4): 64–69.

Giacopassi, D., and R. Winn. 1995. "Alcohol Availability and Alcohol-Related Crashes: Does Distance Make a Difference?" *American Journal of Drug and Alcohol Abuse* 21 (3): 407–16.

Gliksman, L., D. McKenzie, E. Single, R. Douglas, S. Brunet, and K. Moffatt. 1993. "The Role of Alcohol Providers in Prevention: An Evaluation of a Server Intervention Programme." *Addiction* 88 (9): 1195–1203.

Godfrey, C. 1988. "Licensing and the Demand for Alcohol." *Applied Economics* 20:1541–58.

Goldberg, J. M. 1987. "One for the Road: Liquor Liability Broadens." *American Bar Association Journal* 73 (6): 84–88.

Goodman, R. A., G. R. Istre, F. B. Jordan, L. Joy, and J. Kelaghan. 1991. "Alcohol and Fatal Injuries in Oklahoma." *Journal of Studies on Alcohol* 52 (2): 156–61.

Gordis, E. 1996. "Alcohol Research and Social Policy: An Overview." *Alcohol Health and Research World* 20 (4): 208–12.

Greenfeld, L. A. 1998. *Alcohol and Crime: An Analysis of National Data on the*

Prevalence of Alcohol Involvement in Crime. Washington D.C.: U.S. Department of Justice.

Grogger, J. 1991. "Certainty vs. Severity of Punishment." *Economic Inquiry* 29 (2): 297–309.

Grube, J. W. 1997. "Preventing Sales of Alcohol to Minors: Results from a Community Trial." *Addiction* 92 (2): S251–60.

Grube, J. W., and R. B. Voas. 1996. "Predicting Underage Drinking and Driving Behaviors." *Addiction* 91 (12): 1843–50.

Gruenewald, P. J., and W. R. Ponicki. 1995. "The Relationship of the Retail Availability and Alcohol Sales to Alcohol-Related Traffic Crashes." *Accident Analysis and Prevention* 27 (2): 249–59.

Gruenewald, P. J., W. R. Ponicki, and H. D. Holder. 1993. "The Relationship of Outlet Densities to Alcohol Consumption: A Time Series Cross-Sectional Analysis." *Alcohol Clinical Experimental Research* 17 (1): 38–47.

Gruenewald, P. J., A. J. Treno, and P. R. Mitchell. 1996. "Drinking Patterns and Drinking Behaviors: Theoretical Models of Risky Acts." *Contemporary Drug Problems* 23 (3): 407–40.

Gusfield, J. R., P. Rasmussen, and J. H. Kotarba. 1984. "The Social Control of Drinking-Driving: An Ethonographic Study of Bar Settings." *Law and Policy* 6 (1): 45–66.

Harris, D., M. Maclean, H. Genn, S. Lloyd-Bostock, P. Fenn, P. Corfield, and Y. Brittan. 1984. *Compensation and Support for Illness and Injury.* Oxford: Clarendon Press.

Heard, S. 1986. "The Liability of Purveyors of Alcoholic Beverages for Torts of Intoxicated Consumers." *Montana Law Review* 47:495–512.

Hensler, D. R., et al. 1991. *Compensation for Accidental Injuries in the United States.* Santa Monica, Calif.: RAND Corporation.

Hingson, R. 1996. "Prevention of Drinking and Driving." *Alcohol Health and Research World* 20 (4): 219–26.

Hirshi, T. 1969. *Causes of Delinquency.* Berkeley: University of California Press.

Holder, H. D., K. Janes, J. Mosher, R. Saltz, S. Spurr, and A. C. Wagenaar. 1993. "Alcoholic Beverage Server Liability and the Reduction of Alcohol-Involved Problems." *Journal of Studies on Alcohol* 54 (2): 23–26.

Holder, H. D., and R. I. Reynolds. 1997. "Application of Local Policy to Prevent Alcohol Problems: Experiences from a Community Trial." *Addiction* 92 (2): S285–92.

Holder, H. D., R. F. Saltz, J. W. Grube, A. J. Treno, R. I. Reynolds, R. B. Voas, and P. J. Gruenewald. 1997. "Summing Up: Lessons from a Comprehensive Community Prevention Trial." *Addiction* 92 (2): S293–301.

Holder, H. D., R. F. Saltz, J. W. Grube, R. B. Voas, P. J. Gruenewald, and A. J. Treno. 1997. "A Community Prevention Trial to Reduce Alcohol-Involved Accidental Injury and Death: Overview." *Addiction* 92 (2): S155–71.

Holder, H. D., and A. C. Wagenaar. 1994. "Mandated Server Training and Reduced Alcohol-Involved Traffic Crashes: A Time Series Analysis of the Oregon Experience." *Accident and Prevention* 26 (1): 89–97.

Holder, H. D., A. C. Wagenaar, R. Saltz, J. Mosher, and K. Janes. 1990. "Alcoholic Beverage Server Liability and the Reduction of Alcohol-Related Problems:

Evaluation of Dram Shop Laws." Final Report, U.S. Department of Transportation, National Highway Traffic Safety Administration. Springfield, Va.: National Technical Information Service.

Houchens, R. L. 1985. *Automobile Accident Compensation.* Volume 3. *Payments from All Sources.* Santa Monica, Calif.: RAND Corporation.

Howard-Pitney, B., M. D. Johnson, D. G. Altman, R. Hopkins, and N. Hammond. 1991. "Responsible Alcohol Service: A Study of Server, Manager, and Environmental Impact." *American Journal of Public Health* 81 (2): 197–99.

Huber, P. W. 1988. *Liability: The Legal Revolution and Its Consequences.* New York: Basic Books.

Hwang, S. L. 1999. "Light Brigades: Tobacco Companies Enlist the Bar Owner to Push Their Goods." *Wall Street Journal,* April 21, A1 and A6.

Jacobs, James B. 1989. *Drunk Driving: An American Dilemma.* Chicago: University of Chicago Press.

Jolls, C., C. R. Sunstein, and R. Thaler. 1998. "A Behavioral Approach to Law and Economics." *Stanford Law Review* 50:1471–1514.

Jones-Webb, R., T. L. Toomey, B. Short, A. Wagenaar, and M. Wolfson. 1997. "Relationships among Alcohol Availability, Drinking Location, Alcohol Consumption, and Drinking Problems in Adolescents." *Substance Use and Misuse* 32 (10): 1261–85.

Joost, R. H. 1992. *Automobile Insurance and No-Fault Law.* Deerfield, Ill.: Clark Boardman Callaghan.

Kelleher, K. J., S. K. Pope, R. S. Kirby, and V. I. Rickert. 1997. "Alcohol Availability and Motor Vehicle Fatalities." *Journal of Adolescent Health* 19:325–30.

Kenkel, D. S. 1993. "Drinking, Driving, and Deterrence: The Effectiveness and Social Costs of Alternative Policies." *Journal of Law and Economics* 36 (2): 887–911.

Kessler, D. 1995. "Fault Settlement and Negligence Law." *RAND Journal of Economics* 26 (2): 296–313.

Kinkade, P. T., Leone, M. C., and Welsh, W. N. 1995. "Tough Laws: Policymaker Perceptions and Commitment." *Social Science Journal* 32:157–78.

Kochanowski, P. S., and M. V. Young. 1985. "Deterrent Aspects of No-Fault Automobile Insurance: Some Empirical Findings." *Journal of Risk and Insurance* 52 (2): 269–88.

Kornhauser, L. A. 1982. "An Economic Analysis of the Choice between Enterprise and Personal Liability for Accidents." *California Law Review* 70:1345–92.

Kraakman, R. 1998. "Third-Party Liability." In *The New Palgrave Dictionary of Economics and the Law,* ed. P. Newman, 3:583–87. London: Macmillian Reference.

Krout, J. A. 1925. *The Origins of Prohibition.* New York: A. A. Knopf.

Lagenbucher, J., and P. Nathan. 1983. "Psychology, Public Policy, and the Evidence for Alcohol Intoxication." *American Psychologist* 38 (10): 1070–77.

Landes, E. M. 1982. "Insurance, Liability, and Accidents: A Theoretical and Empirical Investigation of the Effect of No-Fault Accidents." *Journal of Legal Studies* 25:49–65.

Lawrence, M. D. 1988. "The Legal Context in the United States." In *Social Con-*

trol of the Drinking Driver, ed. M. D. Laurence, J. R. Snortum, and F. E. Zimring. Chicago: University of Chicago Press.

Leamer, E. 1983. "Let's Take the Con out of Econometrics." *American Economic Review* 73 (1): 31–43.

Lemaire, J. 1985. *Automobile Insurance: Actuarial Models.* Boston: Kluwer-Nijhoff.

Lessig, L. 1998. "The New Chicago School." *Journal of Legal Studies* 27:661–92.

Leung, S., and C. E. Phelps. 1993. "My Kingdom for a Drink . . . ? A Review of Estimates of the Price Sensitivity of Demand for Alcoholic Beverages." In *Economics and the Prevention of Alcohol-Related Problems,* ed. M. E. Hilton and G. Bloss, 1–31. NIAAA Research Monograph no. 25, NIH Publication no. 93–3513. Bethesda, Md.: National Institutes of Health.

Levitt, S. D. 1998. "Why Do Increased Arrest Rates Appear to Reduce Crime: Deterrence, Incapacitation, or Measurement Error?" *Economic Inquiry* 36 (3): 353–72.

Levitt, S. D., and J. Porter. 1999. "Estimating the Effect of Alcohol on Driver Risk Using Only Fatal Accident Statistics." Working Paper no. 6944. Cambridge, Mass.: National Bureau of Economic Research.

Levy, D. T., and T. R. Miller. 1995. "A Cost-Benefit Analysis of Enforcement Efforts to Reduce Serving Intoxicated Patrons." *Journal of Studies on Alcohol* 56 (2): 240–47.

Liang, K.-Y., and S. L. Zeger. 1986. "Longitudinal data analysis using generalized linear models." *Biometrika* 73:13–22.

Loftin, C., M. Heumann, and D. McDowall. 1983. "Mandatory Sentencing and Firearms Violence: Evaluating an Alternative to Gun Control." *Law and Society Review* 17:287–318.

Loftin, C., and D. McDowall. 1984. "The Deterrent Effects of the Florida Felony Firearm Law." *Journal of Criminal Law and Criminology* 75:250–59.

Lott, J. R., Jr. 1990. "A Transaction-Costs Explanation for Why the Poor Are More Likely to Commit Crime." *Journal of Legal Studies* 19:243–45.

Lott, J. R., Jr., and D. B. Mustard. 1997. "Crime, Deterrence, and Right-to Carry Concealed Handguns." *Journal of Legal Studies* 26:1–68.

———. 1998. "Crime, Deterrence, and the Right-to-Carry Concealed Handguns." *Journal of Legal Studies* 26:221–43.

Low, S., and J. K. Smith. 1995. "Decisions to Retain Attorneys and File Lawsuits: An Examination of the Comparative Negligence Rule in Accident Law." *Journal of Legal Studies* 24:535–57.

Luksetich, W. A. 1975. "A Study of Regulation: The Minnesota Liquor Case." *Southern Economic Journal* 41 (3): 457–65.

MacDonald, S. 1989. "A Comparison of the Psychosocial Characteristics of Alcoholics Responsible for Impaired and Nonimpaired Collisions." *Accident Analysis and Prevention* 21 (5): 493–508.

Maddala, G. S. 1983. *Limited-Dependent and Qualitative Variables in Econometrics.* New York: Cambridge University Press.

Males, M. A. 1986. "The Minimum Purchase Age for Alcohol and Young-Driver Fatal Crashes: A Long Term View." *Journal of Legal Studies* 15:181–211.

Mann, R. E., and Anglin, L. 1990. "Alcohol Availability, per Capita Consumption, and the Alcohol-Crash Problem." In *Drinking and Driving: Advances in Research and Prevention,* ed. R. J. Wilson and R. E. Mann, 205–25. New York: Guilford Press.

Manning, W. G., E. B. Keeler, J. P. Newhouse, E. M. Sloss, and J. Wasserman. 1989. "The Taxes of Sin: Do Smokers and Drinkers Pay Their Way?" *Journal of the American Medical Association* 261:1604–9.

———. 1991. *The Cost of Poor Health Habits.* Cambridge: Harvard University Press.

Mastrofski, S. D., J. B. Snipes, and R. R. R. Ritti. 1994. "Expectancy Theory and Police Productivity in DUI Enforcement." *Law and Society Review,* 28:113–48.

Maynard, A., and C. Godfrey. 1994. "Alcohol Policy—Evaluating the Options." *British Medical Bulletin* 50 (1): 221–30.

McDowall, D., C. Loftin, and B. Wiersema. 1992. "A Comparative Study of the Preventive Effects of Mandatory Sentencing Laws for Gun Crimes." *Journal of Criminal Law and Criminology* 83:378–94.

McGinnis, J. Michael, and William H. Foege. 1993. "Actual Causes of Death in the United States." *Journal of the American Medical Association* 270 (28): 2207–12.

McGuinness, T. 1980. "An Econometric Analysis of Total Demand for Alcoholic Beverages in the U.K., 1965–75." *Journal of Industrial Economics* 29:85–108.

McKnight, A. J. 1991. "Factors Influencing the Effectiveness of Server-Intervention Education." *Journal of Studies on Alcohol* 52 (5): 389–97.

McKnight, A. J., and F. M. Streff. 1994. "The Effect of Enforcement upon Service of Alcohol to Intoxicated Patrons of Bars and Restaurants." *Accident Analysis and Prevention* 26 (1): 79–88.

Meier, S. E., T. A. Brigham, and G. Handel. 1984. "Effects of Feedback on Legally Intoxicated Drivers." *Journal of Studies on Alcohol* 45 (6): 528–33.

Michigan Commissioner of Insurance. 1996. "The Availability and Pricing of Liquor Liability Insurance." Lansing: Insurance Bureau, Department of Consumer and Industry Services.

Miller, T. [R.], D. Lestina, M. Gabraith, T. Schlax, P. Mabery, and R. Peering. 1997. "United States Passanger Vehicle Crashes by Crash Geometry: Direct Costs and Other Losses." *Accident Analysis and Prevention* 29 (3): 343–52.

Miller, T. R., S. Luchter, and C. P. Brinkman. 1989. "Crash Costs and Safety Investment." *Accident Analysis and Prevention* 21 (4): 303–15.

Miron, J. A. 1999. "Violence and U.S. Prohibitions of Drugs and Alcohol." Working Paper no. 6950. Cambridge, Mass.: National Bureau of Economic Research.

Mosher, J. F. 1984. "The Impact of Legal Provisions on Barroom Behavior: Toward an Alcohol-Problems Prevention Policy." *Alcohol* 1:205–11.

———. 1988. *Liquor Liability Law.* New York: Matthew Bender. (Supplement, 1997.)

Moskowitz, H., and C. D. Robinson. 1988. *Effects of Low Doses of Alcohol on Driving Skills: A Review of the Evidence.* DOT-HS-800–599. Washington, D.C.: National Highway Traffic Safety Administration.

Mullahy, J. S., and J. L. Sindelar. 1994. "Do Drinkers Know When to Say When? An Empirical Analysis of Drunk Driving." *Economic Inquiry* 32 (3): 383–94.

National Highway Traffic Safety Administration. 1994. *Fatal Accident Reporting System, 1994.* Washington, D.C.: U.S. Department of Transportation.

Nelson, J. P. 1990. "State Monopolies and Alcoholic Beverage Consumption." *Journal of Regulatory Economics* 2 (1): 83–98.

———. 1999. "Broadcast Advertising and U.S. Demand for Alcoholic Beverages." *Southern Economic Journal* 65 (4): 774–90.

Novak, T. 1998a. "Closing Time for Bars." *Chicago Sun-Times,* July 19, 1A, 4A–5A.

———1998b. "Socializing amid the Suds: Corner Bars Are Also Community Centers." *Chicago Sun-Times,* July 19, 4A–5A.

O'Connell, J., and D. F. Partlett. 1988. "An America's Cup for Tort Reform." *University of Michigan Journal of Legal Reform* 21:443.

O'Donnell, M. A. 1985. "Research on Drinking Locations of Alcohol-Impaired Drivers: Implications for Prevention Policies." *Journal of Public Health Policy* 6 (4): 510–25.

Ornstein, S. [I.], and D. Hanssens. 1985. "Alcohol Control Laws and the Consumption of Distilled Spirits and Beer." *Journal of Consumer Research* 12:200–213.

———. 1987. "Resale Price Maintenance: Output Increasing or Restricting? The Case of Distilled Spirits in the United States." *Journal of Industrial Economics* 36:1–18.

Parker, D. A., M. W. Wolz, and T. C. Harford. 1978. "The Prevention of Alcoholism: An Empirical Report on the Effects of Outlet Availability." *Alcoholism: Clinical and Experimental Research* 2 (4): 339–43.

Peltzman, S. 1976. "Toward A More General Theory of Regulation." *Journal of Law and Economics* 19 (2): 211–40.

———. 1993. "George Stigler's Contribution to the Economic Analysis of Regulation." *Journal of Political Economy* 101 (5): 818–32.

Philipson, T. J., and R. A. Posner. 1996. "The Economic Epidemiology of Crime." *Journal of Law and Economics* 39 (12): 405–33.

Pierce, G. L., and W. J. Bowers. 1987. "The Bartley-Fox Gun Laws Short Term Impact on Crime in Boston." *Annals of the American Academy of Political and Social Science* 455:120–32.

Pitchford, R. 1998. "Judgment-Proofness." In *The New Palgrave Dictionary of Economics and the Law,* ed. Peter Newman, 2:380–83. London: Macmillan Reference.

Polinsky, A. M., and S. Shavell. 1999. "The Economic Theory of Public Enforcement of Law." Working Paper no. 6993. Cambridge, Mass.: National Bureau of Economic Research.

Popham, R. E., W. Schmidt, and J. deLint. 1978. "Government Control Measures to Prevent Hazardous Drinking." In *Drinking: Alcohol in American Society—Issues and Current Research,* ed. J. Ewing and B. Rouse, 239–66. Chicago: Nelson-Hall.

Posner, R. A. 1986. *Economic Analysis of Law.* 3d ed. Boston: Little, Brown.

———. 1997. "Explaining the Variance in the Number of Tort Suits across U.S. States and between the United States and England." *Journal of Legal Studies* 26:477–90.

Pro CD, Inc. 1997. *Select Phone.* CD-ROM. Danvers, Mass.: Acxiom.

Prus, R. 1983. "Drinking as an Activity: An Interactionist Analysis." *Journal of Studies on Alcohol* 44 (3): 460–75.

Rabow, J., and R. K. Watts. 1982. "Alcohol Availability, Alcoholic Beverage Sales and Alcohol-Related Problems." *Journal of Studies on Alcohol* 43 (7): 767–801.

Rabow, J., R. K. Watts, and A. C. R. Hernandez.4 1993. "Alcoholic Beverage Licensing Practices in California: A Study of a Regulatory Agency." *Alcoholism: Clinical and Experimental Research* 17:241–45.

Rea, S. A., Jr. 1987. "The Economics of Comparative Negligence." *International Review of Law and Economics* 7 (2): 149–62.

Reiss, A. J., Jr. 1984. "Consequences of Compliance and Deterrence Models of Law Enforcement for the Exercise of Police Discretion." *Law and Contemporary Problems* 47 (4): 83–122.

Rice, D. P. 1993. "The Economic Cost of Alcohol Abuse and Alcohol Dependence: 1990." *Alcohol Health and Research World* 17 (1): 10–11.

Room, R. 1984. "Alcohol Control and Public Health." *Annual Review of Public Health* 5:293–317.

Ross, H. L. 1987. *Deterring the Drinking Driver: Legal Policy and Social Control.* Insurance Institute for Highway Safety Book. Lexington, Mass.: D. C. Heath.

Ross, H. L., and S. S. Cleary. 1996. "License Plate Confiscation for Persistent Alcohol Impaired Driving." *Accident Analysis and Prevention* 28 (1): 53–61.

Rossman, D., P. Froyd, J. McDevitt, and W. J. Bowers. 1979. *The Impact of the Mandatory Gun Law in Massachusetts.* National Institute of Law Enforcement and Criminal Justice, Law Enforcement Assistance Administration, U.S. Department of Justice. Washington D.C.: U.S. Government Printing Office.

Ruhm, C. J. 1996. "Alcohol Policies and Highway Vehicle Fatalities." *Journal of Health Economics* 15 (4): 435–54.

Runge, J. W. 1993. "The Cost of Injury." *Emergency Medical Clinic of North America* 11:241–53.

Runge, J. W., C. L. Pulliam, J. M. Carter, and M. H. Thomason. 1996. "Enforcement of Drunken Driving Laws in Cases Involving Injured Intoxicated Drivers." *Annals of Emergency Medicine* 27 (1): 66–72.

Russ, N. W., and E. S. Geller. 1987. "Training Bar Personnel to Prevent Drunken Driving: A Field Evaluation." *American Journal of Public Health* 77 (8): 952–54.

Saffer, H. 1991. "Alcohol Advertising Bans and Alcohol Abuse: An International Perspective." *Journal of Health Economics* 104:65–79.

Saffer, H., and M. Grossman. 1987. "Beer Taxes, the Legal Drinking Age, and Youth Motor Vehicle Fatalities." *Journal of Legal Studies* 16:351–74.

Saffer, H., M. Grossman, and F. Chaloupka. 1998. "Alcohol Control." In *The New Palgrave Dictionary of Economics and the Law,* ed. Peter Newman, 1:44–48. London: Macmillan Reference.

Saltz, R. F. 1987. "The Roles of Bars and Restaurants in Preventing Alcohol-Impaired Driving; An Evaluation of Server Intervention." *Evaluation and Health Professions* 10 (1): 5–27.

———. 1989. "Research Needs and Opportunities in Server Intervention Programs." *Health Education Quarterly* 16 (3): 429–38.

———. 1993. "The Introduction of Dram Shop Legislation in the United States and the Advent of Server Training." *Addiction* 88 (suppl.): S95–103.

Saltz, R. F., and P. Stanghetta. 1997. "A Community-Wide Responsible Beverage Service Program in Three Communities: Early Findings." *Addiction* 92 (2): S237–49.

Schlesinger, H., and E. Venezian. 1986. "Insurance Markets with Loss Prevention Activity: Profits, Market Structure, and Consumer Welfare." *RAND Journal of Economics* 17 (2): 227–38.

Schuck, P. H., ed. 1991. *Tort Law and the Public Interest—Competition, Innovation, and Consumer Welfare.* New York: W. W. Norton.

Schulhofer, S. J. 1988. "Criminal Justice Discretion as a Regulatory System." *Journal of Legal Studies* 17:43–82.

Schwartz, G. T. 1994. "Reality in the Economic Analysis of Tort Law: Does Tort Law Really Deter?" *UCLA Law Review* 42 (2): 377–444.

———. 1997. "Mixed Themes of Tort Law: Affirming Both Deterrence and Corrective Justice." *Texas Law Review* 75 (7): 1801–34.

———. 1998. "Insurance, Deterrence, and Liability." In *The New Palgrave Dictionary of Economics and the Law,* ed. P. Newman, 2:335–39. London: Macmillan References.

Scribner, R. A., D. P. MacKinnon, and J. H. Dwyer. 1994. "Alcohol Outlet Density and Motor Vehicle Crashes in Los Angeles County Cities." *Journal of Studies on Alcohol* 55 (4): 47–53.

———. 1995. "The Risk of Assaultive Violence and Alcohol Availability in Los Angeles County." *American Journal of Public Health* 85 (3): 335–40.

Seeley, J. R. 1960. "Death by Liver Cirrhosis and the Price of Beverage Alcohol." *Canadian Medical Association Journal* 83:1361–66.

Shapiro, P., and H. L. Votey Jr. 1984. "Deterrence and Subjective Probabilities of Arrest: Modeling Individual Decisions to Drink and Drive in Sweden." *Law and Society Review* 18:583–604.

Shavell, S. 1980. "Strict Liability vs. Negligence." *Journal of Legal Studies* 9:1–25.

———. 1982. "On Liability and Insurance." *Bell Journal of Economics* 13 (1): 120–32.

———. 1984. "Liability for Harm versus Regulation of Safety." *Journal of Legal Studies* 13:357–74.

———. 1987. *Economic Analysis of Accident Law.* Cambridge , Mass.: Harvard University Press.

Shipman, G. A. 1940. "State Administrative Machinery for Liquor Control." *Law and Contemporary Problems* 7 (4): 600–620.

Simon, H. A. 1982. *Models of Bounded Rationality.* Cambridge: MIT Press.

Simon, J. L. 1966. "The Economic Effects of State Monopoly of Packaged-Liquor Retailing." *Journal of Political Economy* 74 (2): 188–94.

Simon, J. L., and D. M. Simon. 1996. "The Effects of Regulations on State Liquor Prices." *Empirica* 23:303–16.

Slade, M. E. 1998. "Beer and Tie: Did Divestiture of Brewer-Owned Public Houses Lead to Higher Beer Prices?" *Economic Journal* 108 (448): 565–602.

Sloan, F. A., R. R. Bovbjerg, and P. B. Githens. 1991. *Insuring for Medical Malpractice.* New York: Oxford University Press.

Sloan, F. A., and P. B. Githens. 1994. "Drinking, Driving and the Price of Automobile Insurance." *Journal of Risk and Insurance* 61 (1): 33–58.

Sloan, F. A., B. A. Reilly, and C. M. Schenzler. 1994a. "Effects of Prices, Civil and Criminal Sanctions, and Law Enforcement on Alcohol-Related Mortality." *Journal of Studies on Alcohol* 55 (4): 454–65.

———. 1994b. "Tort Liability versus Other Approaches for Deterring Careless Driving." *International Review of Law and Economics* 14 (1): 53–71.

———. 1995. "Effects of Tort Liability and Insurance on Heavy Drinking and Drinking and Driving." *Journal of Law and Economics* 38 (1): 49–78.

Smart, R. G., and E. M. Adlaf. 1986. "Banning Happy Hours: The Impact on Drinking and Impaired-Driving Charges in Ontario, Canada." *Journal of Studies on Alcohol* 47 (3): 256–58.

Smart, R. G., and R. E. Mann. 1991. "Factors in Recent Reductions in Liver Cirrhosis Deaths." *Journal of Studies on Alcohol* 52 (3): 232–40.

Smith, J. K. 1982. "An Analysis of State Regulations Governing Liquor Store Licenses." *Journal of Law and Economics* 25 (2): 301–19.

Snortum, J. R. 1988. "Deterrence of Alcohol-Impaired Driving: An Effect in Search of a Cause." In *Social Control of the Drinking Driver,* ed. M. D. Laurence, J. R. Snortum, and F. E. Zimring. Chicago: University of Chicago Press.

Snortum, J. R., and D. E. Berger. 1989. "Drinking-Driving Compliance in the United States: Perceptions and Behavior in 1983 and 1986." *Journal of Studies on Alcohol* 50 (4): 306–19.

Snortum, J. R., D. E. Berger, and R. Hauge. 1988. "Legal Knowledge and Compliance: Drinking and Driving in Norway and the United States." *Alcohol, Drugs and Driving* 4 (3–4): 251–63.

Snow, R. W., and B. J. Anderson. 1987. "Drinking Place Selection Factors among Drunk Drivers." *British Journal of Addiction* 82 (1): 85–95.

Snow, R. W., and J. W. Landrum. 1986. "Drinking Locations and Frequency of Drunkenness among Mississippi DUI Offenders." *American Journal of Drug Alcohol Abuse* 12 (4): 389–402.

Stigler, G. J. 1971. "The Theory of Economic Regulation." *Bell Journal of Economics and Management Science* 2:3–21.

Stockwell, T., P. Rydon, S. Giannatti, et al. 1992. "Levels of Drunkenness of Customers Leaving Licensed Premises in Perth, Western Australia: A Comparison of High and Low 'Risk' Premises." *British Journal of Addiction* 87 (6): 873–81.

Sugarman, S. D. 1989. *Doing Away with Personal Injury Law.* New York: Quorum Books.

Tauchen, H., A. D. Witte, and H. Griesinger. 1994. "Criminal Deterrence: Revisiting the Issue with a Birth Cohort." *Review of Economics and Statistics* 76 (3): 399–412.

Thomann, G. 1887. *Colonial Liquor Laws.* New York: United States Brewers' Association.

Thun, M. J., R. Peto, A. D. Lopez, J. H. Monaco, S. J. Henley, C. W. Heath Jr., and R. Doll. 1997. "Alcohol Consumption and Mortality among Middle-Aged and Elderly U.S. Adults." *New England Journal of Medicine* 337 (24): 1705–14.

Tonry, M. H. 1996. *Sentencing Matters.* New York; Oxford University Press.

Trebilcock, M. J. 1989. "Incentive Issues in the Design of a No-Fault Compensation System." *Law Journal* 2 (1): 19–54.

Turissi, R., B. Nicholson, and J. Jaccard. 1999. "A Cognitive Analysis of Server Intervention Policies: Perceptions of Bar Owners and Servers." *Journal of Studies on Alcohol* 60 (1): 37–46.

U.S. Bureau of the Census. 1997. *Statistical Abstract of the United States: 1997.* 117th ed. Table 478, Washington, D.C.: U.S. Government Printing Office.

U.S. Department of Health and Human Services. 1998. "Economic Costs of Alcohol and Drug Abuse Estimated at \$246 Billion in the United States." National Institute on Drug Abuse (NIDA) and the National Institute of Alcohol Abuse and Alcoholism (NIAA):< http://silk.nih.gov/silk/niaaa1/releases/economic.htm>.

U.S. Department of Transportation. 1991. *Digest of State Alcohol-Highway Safety Related Legislation.* 9th ed. Current as of January 1, 1991. Washington, D.C.: Department of Transportation (also available for other years).

U.S. Executive Office of the President, Office of Management and Budget. 1987. *Standard Industrial Classification Manual, 1987.* Springfield, Va.: National Technical Information Service.

U.S. Federal Bureau of Investigation. 1992. *Uniform Crime Reports for the United States.* Washington, D.C.: U.S. Government Printing Office.

Van Houten, R., P. Nau, and B. Jonah. 1985. "Effects of Feedback on Impaired Driving." In *Conference on Alcohol, Drugs and Traffic Safety—San Juan, Puerto Rico, 1983,* ed. S. Kaye and G. W. Meier, 814:1375–94. DOT-HS-806. Washington, D.C.: U.S. Department of Transportation.

Van Munching, P. 1997. *Beer Blast.* New York: Random House.

Viscusi, W. K. 1986. "The Risks and Rewards of Criminal Activity: A Comprehensive Test of Criminal Deterrence." *Journal of Labor Economics* 3 (part 1): 317–40.

Voas, R. B., Holder, H. D., and Gruenewald, P. J. 1997. "The Effect of Drinking and Driving Interventions on Alcohol-Involved Traffic Crashes within a Comprehensive Community Trial." *Addiction* 92 (suppl.) 2:S221–36.

Von Weyer, P. 1997. "Das Vernebelite Risiko." *Stern* 43:42–48.

Wagenaar, A. C., and M. Wolfson. 1994. "Enforcement of the Legal Minimum Drinking Age in the United States." *Journal of Public Health Policy* 15 (1): 37–53.

Waldfogel, J. 1993. "Criminal Sentences as Endogenous Taxes: Are They 'Just' or 'Efficient'?" *Journal of Law and Economics* 364 (1): 139–51.

Warburton, C. 1932. *The Economic Results of Prohibition.* New York: Columbia University Press.

Waring, M. L., and I. Sperr. 1982. "Bartenders: An Untapped Resource for the Prevention of Alcohol Abuse?" *International Journal of the Addictions* 17 (5): 859–68.

Watts, R. K., and J. Rabow. 1983. "Alcohol Availability and Alcohol-Related Problems in 213 California Cities." *Alcoholism: Clinical and Experimental Research* 7:47–58.

Weiler, P. 1991. *Medical Malpractice on Trial.* Cambridge: Harvard University Press.

White, M. M. 1989. "An Empirical Test of the Comparative and Contributory Negligence Rules in Accident Law." *RAND Journal of Economics* 20 (3): 308–30.

Wieczorek, W., B. Miller, and T. Nochanjski. 1989. "Bar versus Home Drinkers: Different Subgroups of Problem-Drinker Drivers." Research Note 89–6. New York State Division of Alcoholism and Alcohol Abuse.

Wilkinson, J. T. 1987. "Reducing Drunk Driving: Which Policies Are Most Effective?" *Southern Economic Journal* 54 (2): 322–34.

Wilson, R. J. 1992. "Convicted Impaired Drivers and High-Risk Drivers: How Similar Are They?" *Journal of Studies on Alcohol* 53 (4): 335–44.

Wilson, R. J., and B. Jonah. 1985. "Identifying Impaired Drivers among the General Driving Population." *Journal of Studies on Alcohol* 46 (6): 531–37.

Wittman, D. 1986. "The Price of Negligence under Differing Liability Rules." *Journal of Law and Economics* 29 (1): 151–63.

Yu, J., and W. R. Willford. 1995. "Drunk Driving Recidivism: Predicting Factors from Arrest Context and Case Disposition." *Journal of Studies on Alcohol* 56 (1): 60–66.

Zador, P. L. 1991. "Alcohol-Related Relative Risk of Fatal Driver Injuries in Relation to Driver Age and Sex." *Journal of Studies on Alcohol* 52 (4): 302–10.

Zador, P. [L.], and A. Lund. 1986. "Re-analysis of the Effects of No-Fault Automobile Insurance on Fatal Crashes." *Journal of Risk and Insurance* 53 (2): 226–41.

Author Index

Subject Index

ABC Survey, 24, 36, 54, 79, 119, 178, 210
abstainers, 5
accidents, 22, 40, 68, 91, 111, 166, 217, 218, 222, 243, 244, 255, 257
actuarial value, 103, 104
administrative law, 22, 25, 46, 216
adults, 2, 12, 40, 79, 93, 121, 149, 212, 219 220, 248
advertising, 5, 10, 32, 35, 42, 113, 221, 225, 241, 247
alcohol-training, 160
All-Industry Research Advisory Council, 99
ambience, 43
American Law Institute, 121
American Temperance Society, 28
American Yellow Pages, 24
Amherst, 29
amusements, 27
anticonsumption laws, 231, 236
Anti-Saloon League, 29, 30
associations, 29, 49, 50, 133, 147
attorneys, 81, 140, 144, 146, 159
Australia, 106, 113
Austria, 105

BAC (blood alcohol content), 89, 112, 131, 230
bankruptcy, 13, 162, 252, 256
Baptists, 27, 55, 57, 223, 229
barhopping, 43, 121, 257
beer, 2, 5, 24, 26, 30, 32, 49, 51, 96, 124, 127, 131, 133, 178, 202, 221, 225, 241, 247
binge drinking, 2, 16, 20, 106, 108, 110, 135, 216, 218, 220, 222, 224, 228, 238
blacks, 55, 57
bouncers, 149, 171
bounded rationality, 70

breweries, 30
Brown, 29
budgets, 38, 74, 76, 80, 81, 83, 85, 250

California, 9, 46, 50, 112, 113, 118, 120, 221
Canada, 105, 106
cancer, 6, 246
care, level of, 167
Catholics, 27, 29, 55, 57, 223
chain stores, 33, 58, 100, 116, 177, 179, 207
Charlotte-Mecklenburg, N.C., 49
checkpoints, 15
cigarettes, 113, 221
cirrhosis, 6, 48, 49, 50, 51, 135, 143
citations, 106, 132, 139, 187, 207
Civil War, 29
closed claims, 258
cocktails, 24, 132
coffee, 172, 203
common law, 10, 101, 112, 115, 118, 120
comparative negligence, 105, 106, 108, 110 126, 140, 218, 222, 255
compensation, 10, 103, 114, 147, 212, 256
competition, 5, 24, 35, 43, 44, 128, 165, 167, 177, 179, 187, 190, 194, 207, 211, 216, 254, 257
convenience, 9, 43, 113, 169, 238
courts, 26, 70, 98, 115, 246
crashes, 6, 50, 92, 112
custom, 26

dancers, 149
Dartmouth, 29
decoys, 38, 127, 174, 184
density, bar, 42, 225, 240, 249
deterrence, 10, 12, 15, 68, 69, 70, 73, 74, 101, 114, 244, 245, 254

prostitution, 49, 68
Protestants, 29, 55, 223

Quakers, 27
Quebec, 106, 107

race, 153, 220, 257
Raleigh News and Observer, 49
rationality, 15, 70
redlining, 153
refresher courses, 175
rehabilitation, 6, 68, 69
religion, 27, 223, 238
repeat offenders, 95, 96
response rate, 252
Responsible Beverage Training Program
   (RBS), 131, 133
retail sales, 23, 35, 52, 118, 152, 221
retribution, 10, 68, 69, 243
rides, 149, 173, 199, 216, 252, 253
rights, 9, 32, 238
risk aversion, 103
risk loving, 72
Rockefeller Commission, 32, 33
rowdiness, 32, 57, 82, 171
rural areas, 29, 223, 229
Russia, 105

schooling, 210, 219
self-inflicted loss, 6, 114
self-protection, 75
server training, 40, 127, 131, 132, 134, 143,
   148, 149, 155, 159, 160, 165, 174, 175, 195,
   204, 251
Simon, Herbert, 70
single-vehicle crashes, 50, 101, 132
social hosts, 12, 111, 120, 222, 228, 252, 257
Spain, 105
stakeouts, 79
Standard Industrial Classification (SIC), 24
Standard Metropolitan Statistical Areas
   (SMSAs), 55, 57, 80
state-owned stores, 35
strict liability, 126, 129
students, 11, 58, 70, 164, 210
suicides, 114

suits, 108, 115, 158. *See also* malpractice
   suits
Sweden, 34, 96, 106
Switzerland, 105

tabs, 128, 169, 251
taxation, 10, 11, 14, 22, 103, 134, 218, 241,
   245, 254
taxicabs, 127, 132, 165, 198, 223
television, 53, 167
temperance movement, 118
tips, 16, 71, 128, 131, 174, 197, 251, 253
tobacco, 12, 46, 113
trends, 2, 106, 120, 220, 229, 236, 241
Twenty-first Amendment, 31, 119

uncertainty, 74, 129
unconstitutionality, 66
underage drinking, 13, 79, 93, 133, 231
underclaiming, 13
underwriting, 148, 257
United Kingdom, 6, 23, 48, 91, 105
U.S. Bureau of the Census, 23
U.S. Department of Health and Human
   Services, 91
U.S. Executive Office of the President, 24
U.S. Federal Bureau of Investigation, 239
utility, 71, 96, 223, 246

value, 29, 43, 64, 68, 100, 173
Volstead, Andrew, 31

warnings, 132, 184
water, 5, 168
watering drinks, 165
wealth, 27, 100, 244
whiskey, 119, 202
willpower, 70, 129
wine, 2, 5, 24, 178, 221
Women's Christian Temperance Movement, 29

Yale, 29
yuppies, 166

zoning, 38, 134, 240